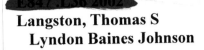

# AMERICAN PRESIDENTS REFERENCE SERIES

- *Lyndon Baines Johnson*
  Thomas S. Langston

- *Abraham Lincoln*
  Matthew Pinsker

- *Franklin Delano Roosevelt*
  Robert S. McElvaine

# Lyndon Baines Johnson

THOMAS S. LANGSTON

*Tulane University*

CQ PRESS

A Division of Congressional Quarterly Inc.
Washington, D.C.

To Jessica

CQ Press
1255 22nd Street, N.W., Suite 400
Washington, D.C. 20037

202-729-1900; toll-free, 1-866-4CQ-PRESS (1-866-427-7737)

www.cqpress.com

⊗ The paper used in this publication meets the minimum requirements of the American National Standard for Information Sciences—Permanence of Paper for Printed Library Materials, ANSI Z39.48-1992.

Cover illustration by Talia Greenberg
Design and composition by Karen Doody
Editorial development by the Moschovitis Group, Inc.,
    New York, N.Y.
Photos courtesy of Lyndon Baines Johnson Presidential Library,
    Austin, Tex.

Printed and bound in the United States of America

06  05  04  03  02      5  4  3  2  1

Library of Congress Cataloging-in-Publication Data

Langston, Thomas S.
    Lyndon Baines Johnson / Thomas S. Langston.
        p. cm. — (American presidents reference series)
Includes bibliographical references and index.
    ISBN 1-56802-703-6 (hardcover : alk. paper)
    1. Johnson, Lyndon B. (Lyndon Baines), 1908–1973. 2.
Presidents—United States—Biography. 3. United States—Politics and government—1963–1969. 4. United States—Foreign relations—1963–1969.
I. Title. II. Series.
    E847 .L36 2002
    973.923'092—dc21                                    2002010381

# Contents

# Preface

Lyndon Johnson's dream was to be somebody. From childhood, he displayed a keen sense of power and an urgent need to dominate people. But Johnson did not want power for power's sake; he wanted it to set things right. His father was a member of the Texas state legislature, and Johnson saw how he used that office to improve life for people in his county. Lyndon's horizon extended further. His vision was to improve life for ordinary people throughout the country, beginning with the South.

When Johnson became president, suddenly and tragically on November 22, 1963, he was at last in a position to do the big things he had spent a long career in politics dreaming about. He got off to a quick start and even proclaimed an unconditional war on poverty. When Johnson won election in his own right in November 1964, he felt that the American people were finally embracing him and his vision.

The love did not last. The president who wanted more than anything to unify the country and bask in its praise came to feel like a hostage in the White House. Intellectuals caricatured him as a hick from the sticks; African Americans protested the limitations of mainstream civil rights legislation; and middle-class suburban voters resented his devotion to the problems of the poor. And then there was Vietnam: Johnson had carried on Kennedy's get-tough foreign policy, but as battle deaths mounted, so did the public's opposition.

Johnson, the would-be unifier, left office after declining to run in 1968. The nation he left to Richard Nixon was divided, and more often than not divided in response to a policy implemented or pursued by Lyndon Johnson. In the immediate aftermath of his presidency, it seemed that his legacy would be a bitter one. The decades since have offered numerous occasions to reconsider Johnson's leadership and its consequences. In assessing what his life and leadership have meant to the United States and to the world, it is essential to have a comprehensive and accurate picture of his life and times. This volume is intended to offer such a portrayal.

Readers will find in the chapters of this book a succinct biography of a pivotal figure in twentieth-century politics. In the documents that accompany the chapters, readers will get a sense of the social and political environment within which Johnson made his decisions. Readers will also understand the texture of life in Johnson's boyhood home, the humiliation he felt in taking the vice presidency, the exhilaration he experienced when he became president in his own right, and the solace he took in life at his ranch in Texas during retirement.

The book is organized thematically and chronologically. Following the Introduction, Chapter 1 provides a biographical sketch of Johnson. Chapter 2 covers Johnson's campaigns and elections. Chapter 3 details the policies of the Johnson presidency, organized by subject area. Chapter 4 looks at how Johnson handled the two biggest crises of his presidency: his assumption of office after Kennedy's assassination and the Vietnam War. Chapter 5 examines the president's relationship with key segments of government and society, from the media and the military to protest groups and the Supreme Court. Chapter 6 follows the president into retirement. Appendixes offer a chronology of events in Johnson's life and brief biographical profiles of key figures in his presidency. A section of documents follows each chapter, and each document—whether letter, speech, or interview—is introduced by a headnote that puts it in the context of the book's narrative. Annotated bibliographical entries also accompany each chapter. The researcher who needs to know just one, or a few, or many things about Lyndon Johnson can dip into this book and quickly locate the pertinent information.

A number of people helped with the creation of this book, and it is a pleasure to thank them now without, of course, imparting any responsibility for errors that remain. Michael Lind helped me think through the reality and the legacy of the Johnson presidency. George Edwards encouraged me to consider how political science and biography might usefully intersect in this project and future ones. Michael Sherman provided invaluable research assistance at all phases of the manuscript's production. The archivists at the Johnson presidential library tracked down information, documents, and photographs. Valerie Tomaselli, Glenn Perkins, and Sonja Matanovic edited the work with care and thoughtfulness. Molly Lohman shepherded the volume through production with tact and professionalism.

*Johnson meets with his cabinet, August 23, 1967.*

# Introduction

Lyndon Johnson pursued consensus as president and could not find it. Since the end of his term in office, there has likewise been no consensus on the nature of his presidency or on the man himself. "What's not to loathe?" asked Robert Sherill in the *Texas Observer* in 1990. The historian Robert Dallek, by contrast, characterized the president as a "flawed giant," the title of the second volume of his comprehensive biography of Johnson. The late president's other major biographer, Robert Caro, describes Johnson as a man consumed by "a hunger for power in its most naked form," a hunger "so fierce and consuming that no consideration of morality or ethics, no cost to himself—or to anyone else—could stand before it" (Caro 1982, xix). Who was Lyndon Johnson to excite such bitter and seemingly never-ending debate?

## WHO WAS LYNDON JOHNSON?

Lyndon Johnson was a complex man of simple beliefs. His complexity has bedeviled those over the years who have tried to describe him for posterity. In Merle Miller's *Lyndon: An Oral Biography,* Johnson's former associates try their best to portray the man they knew. Wilber Cohen, a member of Johnson's cabinet, describes him as "a man of such tremendously different kinds of characteristics that it's difficult, perhaps impossible, to grasp all of his personalities. . . . a combination of Boccaccio and Machiavelli and John Keats" (Miller 1980, xv). The former governor of

3

Texas, John Connally, adds, "There is no adjective in the dictionary to describe him. He was cruel and kind, generous and greedy, sensitive and insensitive, crafty and naïve, ruthless and thoughtful, simple in many ways yet extremely complex, caring and totally not caring; he could overwhelm people with kindness and turn around and be cruel and petty towards those same people; he knew how to use people in politics in the way nobody else could that I know of. As a matter of fact it would take *every* adjective in the dictionary to describe him" (Miller 1980, xvi). "A tormented man," concludes his former press secretary, George Reedy, in *Lyndon B. Johnson: A Memoir.* Johnson was a "bundle of contradictions. . . . not a saint and not a demon but still a towering figure on the landscape of American history" (Reedy 1982, 174).

Amid the complexity, however, some traits stand out clearly. First, Johnson was a man of extraordinary energy and willpower. His work habits as a candidate were legendary. Caro quotes a veteran of many campaigns who said of Johnson, looking back on his first race for Congress, "I never saw anyone campaign as hard as that. I never thought it was *possible* for anyone to work that hard" (Caro 1982, 425).

Johnson's determination is also captured by Warren Woodward in his oral history for the Lyndon B. Johnson Library (LBJL). In 1948 Woodward was the traveling aide to Congressman Johnson. While campaigning for the U.S. Senate, Johnson became ill from kidney stones. Unable to convince him to seek medical treatment, lest the campaign slow down, Woodward waited anxiously in a Houston hotel suite one day while Johnson, who had been in such pain in the morning that he could barely speak or stand, prepared to meet with Stuart Symington, secretary of the Air Force. When the visitor was announced, Woodward watched as Johnson bounded out the door of the bedroom. "Full of energy, ready to go! My God, *will*!" recalls Woodward (LBJL). Johnson, fortunately for his health, was unable to carry off the act for long, and Symington helped persuade him to go to the hospital.

Second, Johnson had considerable talents for leadership and control. In exercising those talents, he could be a terrible bully, publicly humiliating those who were the most devoted to him, including his wife. Richard Neustadt, a political scientist and presidential adviser, observed in an oral history for the Johnson library that Johnson's bullying was "instinctual but not unpurposeful." With a "fine eye for the human vulnerabilities of people he was working with," Neustadt continued,

Johnson demanded, and typically received, absolute devotion from those around him (LBJL).

In dealing with people not on his payroll or living under his roof, Johnson bullied when he could, but more typically he persuaded. Johnson so excelled in the art of persuading that his tactics became widely known as the "Johnson Treatment." He would cajole, plead, threaten, hug, touch, and even cry, as he did once when convincing an old friend and esteemed Washington attorney, James Rowe, to join his Senate staff. Seemingly desperate for help, Johnson tearfully told Rowe that it was "typically selfish" of him not to come to the aid of his friend in this, his hour of deepest need. When Rowe at last relented, Johnson immediately changed tone and told him "Just remember, I make the decisions" (Dallek 1998, 493). The Treatment was as individual as the people to whom it was administered. With Sen. Everett Dirksen, the president would sit close, swap favors, and flatter the proud Republican. With his old mentor, Sen. Richard Russell, Johnson would sometimes wear the older man down, as he once did in an hour-long phone conversation during which Johnson overcame Russell's extreme reluctance to serve on the commission to investigate the assassination of John F. Kennedy.

Even in relaxed settings, Johnson seemed compelled his entire life to exercise control. In Washington in the 1930s, Johnson's friends recall that he would close his eyes and pretend to sleep when the conversation veered away from him. When he "awakened," he would begin talking, loudly, and continue as long as he could hold his audience. As a boy playing baseball in the hill country of Texas, he would literally pick up his ball and go home if the other boys would not let him pitch.

Johnson's energy and passion for control were combined with a third trait—huge ambition. Even as a young man working on a road construction crew, with no plans for college, Johnson would talk of the big future ahead of him, of how he was going to be governor or even president some day. After college, while teaching school for a year before the opportunity to move to Washington, D.C., came along, Johnson performed his job with intense dedication, staying up all night to return student papers the next day or driving all night to get his debate team to another city for a competition.

Johnson always wanted to *be somebody*, but he also wanted to *do something*. If not for this facet of his ambition, all of his bullying and energy would not have attracted to him so many capable men and women. As George Reedy wrote in his memoir of Lyndon Johnson, "Why the members of his staff stuck with him—including me—is a question I cannot answer to this day. It had something to do with a feeling that he was a truly great man and that we owed it to the country to put up with his rampages so he would be there when he was needed. The sentiment may sound squashy to those who have never been close to him but he was capable of generating incredible loyalty" (Reedy 1982, 57). As a member of the U.S. House of Representatives, Senate majority leader, and president, Johnson wanted to achieve great things for himself, but also for the people he represented.

## WHAT JOHNSON WANTED

In a 1958 article for *Texas Quarterly,* Senator Johnson proclaimed himself "a free man, an American, a U.S. senator, and a Democrat, in that order," and also, "in no fixed order, a liberal, a conservative, a consumer, a parent, and a voter" (Lyndon Johnson 1958, 17). As Paul Conkin, an early biographer of Johnson, observed in *Big Daddy from the Pedernales,* "As always when he wanted to talk seriously, he soon fell into vague or moralistic bromides, which he sincerely believed" (Conkin 1986, 129). At the center of this confusing mix of ideas was a vision of himself and of the U.S. government as a fixer of big problems and a fount of generosity. "I believe there is always a national answer to each national problem," Johnson offered in the same article (Lyndon Johnson 1958, 19). Johnson's bluntest statement of what he wanted to achieve through government service was made to Doris Kearns Goodwin, his confidante and biographer, who recorded it in *Lyndon Johnson and the American Dream:* "Some men want power simply to strut around the world and to hear the tune of 'Hail to the Chief.' Others want it simply to build prestige, to collect antiques, and to buy pretty things. Well, I wanted power to give things to people—all sorts of things to all sorts of people, especially the poor and the blacks" (Goodwin 1991, 54).

This does not mean that Johnson saw himself simply as Santa Claus and the government as Santa's helpers. To make sense of Johnson's ambition to give things to people, we have to remember where Johnson came from—a place and time of real need, where only the national government had the strength and the reach to help.

Johnson grew up in an isolated and impoverished part of Texas, without electricity, without a secure economic foundation, and without help from the government. As a young man, Congressman Johnson helped to transform the hill country of Texas using the programs of Franklin D. Roosevelt's New Deal. Through Johnson's initiative, the Rural Electrification Administration brought electricity to isolated homesteads along the Pedernales River; hill country farmers signed up in large numbers to participate in experimental agricultural programs that shored up commodity prices; Texas businessmen received immense contracts to build a series of dams west of Austin, and thousands of Texas voters were employed in government-funded projects. In the New Deal—as interpreted and implemented by Johnson and a host of other policymakers, politicians, and opportunistic businessmen—the American dream of bountiful opportunity was expanded to the South and the West and to segments of the population that had been left behind while others prospered in the Roaring Twenties.

Johnson also believed in the greatness of the American presidency. As a member of Congress, he gave President Roosevelt his absolute support; as Senate majority leader, he cooperated closely with the Republican president, Dwight D. Eisenhower. When he came to the White House as president himself, Johnson seems to have believed that every president was entitled to an unquestioned foundation of support from even his political opponents. After all, as Johnson repeatedly reminded those who came into the Oval Office, "I'm the only president you've got" (Miller 1980, 414).

Finally, the cold war is vital to understanding Johnson's beliefs. He briefly interrupted his congressional service to join the Air Force in World War II, and he witnessed at close hand America's rise to world power under every president from FDR to Kennedy. Like virtually every other American of his generation who came to assume a position of responsibility in the executive branch of government, Johnson believed firmly in America's obligation to the world. He subscribed to the cold war consensus, a set of beliefs held by many U.S. policymakers across a wide-ranging political spectrum. Believers in the consensus were certain that British attempts to appease Adolf Hitler had only encouraged the Nazi dictator to implement his planned assaults on neighboring countries. They were equally convinced that communism was not a congeries of movements, some benign and others harmful, but rather a monolithic threat.

## THE RIGHT MAN?

It would seem that a man with enormous energy, an appetite for leadership, and an ambition to expand government and preserve freedom would be ideally suited for the presidency in the mid-1960s. The U.S. economy was in the midst of an unrivaled expansion, and the intellectual climate favored massive governmental efforts at social reform. In some ways, Johnson clearly was the right man at the right time in the right place. His presidency was one of the most successful in the magnitude of the legislative initiatives he maneuvered through Congress.

President Johnson exercised his leadership skills to engineer a revolution in civil rights, to declare "unconditional war on poverty" in America, and to launch numerous environmental, health, and educational programs designed to build a Great Society on the foundation of American affluence. At the same time, however, he found that the support, and even reverence, for the president that he took for granted was not guaranteed. He attempted to fulfill the promises of a bipartisan foreign policy in Vietnam but ended up leading America into a war that caused a rupture in the cold war consensus.

Even in domestic policy, Johnson's initiatives came under intense criticism before the end of his presidency. Americans' commitment to civil rights was tested by urban riots; antipoverty warriors discovered that their foe was harder to defeat than they had anticipated; and the effort to build a Great Society faced budgetary pressures and waning support from Congress as the war in Vietnam drained the government of resources.

## HOW THINGS WENT BAD

What happened? How did such good intentions and seemingly unassailable assumptions end up with Johnson's decision, made against the backdrop of denunciations of his policies by critics on the left as well as the right, not to seek another term in 1968? How did Johnson's record of accomplishments and failures lead to a history of mixed reviews and contradictory scholarly assessments?

A big part of the answer is that President Johnson's exercise of power undermined his own authority. If he had not pushed so hard for changes in law and society, he would have made fewer enemies. His strong leadership on civil rights drove a wedge between southern conservatives and northern liberals within his party. Ever since Franklin Roosevelt had cobbled together the modern Democratic coalition in the 1930s, southern conservatives had been nervous. Would the northern liberals within the party turn against the southerners on the issue of race? Democratic presidents since Roosevelt had supported civil rights, but no Democratic president before Johnson had actually had the power to push strong civil rights legislation through Congress. When Johnson forced the Democratic Party to take a clear stand on the issue, northern liberals and southern conservatives could no longer ignore their deep differences. Eventually, many southern conservatives would abandon the Democratic Party altogether.

The Democratic Party had been identified with the interests of the less fortunate since the 1930s. But President Johnson's War on Poverty went further than previous programs to help the poor and excited middle-class resentment against the welfare state. In Johnson's military deployments, he similarly acted on principles articulated by a succession of Democratic presidents. The United States, as John F. Kennedy had famously said in his inaugural address, stood ready to "pay any price, bear any burden, meet any hardship, support any friend, oppose any foe, in order to assure the survival and success of liberty." It was Lyndon Johnson's misfortune to be in office when the burden of this commitment became too great for most Americans to bear.

It was not the principle of righting racial injustices that made Johnson a target of those who thought he was moving too fast or too slowly; it was his success in actually moving at all. Because of his success in passing legislation on behalf of civil rights, the pro– and anti–civil rights blocs within the party came into open conflict, weakening the party and its president. It was not the principle of anticommunism that undermined Johnson's presidency in 1968; it was the president's application of that principle in a challenging situation.

As president, Johnson was blessed with the opportunity to put to the test his party's commitments to security and justice at home and abroad. This blessing was also a curse. If Johnson had not tried so hard as president, he would have stood a better chance at preserving popular support. But then he would not have been Lyndon Johnson; he would not have been true to his party's beliefs and hopes or to his own ambition.

## JOHNSON'S LEGACY

What is Lyndon Johnson's legacy as president? In politics, the Democratic Party's commitment to civil rights, and its reliance on African Americans as core voters, is a legacy of Johnson's presidency. In addition, the New Deal legacy of Johnson's idol, Franklin Roosevelt, was cemented into place in the Johnson administration with the expansion of Social Security and the addition of Medicare and Medicaid as tenets of the informal social contract the American people have with their government.

Moreover, the United States is more unified than it would have been without Johnson's presidency, a conclusion that might surprise many, given the tumultuous times in which he governed. Johnson was, in the words of Robert Dallek, a "liberal nationalist" (Dallek 1991, 509). He used the power and money of the government to promote the economic development of the South and West, through such means as government contracts for defense bases and armaments, space exploration and scientific research, and the building of dams, highways, and power lines. Through government spending, the South and West were brought closer to the level of the North and Midwest in terms of economic development. Moreover, by forcing the Deep South to rid itself of Jim Crow segregation, Johnson enhanced the South's standing within the nation, as well as its attractiveness as a site for business investment.

The tumult of the 1960s is also considered part of Johnson's legacy, the negative side, including antiauthority turmoil and the exhaustion of liberalism. The culture wars of the 1980s and 1990s were a response to the shock waves of the 1960s. Perhaps the flowering of antiauthority beliefs and lifestyles was set to happen in the 1960s regardless of the policies of the Johnson administration. If the Vietnam War had not happened, in other words, the radicals of the 1960s may well have organized in protest against something else. But the war was there, and the commander in chief was an easy target for protestors.

In *War, Presidents, and Public Opinion*, John Mueller makes clear that the protestors were never popular in America (Mueller 1973, 164). But the protest against the protestors—the backlash of Richard Nixon's "silent majority"—came too late to help President Johnson retain power, while it divided the nation in the 1970s in uncomfortable ways. Divisions of lifestyle, attitudes toward authority, and opinions on social and moral issues deepened in America as a legacy, at least in part, of the Johnson presidency.

Johnson's leadership during the Americanization of the Vietnam War has also left a legacy in American politics, policy, and culture. In popular culture, President Johnson is sometimes demonized as a warmonger even today. In political debate over post–cold war military operations, the worst thing that can still be said of a proposed course of action is that it would lead the nation into "another Vietnam." The shadow of Vietnam has its most powerful influence perhaps in military policy, where the U.S. officer corps is just now emerging from its resentment against an allegedly uncaring and deceitful civilian leadership. American presidents since the Johnson years have faced a more resistant and less deferential military leadership, thanks to memories of President Johnson's bullying of the military in Vietnam.

How does this all add up? Johnson was not the president he so desperately wanted to be—greater than Roosevelt, with the entire nation united behind him. But he was indisputably a highly consequential president. His problems as president were in part of his own making, and they were exacerbated by his oversized personality. But his presidency was not mysterious, as the various historical analyses of it might imply. Lyndon Johnson's presidency—the vastness of its reach and the looseness of its grasp—was perhaps just what one should have expected given the values and ideas that he brought into office with him and the difficulty of the tasks he set out to achieve.

BIBLIOGRAPHY

The only complete, major study of Lyndon Johnson's life is Robert Dallek's two volumes, *Lone Star Rising: Lyndon Johnson and His Times, 1908–1960* (New York: Oxford University Press, 1991); and *Flawed Giant: Lyndon Johnson and His Times, 1960–1973* (New York: Oxford University Press, 1998). Dallek portrays Johnson as a man of his times, with serious virtues as well as vices. Robert A. Caro has devoted the better part of his adult life to a comprehensive biography of Johnson. The first three volumes are *The Years of Lyndon Johnson: The Path to Power* (New York: Knopf, 1982); *The Years of Lyndon Johnson: Means of Ascent* (New York: Knopf, 1990); and *The Years of Lyndon Johnson: Master of the Senate* (New York: Knopf: 2002). All students of Johnson's life are indebted to Caro for his exhaustive research, but his surmises and deductions should be approached with caution. As Dallek told Robert McNamara, in the course of conducting an oral history interview with Johnson's former secretary of defense, archived in the Johnson presidential library, Caro "beats up on" Johnson in his biography with an unceasing will that Johnson himself might have admired, though not appreciated.

Johnson's White House memoirs are turgid and less than candid. They are highly useful nonetheless. See Lyndon Johnson, *The Vantage Point: Perspectives on the Presidency, 1963–1969* (New York: Holt, Rinehart, and Winston, 1971). Doris Kearns Goodwin worked at the Johnson ranch on the president's memoirs. Johnson seems to have poured out to her all the stories and emotions that he refused to put down on paper himself for his own account of his presidency. The result is Goodwin's best-selling *Lyndon Johnson and the American Dream* (New York: St. Martin's, 1991), originally published under the author's maiden name, Doris Kearns, in 1976.

Other valuable studies of Johnson's life are Merle Miller, *Lyndon: An Oral Biography* (New York: Ballantine, 1980); Ronnie Dugger, *The Politician: The Life and Times of Lyndon Johnson: The Drive for Power— from the Frontier to Master of the Senate* (New York: Norton, 1982); and Paul K. Conkin, *Big Daddy from the Pedernales: Lyndon Baines Johnson* (Boston: Twayne, 1986).

Three more specialized books provide useful starting points for a study of the Johnson presidency. Vaughn Davis Bornet, *The Presidency of Lyndon B. Johnson* (Lawrence: University Press of Kansas, 1983), is one of the finest volumes in a series of presidential studies published by the University Press of Kansas. Harry Middleton, the longtime director of the Johnson presidential library, is the compiler and annotator of an outstanding collection of photographs, mostly by White House photographer Yoichi Okamoto, *LBJ: The White House Years* (New York: Abrams, 1990). Stephen Skowronek, a professor of political science at Yale University, is the author of *The Politics Presidents Make: Leadership from John Adams to George Bush* (Cambridge: Belknap Press of Harvard University Press, 1993). Skowronek presents an insightful account of President Johnson's difficult leadership environment and compares Johnson to other presidents (including James Monroe and James K. Polk) who unwittingly, and perhaps unavoidably, undermined their authority by exercising their power.

Family members have offered their insights as well. See Lady Bird Johnson, *A White House Diary* (New York: Holt, Rinehart, and Winston,

1970); Sam Houston Johnson, *My Brother Lyndon,* ed. Enrique Hank Lopez (New York: Cowles, 1969); and Rebekah Baines Johnson, with an introduction by President Lyndon Baines Johnson, *A Family Album,* ed. John S. Moursund (New York: McGraw-Hill, 1965).

Billy Lee Brammer's set of novellas, published as *The Gay Place* (Austin: Texas Monthly Press, 1978), provides a compelling fictionalized treatment of Johnson, for whom Brammer worked before his writings resulted in his ostracism. Another fictional account, more endearing to the Johnson family, is Lawrence Luckenbill's *Lyndon,* a one-man play by James Prideaux, published on VHS in 1993 by Arluck Entertainment and available from the Johnson library. The Public Broadcasting System's biography, "LBJ," part of the *American Experience* series, contains worthwhile footage from every stage of Johnson's life. It was produced by WGBH, Boston, and is also available from the Johnson library.

Other works cited in this chapter are Lyndon Johnson, "My Political Philosophy," *Texas Quarterly* 1 (winter 1958); John E. Mueller, *War, Presidents, and Public Opinion* (New York: Wiley, 1973); and George Reedy, *Lyndon B. Johnson: A Memoir* (New York: Andrews McMeel, 1982).

*The young Lyndon Johnson, circa 1915.*

# CHAPTER ONE

# From the Hill Country to Washington and Back Again

## *A Biographical Sketch*

Lyndon Baines Johnson was born August 27, 1908, in Stonewall, a town deep in the Texas hill country (see Document 1.1). He would talk often in later years of his impoverished upbringing, going so far as to tell writers Theodore White *(The Making of the President, 1964)* and Alfred Steinberg *(Sam Johnson's Boy)* the yarn that he was a "hobo at sixteen" when he "wandered off" to California but was happy because "it meant one less mouth for my poor daddy to feed." At the same time, Johnson would boast occasionally in retirement, as he did his entire life, of his family's heritage. He would remind acquaintances and reporters that his ancestors and relations included a number of accomplished men and women—a college president, numerous teachers, preachers, lawyers and other professionals. In fact, the publishers of Burke's *Peerage and Baronetage* conclude that "Johnson was of better family" than his predecessor in the White House (Brogan and Mosley 1993, 689–690).

What was the reality? The Johnson family was poor but seldom if ever needy. Even in hard times, the family kept a car. And when Lyndon Johnson's father did lose everything he owned, and a lot more that he had borrowed, in a risky real estate venture, his relations came to his aid, enabling the family to retain the appearance of independence. Moreover, Lyndon Johnson did descend from accomplished forebears, and he grew up delighting in tales of his family's great deeds.

## PRIDE AND SHAME: GROWING UP A JOHNSON IN JOHNSON CITY

Johnson City was founded in 1879 by James Polk Johnson, Lyndon Johnson's first cousin once removed. Lyndon's paternal grandfather, the uncle of James Polk Johnson, was famous in central Texas. After the Civil War he had driven huge herds of cattle along the Chisolm Trail, becoming gloriously rich before losing everything on one last drive, when prices plummeted. Sam's wife, Eliza Bunton Johnson, survived one of the last Comanche raids in the Texas hill country and was included in *Heroines of the Highlands of Southwest Texas* (1940). Lyndon's maternal grandfather, Joseph Wilson Baines, served in the Texas House of Representatives and was elected Texas's secretary of state in 1883.

Lyndon's parents were Sam and Rebekah Johnson (see Document 1.2). Rebekah (b. 1881) seems to have felt that she married beneath her, and many of Johnson's biographers have commented on her domineering presence in his life. Lyndon's father, Sam Ealy Johnson Jr. (b. 1877), was a hard-drinking man of high ideals. He served from 1917 to 1924 in the Texas House of Representatives, in the seat vacated by his father-in-law, Joseph W. Baines, and earned a reputation in Austin, the state capital, both for his integrity and for his way of persuading other members to vote with him. Sam would edge closer and closer to a man until their noses were almost touching; he would grasp shoulders and arms and jab a finger into a man's chest. Sometimes at his side during these performances was Lyndon, who enjoyed traveling to Austin with his father. Sam's crowning achievements as a legislator were the Johnson Blue Sky Law and the Alamo Purchase Bill (see Document 1.3).

Sam Jr. went bankrupt like his father before him. Operating out of an office in the town of Blanco, he had made good money in small land investments, but in trying to keep the family farm along the Pedernales River intact after his mother died, Sam took on debts that he could not repay. The price of cotton collapsed in the fall of 1920, just months after Johnson had gone deep into debt to purchase his siblings' shares of the family cotton farm. By 1922 Sam had fallen behind in his loan payments and had to sell the farm. There was no longer a "Johnson farm" in Blanco County, and Sam still owed as much as $40,000 to merchants and banks all along the Pedernales valley. Lyndon would eventually have to settle some of those debts after his father's death many years later. His father's fall from financial security happened when Lyndon was twelve.

Lyndon Johnson grew up prideful, then, but perhaps with a bit of shame as well. During his adolescence, he was openly competitive with his father and rebelled against him. According to his biographer Robert Caro, Johnson grew determined not to repeat the family misfortune, which Caro ties to sentimentality and idealism. Indeed, it was Sam Jr.'s sentimental quest to preserve the family homestead that led to his financial ruin. Moreover, Caro suggests, if Sam, like most other legislators, had gone along with the lobbyists in Austin, he could have taken home much more income than his meager salary. According to Caro's interpretation, Johnson was compelled not just to "make it" as an adult but to let people know he had done so by being hard and at least a little bit crooked, unlike his honest but soft father (Caro 1990, 8).

Other biographers, including Doris Kearns Goodwin, are equally certain that Johnson's mother played the crucial role in shaping her oldest son. Letters between the two indicate that Rebekah and her son shared their hopes and concerns throughout Johnson's career (see Document 1.4). Her attention could, however, be overbearing at times, and her habit of withdrawing affection when her son displeased her may have left Johnson with a lifelong need to prove his worthiness through devotion to his mother's Victorian morality.

Regardless of the validity of these speculations, many of the future president's traits emerged in his late adolescence and early adulthood. Johnson graduated from Johnson City High School (which offered instruction only through the eleventh grade) as president of his "senior" class (which comprised four girls and two boys). The class prophecy for Johnson was that he would be governor of Texas. The evening of his graduation, Johnson and his mother fought at home, after he announced that he was through with book learning for good. His mother was angry enough to repeat a prophecy starkly different from the one with which his classmates had honored him: she echoed his grandmother, who often prophesied that he would land in the penitentiary, "mark my word" (Caro 1982, 102).

## Not to College but to California

In 1924 Johnson set out, not to college but to California. He and some older friends sneaked out of town and headed west. When they arrived,

Johnson and one of his companions went to work for Johnson's cousin, Tom Martin, a divorce attorney in San Bernadino. Martin told Johnson that, with his help, Johnson could be admitted to the Nevada, then the California bar, without ever having to go to college, much less to law school. Eventually, Johnson learned that his cousin had left out some important details regarding how many years it would take to make this scheme work and about Nevada's plans to raise its standards for bar admission. In the summer of 1925 Martin's wife left town to visit with her family, and the attorney went on a two-month spree, leaving Johnson and his friend to run the law firm by themselves. Realizing that his California dream had gone bust, in November 1925 he hitched a ride back home with another of his many relatives, to the derision of his childhood friends, who teased him about having to return "C.O.D." (or "Call On Dad").

For the next two years, Johnson continued to resist his parents' entreaties to enroll in college. Instead, he did manual labor on a road construction crew, a political patronage job in those days. Finally, he decided he had no more alternatives to college. His job, as unattractive to Johnson as it was, was going to be lost in the change of gubernatorial administrations, and his pretensions of being a man to reckon with were damaged in a barroom brawl with a stronger man. So in the winter of 1927 Johnson went off to Southwest Texas State Teacher's College in San Marcos to take remedial courses in preparation for the start of the spring quarter.

## SAN MARCOS, COTULLA, AND HOUSTON

Johnson's career at San Marcos encompassed two big events that shaped his life. First, he ingratiated himself with the president of the college and maneuvered into a position of considerable behind-the-scenes influence around campus. Through his association with Cecil ("Doc") Evans, Johnson could dispense student jobs throughout the campus. As a big man on campus, he made enemies as well as friends, but there was no denying his influence. He used it to mobilize a secret society, the "White Stars," to overthrow the athletes who made up the "Black Stars" and dominated campus life (see Document 1.5). Through this organization, Johnson gained experience in practical politics. He and his co-conspirators used a variety of methods, some fair and some foul, to win elections and dominate events in what, in a visit to campus after leaving the presidency, he called his "first real Hitlerized operation" (Caro 1982, 190). Through his efforts, the athletic department was forced to share campus funds with nonathletic extracurricular organizations, and the White Stars took charge of the campus newspaper.

Second, though Johnson never excelled as a student, he discovered that he was a tremendous teacher. In the 1928–1929 academic year, he kept up with his studies by correspondence while serving as a full-time teacher and the principal of a Mexican-American school in Cotulla, Texas, between San Antonio and the border with Mexico. This was the site of his first success in the adult world. When the other teachers threatened to strike rather than obey Principal Johnson's instructions to supervise games at recess, he countered their threat by assuring the school board that he could replace the teachers with friends from San Marcos. The teachers backed down, and the children of the school had an unforgettable year (see Document 1.6). Johnson organized activities for recesses and after school hours, began a debate team, recruited parents to carpool students to compete in athletic and nonathletic events in nearby cities, and personally tutored the janitor in English. People who knew him then recall he approached his work, "as if his life depended on it" (Caro 1982, 207). The phrase would be a refrain throughout the rest of Johnson's life.

After graduating from San Marcos in August 1930, Johnson took a job teaching at Sam Houston High School, in Houston, Texas. He lived in a house with an uncle and six other relatives and taught public speaking. Johnson was once again a star teacher, leading the debate team to an unprecedented string of victories and coming one victory away from a state championship. Along the way, he secured publicity for his debaters and himself from the Houston newspapers and gained new experience in mobilizing human talent. He worked his debate team the way a particularly hard-nosed coach might work his football team. As Robert Dallek notes in the first volume of his biography of Johnson, the future president boasted of his teaching style: "I'd just try to run 'em underground, just almost stomp 'em, but would always make it clear that I loved them, where they'd never run completely off. I would humiliate 'em and embarrass 'em and make fun of 'em . . . until they got to the point where they could take care of themselves, which they did" (Dallek 1991, 40). The effect on his students was mesmerizing. One of his former students recalled that he made them feel "the world's going to open. God, he made you believe. . . . You were people who were going to succeed" (Caro 1982, 210).

Johnson's next big step came the following year, when he got a call from the office of newly elected U.S. representative Richard (Dick) Kleberg, a member of the family that owned and operated the legendary King Ranch. Larger than the state of Rhode Island, the King Ranch was the historic home of Texas ranching and one of the world's largest parcels of private property. A young member of the Texas senate, Welly Hopkins, had recommended Johnson to Kleberg, based on the campaign work that Johnson had done for him on a volunteer basis in a special election in 1930. Sam Jr., according to Lyndon's mother's and brother's recollections (recounted in *A Family Album* and *My Brother Lyndon*), was also instrumental in setting up the interview with Kleberg. Regardless of who opened the door, Lyndon Johnson walked right in and quickly made himself at home in a new environment, Washington, D.C.

## SECRETARY TO A PLAYBOY CONGRESSMAN

As Representative Kleberg's secretary, Johnson displayed his enormous capacity for work and his talent at getting the most out of his staff (see Document 1.7). Years later, one of his associates recalled for Robert Caro that Johnson would literally run to his office as soon as the Capitol dome came into view. He treated his staff much the same way that he had treated his debate team—which made sense because two of the original members of his staff were his star debaters from Sam Houston High. Lyndon also demonstrated, upon a wider stage, the talent he had shown back in San Marcos when he had made himself indispensable to the college's president.

Johnson studied how things worked in Washington and quickly put his knowledge to work for Kleberg's constituents. Writing letters to constituents became the obsession of Johnson's small staff, while Johnson spent his days lobbying executive branch agencies. Johnson had the good fortune to be an ambitious young man working for an older man who had no ambition at all. Kleberg just wanted to play golf and have drinks, leaving his work to Johnson. Because Johnson loved work as much as Kleberg detested it, they made an odd but effective team, and Johnson had wide latitude to exercise his influence, sometimes impersonating his boss himself in telephone conversations with civil servants throughout the government.

Johnson stood out among the secretaries on Capitol Hill, winning election as speaker of the "Little Congress," an informal club of congressional assistants. As speaker, Johnson brought one of his heroes, Huey Long of Louisiana, to address the club, and he took the Little Congress's leadership on an expenses-paid junket to New York City. Johnson's obvious ambition for himself eventually caused friction with his boss, and his boss's wife, to whom Johnson had been writing the congressman's "personal" letters as part of his regular work. Johnson wanted to move on, and up, and would not stay on as Kleberg's secretary for many years. He stayed only until his next political opportunity arrived, in 1935.

## Marriage, Courtship, and the National Youth Administration

Johnson's path from the Little Congress to the real Congress lay, indirectly, through his marriage to Claudia ("Lady Bird") Taylor and his courtship of Sam Rayburn. First came Lady Bird. A shy but adventurous young graduate of the School of Journalism at the University of Texas, she was visiting a friend's office at the Texas Railroad Commission at the end of the workday on August 30, 1934, when Lyndon Johnson walked into the room to keep a date with another girl. Surreptitiously arranging a date with "Bird" for the next morning, Johnson began their whirlwind romance. On their first full day together he briefed Lady Bird on his background, ambitions, net worth, goals and values, and he told her they were going to be married. Lady Bird was hesitant but intrigued. She had studied journalism to see the world and meet interesting people. Here was an interesting person who seemed to be headed places; if he fulfilled even half of his dreams, he could show her more of the world than she could ever see from the veranda of her father's mansion in a remote east Texas town. In a hastily arranged ceremony, the two were married on November 17, 1934, in San Antonio.

Lady Bird was of great help to Lyndon Johnson throughout his political career, even at the beginning. Soon after returning to Washington together, Lady Bird became fast friends with one of the most senior members of the Democratic Party, Sam Rayburn. "Mr. Sam" was a lifelong bachelor, and though he had a reputation for being stern and aloof, Lady Bird seems to have recognized his loneliness, and she and her husband were soon sharing quiet Sunday mornings with the future Speaker of the House.

When the National Youth Administration (NYA) was created, Mr. Sam went to the White House to secure for Johnson the job of Texas NYA director, making Johnson the youngest state director in the NYA. In Texas, Johnson and a staff that he recruited heavily from among his associates in San Marcos had a daunting task. In the spring of 1935 one-fifth of the nation's youth had quit school and were either on relief or were looking for work. The job of the NYA was to get them back into school by offering part-time jobs on campus or to teach them vocational skills so that they could find decent jobs right away. Johnson took the position on July 25 and intended to implement a program before the school year began in September.

Johnson's staff worked around the clock to devise programs to encourage young people to stay in school. One program provided jobs to high-school-age children whose families were on relief. The intention was to increase family income so that children might be both breadwinners and students at the same time. For college-age students, the Texas NYA established an early form of work study and set up "Freshmen College Centers" so that poor students who could not afford to enroll year-round could start on a college education by taking a few classes in the summer.

Typically, at the end of the day the office staff would assemble at the Johnson's Austin home. Lady Bird, uncomplainingly, would prepare a meal for however many people Lyndon had brought home with him that night. The night would close with Lyndon musing about the NYA's part in "making history" and, as Dallek records, exhorting his staff to work harder, to "put them to work! Get them out of the boxcars!" (Dallek 1991, 132). Through his hard work, Johnson built a highly regarded organization and made statewide contacts that he would build upon as he entered elective politics.

## REPRESENTATIVE JOHNSON

Johnson's career as an elected politician began two years into his term as director of the Texas NYA. A special election was to be held to fill the seat of James Buchanan, the representative from Texas's Tenth Congressional District, who had died in February 1937. Newspaper reports indicated that the representative's widow might announce for the seat. Lyndon hesitated to run against the widow, but he received some shrewd advice from his aging father. She won't enter if she knows she'll have to fight, Sam told his son; announce now. Lyndon followed his father's suggestion, and Buchanan's widow quickly put an end to talk of her possible candidacy.

In a crowded field, Johnson outworked the competition and relied on the help of some powerful men whom he had befriended in Austin, most notably Alvin Wirtz, a onetime member of the Texas senate and a politically connected lawyer. Running as a hundred-percent New Dealer, promising President Franklin Delano Roosevelt support for all his policies, including the controversial presidential plan to expand the Supreme Court, Johnson won the election and the notice of the president (see Document 1.8). On a trip to Texas shortly after the election, Roosevelt invited Johnson to ride along with him on his train trip to Fort Worth from Galveston. Impressed with the young congressman-elect, Roosevelt told Johnson to call "Tommy," meaning his close aide, Thomas Corcoran, when he got to Washington; Corcoran would be able to help him obtain a plum committee assignment in the House.

Johnson needed all the help he could get because the men who had provided the critical financing for his election—after Lady Bird had put in $10,000, secured overnight from her father—needed action from their representative. They needed, moreover, the sort of action that freshman members of Congress are usually poorly suited to provide.

When Buchanan died, he had been steering through the government a complex tangle of laws and regulatory rulings for building a massive hydroelectric and flood-control dam in the hill country. Johnson was now to be the district's champion for this project. The attorney for the project was none other than Johnson supporter Alvin Wirtz. The contractors were George and Herman Brown, the leaders of the Brown and Root Construction Company. With characteristic energy, Representative Johnson obtained approval for the project.

In Washington, Johnson got help from established friends like Mr. Sam and from an assortment of new friends and associates. In his capacity as an up-and-coming Democratic member of Congress, Johnson became particularly close to the city's young New Dealers. Years later, they remembered him in their oral histories for the Johnson presidential library and in other reminiscences with fondness. Johnson was, said the legendary "White House Tommy" Corcoran, "long, loud and unstoppable." Elizabeth Rowe, the wife of Johnson's New Deal compatriot James Rowe, remembered Lyndon as "always more fun to be with than anybody else" (LBJL). Johnson's friends in the New Deal extended even to President Roosevelt himself, who did not often share his scarce time with novices.

Johnson won the dam, really a series of dams and related projects, for his backers, but what he most wanted for his hill country constituents was the electricity that would flow from the dam and from existing power plants. The government, under the aegis of a New Deal program, the Rural Electrification Association (REA), was selectively subsidizing power delivery to impoverished areas, as those areas met certain criteria specified under law.

In Johnson's first scheduled meeting with the president, he meant to lobby Roosevelt for a waiver of REA rules for his district, but he never got the chance. As Dallek tells the story, Roosevelt distracted Johnson in classic fashion, asking the startled representative before he could even sit down, "Lyndon, have you ever seen a Russian woman naked?" After listening to the president ramble on about this and other topics for their allotted time together, Johnson was ushered out of the Oval Office by one of the president's aides. Johnson rescheduled, with some difficulty, and this time came prepared. He took control of the conversation and showered the president with graphs, figures, and photographs to back up his verbal plea. With Johnson still in his office, the president got his REA administrator on the phone and instructed him to "just go on and approve this and charge it to my account" (Dallek 1991, 179–180).

Through such means, Lyndon Johnson became one of, if not the very best, New Deal legislators ever. But, no matter how he excelled, as a member of the House with no formal leadership position, Johnson was just one of many junior representatives with limited power. In 1940 he sought to distinguish himself by securing a formal leadership position to raise funds for the Democratic congressional campaigns of that year. He knew that he could tap Brown and Root and Wirtz and their friends in the growing Texas petrochemical industry to help out the Democratic Party. The party was having trouble competing with the Republicans in fund raising, and the formal Democratic Party campaign apparatus was not effective in closing the gap. Roosevelt worried that giving Johnson a formal role in the campaign would wound the pride of the Democrats' campaign managers. Nonetheless, the president had confidence in Johnson, and his party needed all the help it could get in the upcoming election. Consequently, in a White House meeting, Roosevelt gave Johnson a vague unofficial mandate to raise money for fellow Democrats. That afternoon, Representative Johnson rented office space and got on the phone to his rich backers in Texas.

By the end of the congressional campaign, Johnson had spread his (and Texas's) largesse where it was needed most—to Democrats in close races across the nation, where the timely infusion of a few thousand, or even a few hundred, dollars might make the difference. Despite the lack of a formal position with the campaign, Johnson made many new friends among his colleagues in the House and was thereafter treated with more respect than his scant seniority demanded.

Roosevelt was grateful, too, and he even played along as Lyndon competed with Sam Rayburn for the unofficial title of Roosevelt's man in Texas. When a special Senate race was announced in 1941 in Texas, Johnson entered and received the president's jocular nonendorsement endorsement in an April 22 press conference. "I can't take part in a Texas primary," the president protested to reporters. "If you ask me about Lyndon himself, I can't take part in his election. I can only say what is perfectly true—you all know he is a very old and close friend of mine . . . now don't try to tie those things together!" (Roosevelt 1972, 122).

Johnson did not win that campaign. He was beaten by a Texas folk celebrity and former spokesman for a flour company, "Pass the Biscuits Pappy" O'Daniel. In his campaign, O'Daniel, the incumbent governor, promised to crack down on gambling and drinking and began to appoint prohibitionists to the state's Liquor Control Board. In the final weeks of the Senate race, O'Daniel received critical behind-the-scenes support from gambling and liquor interests who wanted the troublemaking O'Daniel out of Texas. Roosevelt, uncharacteristically, stood by Johnson after his failure and continued to support him. He did so, moreover, even as Johnson drifted to the right with his state in wartime politics. During the war, as the lengthy depression of the 1930s finally gave way to good economic times, the New Deal became increasingly unpopular in Texas. Representative Johnson now showed a sterner face to his constituents. He spoke out against big government and introduced legislation that would have required employers to report to local draft boards the absenteeism records of potential draftees. Nevertheless, when the Johnson's first child, Lynda, was born in 1945, a White House car arrived at the Johnson home with a copy of a book about the president's dog, Fala. The book was inscribed by the president, "From the Master, to the Pup."

World War II was occasion for a brief interlude in Johnson's political career, though in some ways his military service during this time was more political than anything else. He spent his service as an Air Force officer inspecting California war plants and elbowing his way into a combat zone in the Pacific. On an inspection tour to New Guinea, he insisted on accompanying troops on a bombing run. It was a risky decision. At this stage of the war in the Pacific, losses of one-quarter of the planes and crew members were not uncommon on bombing missions. Johnson's B-26 came under intense fire as it dropped to 10,000 feet to release its munitions, and he and the rest of the crew survived, thanks only to the skill and courage of the pilot. Johnson, and only Johnson, was awarded the Silver Star for his part in the combat mission. (If Johnson had not lost his spot in the first B-26 he boarded that day—so he could rush to relieve himself before the flight—he would have received his medal posthumously.)

Back stateside, Johnson was becoming bored with his congressional career. He would turn forty in 1948, and though he was acknowledged as a master political operator, he was a long way from national power. His ultimate patron, President Roosevelt, died before the war ended in the summer of 1945; his old New Deal friends were scattered about town, most of them no longer working for the government; his own state had become increasingly conservative; and his self-important manner had alienated many colleagues. As a member of the House, especially after Roosevelt's death, Johnson lacked the prestige that had come from intimate association with the president. His congressional and presidential aide George Reedy wrote that Johnson's "manners were atrocious—not just slovenly but frequently calculated to give offense" (Reedy 1982, x). His associates on Capitol Hill would put up with Johnson's domineering ways as long as he had the power to make things—like their reelection—happen, but without power to back it up, Johnson's arm twisting and boasting inspired derision rather than respect.

The 1940s was the decade in which Johnson began to make a fortune. Conscious of the fact that he might eventually have to leave politics, Johnson did not want to leave poor as his father had done. So, in 1942, he used his influence and his wife's inheritance to acquire KTBC, a radio station in Austin. KTBC was the nucleus of what became a successful and, for a time, monopolistic television and radio empire (see Document 1.9).

## SENATOR JOHNSON

Johnson's best opportunity to move up would come in 1948, when the Senate seat occupied since 1941 by "Pass the Biscuits Pappy" O'Daniel, the hillbilly flour salesman turned senator, would be open for competition. Preparing for that race, Representative Johnson began to address his constituents on national and even global events (see Document 1.10). He also sought to reposition himself as a moderate, not a liberal. "The term New Dealer is a misnomer," Johnson informed his statewide audience. He had won his first race for the House and had kept the seat secure in subsequent campaigns by outworking the competition, traveling the byways, and personally meeting and greeting an enormous number of his constituents. But Texas was a big state, and Johnson could not, no matter how hard he worked, shake every voter's hand in this election. To counter the advantage of his principal opponent, Gov. Coke Stevenson, who was more widely known throughout the state, Johnson ridiculed Stevenson as a weary old man controlled by others. He also launched a speaking tour that took him, as Caro writes, to the "forks of the creeks" throughout the state (Caro 1982, 422; see Document 1.11).

To add excitement to his speaking tour and to speed the process along, Johnson traveled by helicopter—"the Johnson City windmill" (see Document 1.12). Often as not, a crowd that gathered mainly to see the helicopter would be captivated by the young politician's feisty rhetoric and his accomplished impersonations of the slow-talking, pipe-smoking governor.

Johnson and Stevenson essentially tied in the election of 1948. When Johnson had faced a similar situation in 1941, his side released its vote tallies prematurely, allowing his opponent's workers to make fraudulent recounts in precincts they controlled, knowing just how many votes they needed to steal (and seal) the election. This time, it was Johnson's side that played it smart and did the most effective stealing. As Tom Miller, mayor of Austin during the election, recalled later, the Stevenson Democrats "were stealing votes in East Texas. We were stealing them in South Texas. Only Jesus Christ could say who actually won" (Dugger 1982, 463n). With some creative legal work provided by Abe Fortas, a New Deal associate of Johnson, whom Johnson would eventually place on the Supreme Court, Stevenson's contest of the results was silenced, and "Landslide

Lyndon" claimed his seat as a member of the U.S. Senate. He handily won reelection contests in 1954 and 1960 (see Document 1.13).

The Senate was the perfect environment for Johnson to apply his brand of personal leadership. Ever since his association with the president of Southwest Texas State, Cecil Evans, he had continued the habit of attaching himself to powerful, older men (see Document 1.14). In the House, he had become exceptionally close to Sam Rayburn (see Document 1.15). In the Senate, he cultivated yet another surrogate "daddy," Sen. Richard Russell, a courtly, conservative Democrat from Georgia. By deferring to Russell and by distinguishing himself in numerous small ways before other senators, Johnson made himself useful. In the Senate there is little formal authority. For this reason, a senator who is useful to others—one who can be counted on to be knowledgeable about pending legislation, knowing what is in a bill and who is for it and who is against it, and who can help forge coalitions so that everyone can claim at least a partial victory—automatically becomes leadership material. By studying the other members, their strengths and weaknesses, their states and reelection prospects, their fund-raising abilities and needs, Johnson knew many members' political situations better than they knew them themselves.

Johnson's knowledge gave him power; he knew when another senator could and could not risk a particular vote, and he knew who had done precisely what favors for whom over the years. His desire for leadership meant that he was willing to put his power to use fifteen or more hours a day, counting votes, meeting with members, the press, the administration, and constituents, and, when necessary, giving the famed "Johnson Treatment"—a hands-on, vaudeville show of passion, charm, and bullying—to some recalcitrant senator or member of the press (see Document 1.16).

With his natural affinity for the Senate, Johnson moved up the ladder of leadership posts: majority whip in 1951, minority leader in 1953, and majority leader in 1955. A massive heart attack nearly ended his career, and his life, in the same year he was elected majority leader, but by 1956 he was back at work and touted in the media as a possible presidential contender.

## MAJORITY LEADER JOHNSON

As Senate majority leader, Johnson typically cooperated with the highly popular president, Dwight D. Eisenhower. In the 1950s Eisenhower, a

Republican, and the Democratic Congress institutionalized many of the New Deal innovations of President Roosevelt, such as Social Security, public housing, and unemployment compensation, while paring down the military in the cold war. Liberal Democrats in and out of Congress sometimes complained about Johnson's penchant for compromise, but as Johnson told Doris Kearns, "It is the politician's task to pass legislation, not to sit around saying principled things" (Goodwin 1991, 141). The three items Johnson was most associated with during his leadership years in the Senate were the censure of Republican senator Joseph McCarthy, the Civil Rights Act of 1957, and the launching of the National Aeronautics and Space Administration (NASA) in 1958.

McCarthy was a problem for the Senate for several years before Johnson helped engineer his self-destruction in a series of televised hearings. McCarthy had made himself a highly popular figure in many parts of the country by exposing alleged communists in and out of the government. As leader of his party, Johnson was pressured by his colleagues to quiet the Wisconsin senator. Johnson's replies were typically in the spirit of one of the Texas maxims George Reedy remembers him as favoring: "Don't kill the snake until you've got the hoe in your hands" (Reedy 1982, xv). Dallek recounts how Johnson commiserated with his liberal friend from San Antonio, Maury Maverick, about the "hysteria" that McCarthy had created, but he urged him to be patient. "You have got to realize that atmosphere can be dispelled only by letting it run its course so that people can see for themselves what is really behind all the noise," he wrote to Maverick (Dallek 1991, 453). In Bobby Baker's memoirs, *Wheeling and Dealing,* Johnson's senatorial assistant recalls Johnson's attitude similarly. McCarthy, Johnson said, "can't tie his goddamn shoes," but "he's riding high right now" (Baker 1978, 92–93). Once fevers cooled and McCarthy went too far, then the hoe was in the hands of men like Senator Johnson.

In 1954 McCarthy finally took on the wrong enemy, the U.S. Army (see Document 1.17). A series of charges and countercharges by McCarthy and the army led to a plan whereby Republican Karl Mundt of South Dakota, an ardent supporter of McCarthy, would chair an official Senate investigation. Had McCarthy attempted to get special treatment from the army for a friend of one of his Senate aides? Had the army knowingly granted promotion to communists? Mundt's investigation was supposed to uncover the truth on both sides. It would allow a platform, in other words, for both the McCarthyites and their critics.

Through intermediaries, Johnson persuaded ABC to televise the hearing gavel to gavel. Johnson wanted to "make people see what the bastard was up to" (Dallek 1991, 454). McCarthy agreed, not realizing he was being set up. In a confrontation with the dignified special counsel for the army, McCarthy came across as ill-tempered and reckless. Public opinion in most of the nation turned solidly against the senator, who was thereafter formally censured by his Senate colleagues. In the postinvestigation maneuvers that led to the censure vote, Johnson was instrumental, selecting conservative Democrats to sit on the special bipartisan committee that recommended punishing McCarthy. Moreover, just before the censure vote on the floor, Johnson persuaded his Democratic colleagues not to take a formal partisan stand on the issue but to let all members vote their conscience. In this way, the Republicans would not be able to shift blame for McCarthy's undoing after the fact, should the censure vote ever become unpopular. (As it was, all but one Democrat voted for censure.)

During the Eisenhower years the Civil Rights Act of 1957 proclaimed, but could not enforce, the voting rights of all citizens. It was important, however, for building momentum toward the far more consequential civil rights bills passed when Johnson was president. The 1957 act, according to a modern-day account in the *New York Times,* was "the most significant domestic action of any Congress in this century" (Goodwin 1991, 150). It was certainly a masterful political victory for the majority leader. "Red hot" liberals, as Johnson called them, remained unconvinced by Johnson's show of leadership, but to most observers he had taken a vital step toward making himself a viable national leader. At the same time, Johnson could tell his conservative constituents in Texas that without his leadership an even stronger civil rights bill would have been passed.

Johnson was also instrumental in the bill that established NASA, the National Aeronautics and Space Administration; it was forged first in a subcommittee on preparedness of the Senate Armed Services Committee, a forum that Johnson had chaired during the Korean War. For Johnson, NASA was a "head" issue, not an issue of the "heart." His aides, recalls George Reedy in his memoir, had to push Johnson to stick with

NASA once the press began to lose interest in the issue. After the program succeeded and gained an important place in the nation's consciousness during the 1960s, Johnson came to believe, according to Reedy, that he had been enamored of the space program from day one.

## VICE PRESIDENT JOHNSON

By 1960 Johnson was again becoming restless. His colleagues had benefited from his leadership, but they were tired of the pace, and liberal senators were openly pressing for less bipartisan blurring of lines and more outspoken statement of principles. Johnson began talking to his friends and family about quitting politics altogether and concentrating on his and Mrs. Johnson's growing radio and television interests. Reedy, for one, believes that this time Johnson meant it; he really wanted out. The 1960 campaign for the Democratic presidential nomination, he notes, was the only race in his life that Johnson did not devote his usual manic energies to win. Johnson's old New Deal friends were in position to help him in the behind-the-scenes campaign for the nomination, but Johnson refused to let them help. "F*** all of 'em," Reedy recalls Johnson as saying, while musing on his political obligations and possibilities.

Nevertheless, John F. Kennedy, the junior senator from Massachusetts, offered Johnson the vice presidential spot on the ticket, and he took it. Johnson comforted himself with the thought that "power is where power goes." But even Lyndon Johnson could not transform the vice presidency into a seat of power. Johnson's brother, Sam Houston, notes in *My Brother Lyndon* that he kept away from Washington from 1961 through 1963 because he could not bear to watch the "day-to-day humiliation" of his brother in the vice presidency.

President Kennedy was sensitive to Johnson's feelings as his number two, and he and Johnson maintained a correct and respectful relationship, but other members of the Kennedy White House ridiculed Johnson as "Senator Cornpone," when they did not more deeply wound him by merely ignoring him altogether. Johnson made what he could of the opportunity for foreign travel as vice president (see Document 1.18) and otherwise drank too much, ate too much, and said, for the first time in his life, almost nothing, while he waited to see what the future might bring.

## PRESIDENT JOHNSON

With the assassination of President Kennedy on November 22, 1963, Johnson found himself suddenly in the presidency. His assumption of that office (covered in Chapter 5) assured the nation of the essential continuity of government. As a caretaker president for the rest of Kennedy's elective term, Johnson mobilized an impressive show of public support for the legislative agenda that Kennedy had placed before Congress. In front of the press and the television cameras, President Johnson urged Congress to pass a new civil rights bill and an economic stimulus bill as testaments to the slain leader's memory. Behind the scenes, Johnson assiduously bargained and pleaded with his former colleagues in Congress. In the White House, the theme of the early Johnson presidency was also continuity, as Johnson asked all of Kennedy's cabinet and White House staff to stay on the job.

In foreign affairs, the new president inherited no crises, but there were a few problems, including a growing U.S. commitment to the defense of South Vietnam against a North Vietnamese–controlled insurgency. During the election campaign of 1964, Johnson portrayed himself as the peace candidate while suggesting that his Republican opponent, Sen. Barry Goldwater, might lead the nation into war. American boys, Johnson assured the nation, would not be sent to fight another Asian war (as they had in Korea just over a decade before).

After he was reelected, Johnson set out to eclipse the record of domestic reform legislation passed by his model, Franklin Roosevelt. Under his prodding, the Eighty-ninth Congress, elected in 1964 with heavily Democratic majorities, passed a significant volume of domestic legislation. In addition to Medicare and Medicaid, Congress enacted the Elementary and Secondary Education Act, the Voting Rights Act of 1965, and the Economic Opportunity Act.

Unfortunately for the president, his record of legislative triumphs would soon be overshadowed by the war in Vietnam. In that war, the president never felt free to fight unconditionally. To do so, Johnson believed, would risk causing World War III. Unable to win but unwilling to accept defeat, Johnson was trapped in a debilitating stalemate in Vietnam (see Document 1.19). Seeing no way out, he made a surprise announcement to the nation on the last day of March 1968. He would neither seek nor accept the nomination for reelection by the Democratic Party.

## PRESIDENT JOHNSON IN RETIREMENT

Back at the ranch he had acquired in the 1950s, fulfilling the dream that had eluded his father, President Johnson maintained the imperious habits of a lifetime (see Document 1.20). He would supervise every detail of the ranch's operation and personally intervene to resolve any "crisis" that might develop. When, for instance, a water pump's delivery was delayed, Johnson conferred on the phone with the president of the airline responsible for shipping the item and demanded hourly updates on the status of the delivery until the pump was at hand.

Fortunately for those who worked on the ranch every day, the president had two other interests to which he devoted some of his energy. He worked with a small staff on his White House memoirs and oversaw the organization of the mammoth Lyndon Baines Johnson Presidential Library and Museum on the campus of the University of Texas. His final public appearance, just weeks before his death, was at his library, where he spoke to conferees on civil rights, perhaps the issue closest to his heart as president. Johnson died of a heart attack on January 22, 1973. He is buried along the Pedernales River, on the Johnson ranch, now a property of the National Parks Service.

BIBLIOGRAPHY

On Johnson's life before the presidency, the most comprehensive references are those listed at the end of the Introduction, especially Robert Dallek's two volumes. A more truncated work published in midpresidency is Rowland Evans and Robert Novak, *Lyndon B. Johnson: The Exercise of Power* (New York: New American Library, 1966). See also William E. Leuchtenburg, *In the Shadow of FDR: From Harry Truman to Ronald Reagan* (Ithaca: Cornell University Press, 1983); and Harry McPherson, *A Political Education: A Washington Memoir* (Austin: University of Texas Press, 1995), originally published in 1972.

On "Mr. Sam," see D. B. Hardeman and Donald C. Bacon, *Rayburn: A Biography* (Austin: University of Texas Press, 1987). Insight into particular stages of Johnson's early career can be gained from Katie Louchheim, *The Making of the New Deal: The Insiders Speak* (Cambridge: Harvard University Press, 1983); Betty and Ernest Lindley, *A New Deal for Youth: The Story of the NYA* (New York: Viking, 1938); and William S.

White, *Citadel: The Story of the U.S. Senate* (New York: Harper, 1957).

Other works cited in this chapter include Bobby Baker, with Larry L. King, *Wheeling and Dealing: Confessions of a Capitol Hill Operator* (New York: Norton, 1978); Hugh Brogan and Charles Mosley, *American Presidential Families* (New York: Macmillan, 1993); Ronnie Dugger, *The Politician: The Life and Times of Lyndon Johnson* (New York: Norton, 1982); and Franklin D. Roosevelt, *The Roosevelt Presidential Press Conferences*, 12 vols. (New York: Da Capo, 1972), vol. 8.

## Document 1.1    Map of Texas Outlining Hill Country

*Johnson City, where the president spent most of his childhood, is in the center of the Texas hill country, a land of rolling, rocky hills at the intersection of two cultures, the east Texas plantation country and the cowboy culture of the American West. As biographer Robert Dallek records in* Lone Star Rising *(New York: Oxford University Press, 1991), during the drought of 1886, one hill country farmer abandoned his home in Blanco County and left a sign that read, "200 miles to the nearest post office; 100 miles to wood; 20 miles to water; 6 inches to hell. God Bless our home! Gone to live with the wife's folks" (20).*

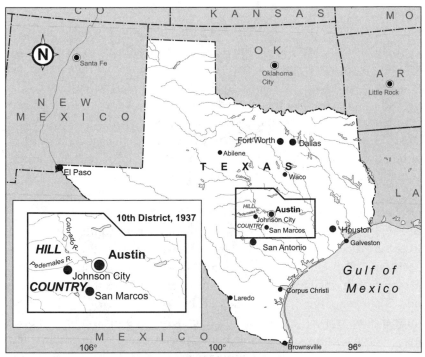

*Source*: Maps.com, http://www.maps.com. Copyright 2002.

**Document 1.2    Family History**
*The excerpts that follow are from* A Family Album, *which Rebekah Johnson gave to her son on Christmas 1954.*

ON LYNDON JOHNSON
It was daybreak, Thursday, August 27, 1908, on the Sam Johnson farm on the Pedernales River near Stonewall, Gillespie County. In the rambling old farmhouse of the young Sam Johnsons, lamps had burned all night. Now the light came in from the east, bringing a deep stillness, a stillness so profound and so pervasive that it seemed as if the earth itself were listening. And then there came a sharp compelling cry—the most awesome, happiest sound known to human ears—the cry of a newborn baby; the first child of Sam Ealy and Rebekah Johnson was "discovering America."

ON REBEKAH JOHNSON
Normally, the first year of marriage is a period of readjustment. In this case, I was confronted not only by the problem of adjustment to a completely opposite personality, but also to a strange and new way of life, a way far removed from that I had known in Blanco and Fredericksburg. Recently, my early experiences on the farm were relived when I saw "The Egg and I"; again I shuddered over the chickens, and wrestled with a mammoth iron stove. However, I was determined to overcome circumstances instead of letting them overwhelm me. At last I realized that life is real and earnest and not the charming fairy tale of which I had so long dreamed.

ON SAM EALY JOHNSON JR.
In August 1907, after a whirlwind courtship of a few months, he married Rebekah Baines, the daughter of his predecessor in the legislature. In disposition, upbringing and background, these two were vastly dissimilar. However, in principles and motives, the real essentials of life, they were one. Their marriage of thirty years broken only by death was based on mutual trust, respect, and love. The chief desire of both was to give their five children a happy comfortable home, the assurance of the interest and love of their parents, the best advantages within their reach, and good educations. Life was often complex and strenuous, but it was full of satisfying constructive work, fond hopes and ambitions and unity of purpose.

He had a sound and sage philosophy which he expressed by a quoted axiom, proverb, or Scriptural passage. He liked to illustrate a situation by relating a remembered incident in history, a humorous anecdote, or a personal experience. He was an interesting conversationalist with a broad knowledge of State and national affairs, political figures and issues, and a deep understanding of people, their ideas, capacities, and desires. He delighted in being of service to those in need, giving sympathy and practical aid freely. Small wonder that "The House by the Side of the Road" was a favorite of his, as he was truly "a friend to man," extending hospitality to the truck driver who broke down in front of his door as graciously as to the Governor of the State who dropped in to talk politics.

*Source:* Rebekah Johnson, *A Family Album* (New York: McGraw-Hill, 1965), 17, 25, 27, 30.

## Document 1.3     Alamo Purchase Bill

*The many jobs of Sam Ealy Johnson Jr. included rancher, teacher, real estate broker, bus inspector, and politician. The career that most intrigued his son was politics. Sam served as the Eighty-ninth District's representative to the Texas House of Representatives in the Twenty-ninth, Thirtieth, Thirty-fifth, Thirty-sixth, Thirty-seventh, and Thirty-eighth legislatures. The pay for legislators was a paltry $5 per day for the first two months the legislature was in session and $2 per day after that. Serving in the capital, however, was not without benefits. Lobbyists munificently treated lawmakers to "beefsteak, bourbon, and blondes," as well as cash payments in exchange for their votes. Sam Johnson took part in the excesses of his time and place but paid for them with his own money.*

*Sam Johnson's crowning achievements in the Texas House of Representatives were the Johnson Blue Sky Law and the Alamo Purchase Bill. The Blue Sky Law sought to regulate the trading of stocks and bonds. The excerpt is taken from the text of the Alamo Purchase Bill, which passed 101–9 in the house and 24–0 in the senate.*

An Act to provide for the purchase and conveyance to the State of Texas of the land in the city of San Antonio known as the Hugo and Schmeltzer Company property, which was part of the Alamo Mission; and for the care and preservation of said property, and of the Alamo church property now owned by the State; and appropriating the sum of Sixty-five Thousand Dollars ($65,000) to carry out the provisions of this Act. . . .

Section 5. The great importance to the people of Texas of conserving the existing monuments of the heroism of their fore-fathers, and the fact that this property must be acquired at once, if at all, creates an emergency and an imperative public necessity for the suspension of constitutional rule requiring bills to be read on three separate days, and said rule is so suspended, and that this Act take effect and be in force from and after its passage; and it is so enacted.

Approved January 26, 1905.

Became a law January 26, 1905.

*Source:* O. K. Shannon, Secretary of State, *General Laws of the State of Texas Passed at the Regular Session of the Twenty-ninth Legislature Convened at the City of Austin, January 10, 1905, and Adjourned April 15, 1905* (Austin: State Printing Company, 1905), 7–8.

## Document 1.4    Letter from Rebekah Johnson to Lyndon Johnson, February 4, 1953

*Johnson's close relationship with his mother is evidenced by the extensive collection of letters between the two. For much of his adult life, Rebekah maintained daily correspondence with her son.*

Dearest Lyndon,

This is just a brief note of thanks. First, I must tell you how delighted I am with the pictures which just arrived. I had hunted up one of you and Eisenhower and all together they make an interesting group of notables. I'm so happy to have them.

It was so dear of you to call me Monday night and I appreciate the call as I do all the many kind and wonderful things you are always doing for the family.

It was a great relief to learn that Sam Houston is under hospital care. I am so glad you put him where he can rebuild his shattered nerves. I know he will cooperate and stay until he is strong and as long as you wish. He must have been in a serious condition.

Whatever you and Bird decide about Josefa will be the best I am sure. I was so glad to talk to her and find her improved. Anything you wish me to do I shall gladly do. Certainly appreciate all Bird is doing for Josefa. There aren't any more Birds as there are no more Lyndons. Again thanks for the call and everything—Dearest love to my precious boy.

—Mother

*Source:* LBJ Library.

## Document 1.5     Johnson the College Student

*Johnson made friends and enemies at Southwest Texas State Teacher's College in San Marcos, at the juncture of the hill country and the coastal plains stretching to the Gulf of Mexico. He befriended the president of the institution, Dr. Cecil Evans, and built a political coalition that realigned the power structure of campus politics. In the process, however, he stepped on many toes. A yearbook cartoon portrayed Johnson as a donkey. The donkey is the historic symbol of the Democratic Party, but that is not the association the yearbook editors intended to make. They meant, rather, to call Lyndon a jackass.*

Chosen editor of the *Star* by the student council in the summer of 1928, he at once began running sketches of people in the administration, and in the editorial about his boss he practices shameless flattery, "Dr. Evans is greatest as a man. . . . With depth of human sympathy rarely surpassed, unfailing cheerfulness, geniality, kind firmness," and so on. Lyndon "was in and out of Dr. Evans's office all the time," as an assistant registrar remembered. Little wonder that Evans took a shine to him. "I was tremendously fond of him," Evans said. "We promoted him to increasingly responsible positions. . . . He could handle people extremely well."

Using the paper as a tool in his personal advancement, Lyndon was laying the basis (in his example to himself) for his lifelong attitude toward newspaper people, judging them according to whether they had the good sense to help him or the stupidity to hurt him. Glomming onto Evans, Johnson was also beginning his practice of the art of protégéship. Older men, seeing his energy, ability, and willingness to serve them without doubts, used him and, in return for his loyalty to them, advanced him. . . .

Lyndon and a football star, Alfred "Boody" Johnson, moved into a tiny room above the president's garage. They slept on cots; since there was no shower they shaved and showered at the men's gym down the road. To help them pay the rent, Evans let them paint the garage, and one spring they painted it three times.

Some of the students began to resent this audacious young man, suddenly so close to power, and students who put together the college annual let him have it. In the spoof section there was a drawing of a jackass made to resemble him, with this caption:

Lyndon Johnson: *As he looks to us on the campus every day* from far away, and we sincerely trust he is going back. Sophistry Club. Master of the gentle art of spoofing the general public. . . .

[Dean Alfred] Nolle said Lyndon wanted to get in Black Stars and tried out as a baseball pitcher so he could be considered an athlete. By a Black Star's account, he was considered for membership because of his influence in the president's office, but there was a blackball. Lyndon believed it was cast by a student about whom he had put a snide item in the paper.

Rejected, he "became somewhat incensed," Nolle said. The Black Stars would rue their mistake. According to his brother, Lyndon figured that only a tenth of the students were jocks and that it stood to reason other students secretly hated and resented them. "Since every practical politician knows that hate and fear offer more forceful tools for organizing than love and respect," Sam Houston said, "Lyndon had a rather fertile field. . . ."

The head of the Black Stars was "Boody" Johnson, Lyndon's roommate, and one night in 1928, while Boody was taking a shower, Lyndon said, the constitution of the outfit "fell out" of something and he read it, naturally. In this way he learned that only football players could belong to it. Boody told him he had no business reading it, but it was too late—"I organized the White Stars."

Six or seven boys, including Lyndon, laid the counterplot, selecting the secret name Alpha and Omega. They decided to choose promising boys, the comers with brains and savvy, but they, too, used the blackball. One of the founders, Horace Richards, said he swore in the first members, including Lyndon, with a candle and a Bible in the dead of night on the banks of the San Marcos River. The ten members that night took vows of brotherhood and secrecy. They had a rule that no more than two of them could be seen together on campus—if three came together without thinking, they would signal with their eyes which one was to leave.

Turning at once to the campus elections, Lyndon's White Stars studied the voting blocs, counted the votes, figured out how they could split up the opposition. They gained a one-vote majority on the student council and, through it, control of the student paper and the annual.

*Source:* Ronnie Dugger, *The Politician: The Life and Times of Lyndon Johnson: The Drive for Power—from the Frontier to Master of the Senate* (New York: Norton, 1982), 112–114.

## Document 1.6    Johnson the Grade-School Teacher

*Johnson was forced to interrupt his studies at Southwest Texas State Teacher's College in September 1928 when he could not afford tuition. Fortunately, he had already completed the five education courses required to obtain an elementary-school teaching certificate. During his one-year furlough from San Marcos, he was a teacher and principal at the Welhausen grade school in Cotulla, Texas; it was an experience that he referred to often in later years. The following excerpt is from President Johnson's remarks at the National Conference on Education Legislation on March 1, 1965.*

I don't know how the final record will look. But I do know that I am proud of this democracy and I do genuinely believe that education is its guardian and is its steward, and that a trained mind is the best possible insurance premium we can buy to preserve our freedoms and our liberties and to keep us from being slaves.

I have said this before and I am not going to bore those of you that may have read it or heard it by any long statements on it, but I came from a family that is interested in public life and in education. My mother was a teacher and my father was a teacher. My great Grandfather, my mother's grandfather, was the second president of Baylor University when it was located down at Washington on the Brazos. . . .

I left college as a sophomore to become the principal of a six-teacher school and I drew the magnificent, munificent salary of $125 a month!

I remember I asked my teachers, in my first year of teaching, to get out and have supervised play activity. I had a little Mexican school. And what they'd all do was go to the bathroom and smoke during recess. And I said: "You take the north corner. And you take the south one. And you take the east one. And you take the west one. And let's have volleyball!" And I took my own first paycheck and bought a volleyball for them and bought a playground softball for them and had some dancing for them out there and some musical instruments to entertain them during recess—these poor people that lived down on the border of Texas. I have never understood it, but the Mexican people have been voting for me ever since. They understand!

Finally one day after I came in one Saturday morning, the school superintendent (he was a Mr. Donaho, he lives down in Floresville, Texas, now; he's retired) he came to me and said I am in trouble. He said, "Every one of your teachers struck on you." And I said, "What is the matter?" "Well," he said, "they don't like that supervised play activity." (One of them was the sister of the mayor, another one was the sister of the postmaster and they kind of had it pretty good—very influential friends around town. One of them was the daughter of one of the important men, one of the bankers.) And he said, "They called on me while you were off supervising the football team for the high school yesterday. They called on me and said they had struck." I said, "What did they say?" And he said, "The Leading lady that was spokesman for them said 'Our traces are down and we have balked.'"

Well, there was a lady in town who was on the schoolboard that had been to Randolph Macon; she was a graduate and she had married one of the local fellows (he had gone up east a little way from Texas a little while and they met and married) and she was on the schoolboard. And she said, "well, they don't like to go through these recesses and hot lunch hours supervising these children. They just let them fight all the time. They have had nothing to play with and they just let them fight." "But," she said, "you just accept every one of their resignations and go back to that teacher college you came from and hire you five more that will come here and supervise." So she made a motion to that effect and the board voted with me. And the teachers were called in and they said, well, we misunderstood what they said to begin with!

*Source: Public Papers of the Presidents of the United States: Lyndon B. Johnson, 1965* (Washington, D.C.: U.S. Government Printing Office, 1965), 1:227, 2229–2230.

## Document 1.7    Letter from Lyndon Johnson to
## Rebekah Johnson, December 1931

*Johnson's personality was well suited to Washington, D.C., where he could immerse himself in politics twenty-four hours a day. When he moved north to work as a secretary for Rep. Richard Kleberg, D-Texas, he took up residence in the Dodge Hotel, home to many congressional staffers. Because the building had communal bathrooms, he took four showers and brushed his teeth five times a day, just so he could "accidentally" meet more of his neighbors. Johnson wrote the following note to his mother less than one week after moving to Washington.*

Dearest Mother:

I don't know when I've been so tired as I am tonight. . . .

To start to tell you how I've worked since I came here would require more time and effort than I feel like expending. I get up at 6 o'clock and go to the office by 7:30, take off 30 minutes sometime during the day for lunch and leave the office about six or seven depending on the correspondence. I *run* the office *force*. Mr. Kleberg doesn't spend an hour a day there and then only signing letters. Frequently I go back at night to finish so I won't get behind. I am learning fast and doing a good job of my work. The only expressions that Mister Dick has made regarding my work go like this: "Great—Good—That's what I want etc." I work for one of the ablest men in Washington and I'm confident the best. He treats me like his brother. Eat, sleep, and work with him. He spares no expense for my comfort, sacrifices everything for my desire. I'm going to move from here before the holidays. Don't know where I'll go but am going to find a nice place.

Am afraid I can't come home Xmas. You don't know how I want to. Am 2,087 miles from S.A. over 1,000 from St. Louis. He may let me go tho'.

Must go. Mr. Kleberg has just come in. I'm placing a call now for him to Mrs. Kleberg in Corpus Christi.

Love to all. Please write. Lyndon Baines.

*Source:* LBJ Library.

## Document 1.8  Texas Tenth Congressional District Elections, 1937–1946

In the 1937 special election for the U.S. House of Representatives, Johnson beat his five opponents, finishing more than ten percentage points ahead of Morton Harris, the runner-up. Johnson maintained the seat for over a decade, running unopposed in four of the next five elections.

| Year | Candidates | Votes | Percentage |
|------|-----------|-------|------------|
| 1937 | Lyndon B. Johnson (D) | 8,280 | 27.7% |
|      | Morton Harris | 5,111 | 17.1 |
|      | Polk Shelton | 4,420 | 14.8 |
|      | Sam V. Stone | 4,048 | 13.5 |
|      | C. N. Avery | 3,951 | 13.2 |
|      | Houghton Brownell | 3,019 | 10.1 |
| 1938 | Lyndon B. Johnson (D) | 14,476 | 100.0 |
| 1940 | Lyndon B. Johnson (D) | 48,442 | 100.0 |
| 1942 | Lyndon B. Johnson (D) | 12,799 | 100.0 |
| 1944 | Lyndon B. Johnson (D) | 44,602 | 92.9 |
|      | A. H. Bartelt (R) | 3,423 | 7.1 |
| 1946 | Lyndon B. Johnson (D) | 16,947 | 100.0 |

*Source:* Compiled from data in *Congressional Quarterly's Guide to U.S. Elections,* 4th ed. (Washington, D.C.: CQ Press, 2001), 1067–1086.

## Document 1.9  Lady Bird Builds a Fortune in Television

*Johnson's meteoric rise from congressional staffer to president of the United States paralleled an equally impressive rise from bankrupt college student to multimillionaire. The foundation of that wealth was a radio station Lady Bird Johnson purchased in 1943. According to the* Wall Street Journal, *KTBC was a struggling enterprise that could not gain the requisite government permits to broadcast at night, gain network affiliation, or have its own wavelength. Soon after Mrs. Johnson purchased the station, it received the full support of the Federal Communications Commission (FCC). When KTBC opened a television station on Thanksgiving Day 1952, it enjoyed an*

*FCC–sanctioned monopoly in the Austin area. Twenty years after Lady Bird purchased the station, the* Wall Street Journal *estimated its assets at more than $3 million, with an annual income of $500,000.*

The LBJ success story comes in two volumes: Public Service and Private Enterprise. Lyndon Baines produced Volume I, from poor boy to Presidency, as everyone knows. Lady Bird is credited with putting together Volume II, the business saga, and in many respects it is equally astonishing . . . .

Today the keystone of the business that Mrs. Johnson built is station KTBC-TV—with its "monopoly" on television broadcasting in Austin, its affiliations with all three networks, its transmitting power boosted with Federal approval, its solitary status protected against competitive invasion by Federal disapproval.

But the tale begins back in 1942, at a time when Lyndon was a 34-year-old Texas Congressman. He'd just finished an active duty stint in the Navy, during which time Mrs. Johnson had kept shop at his House office. That chore complete, she and Lyndon were intrigued when they heard a "for sale" sign was going to appear on KTBC, an Austin radio station serving her husband's constituents, including those in Johnson City.

**FCC Approval.** She bought it in early 1943 and the broadcasting purchase was government approved, as all must be by the Federal Communications Commission after she had recited her service on Capitol Hill and her experience administering her personal inheritance, had offered her personal balance sheet showing a net worth of $63,332, partly liquid and partly in real estate, and had pledged her "full time and energetic efforts."

The fearsome challenge that faced Mrs. Johnson can perhaps be measured by this fact: The broadcasting company had been headed by Robert B. Anderson—a man whose financial genius was sufficient to lift him later to the post of U.S. Secretary of the Treasury under Eisenhower, but insufficient then to keep KTBC out of the red. The outfit had lost $7,321 in 1942 on revenues of $26,795. If he couldn't make the thing pay, who could?

Lady Bird Johnson . . . The basic reasons for financial trouble, recalls one of the former owners, A. W. Walker, were that "we did not have a network affiliation, and couldn't operate at night time." As a matter of fact, KTBC had only left-over hours of broadcasting because all that its original owner had been able to win from the Government after a long struggle was the right to share a transmitting wavelength primarily assigned to Texas A&M College.

*Unlimited Hours Granted.* In a hustle, Mrs. Johnson asked the FCC to grant her station unlimited broadcasting hours, and quadruple its 250-watt transmitting power. Permission was granted for both: the former required FCC allocation of an entirely different wavelength. And quickly Mrs. Johnson pursued valuable network affiliation. An NBC executive who was a friend of Lyndon at the time was regretful that Lady Bird's request for his network's programs had to be turned down because of the objection of a San Antonio affiliate. But she rapidly won affiliation with CBS. So now Lady Bird could go out and get business.

Soon she had mopped up that red ink—achieving in August her first profit, $18—and begun building a profitable broadcasting duchy. By the most conservative measurement, this broadcasting investment has grown more than 200-fold: assets of $3,092,902 are shown on the latest (Feb. 28, 1963) balance sheet on file at the FCC. Experts estimate the actual market value of the enterprise today might be around $7 million. One broadcasting executive who is not associated with the corporation but who has long known the Johnsons indicates that net earnings now exceed $500,000 annually. . . .

Unlike most businesses, a broadcasting enterprise can exist and expand only with Government approval. From the very beginning and repeatedly thereafter, the fate of the Johnson family fortune has inevitably hung not only upon business acumen but also upon favorable rulings by the Federal Communications Commission. Yet FCC public records show not a single intervention by Representative, Senator, Vice President, or President Johnson in quest of a favor for his wife's company.

In 1948, the FCC suspended granting any new TV channel allocations and launched a prolonged national study of where they should go. It was in this same year that Lyndon Johnson was elected to the Senate; he promptly moved on to the Commerce Committee which is the Senatorial overseer of the FCC and the body to which all communications bills are referred; by 1951 he had in addition become Democratic Whip, thus holding his party's No. 2 power position in the Senate. In 1952, the FCC unrolled the map showing the conclusions of its study, and lifted the freeze on net station grants.

It turned out the Austin area was awarded just one standard (very high frequency) channel, while the Fort Worth-Dallas area got five and some other cities in this slice of Texas also received multiple standard channels. The FCC emphasizes that technical considerations prevailed. Any two stations transmitting on the same channel had to be spaced far enough apart to avoid signal interference. With that guideline, cities were granted stations on the basis of population in the 1950 census. So Austin, with a population of 132,459 deserved just one.

Around the nation a lot of other towns received similar slim rations: there are today nearly 150 from Manchester, N.H., to Chico, Calif., which depend on a single standard station. But FCC experts say Austin is "among the top four or five single-station markets." Triple network affiliation can be taken as the badge of a rich market for a solitary broadcaster; recent research by one network shows that among those thus linked to CBS, NBC and ABC, the Austin station boasted the largest audience—203,500 homes with TV sets....

***Corpus Christi Station.*** Looking back, there seem to have been some quirks. To the south of Austin is Corpus Christi; it had within city limits a smaller population, 108,287, and yet the Government study from the beginning projected two standard stations for Corpus Christi and not considering that sufficient, the Federal allocators later added another channel. Furthermore, far from being demonstrably free from any signal-interference problem, this third channel was involved in an interference problem with Mexico which could not be resolved until 1960; the third Corpus Christi station has not gone into broadcasting even yet.

After deciding one station would handle all standard television in Austin, FCC had no difficulty choosing who should have it. The agency announced on April 14, 1952, its formal verdict that Austin would get channel 7; Mrs. Johnson's company had filed for exactly that channel one month earlier, and had already nailed down network affiliation....

No rival applicant had contested Mrs. Johnson's TV quest. And by then her record in radio left no doubt of her qualifications. As one male associate has since observed, she was "any man's equal: she read a balance sheet like most women examine a piece of cloth." ...

As a footnote, it must be observed that there were other people who did want to televise from Austin. FCC had also allocated two non-standard (ultra high frequency) channels to the city; application for both of these were filed, and granted in the summer of 1952.

Why didn't such groups instead seek the choice standard television channel? An FCC aide remarks it "looks funny now," but explains that "apparently" they were not eager to do battle against the strong Johnson bid before a Federal agency, when the UHF channels were available as an alternative—and at a time when the UHF's competitive disadvantages had not become apparent.

One recipient of an Austin UHF channel was Tom Potter, who boasts he had built the first Texas TV station, WFAA, in Dallas and obtained its FCC permit before the '48 freeze. His explanation of why no one vied against the Johnson application for Austin's standard channel is simple, "Lyndon was in a favorable position to get that station even if somebody had contested it. Politics is politics."

*Source:* Louis M. Kohlmeiher, "How the President's Wife Built $17,500 into Big Fortune in Television." *Wall Street Journal,* March 23, 1964, A1.

_____

### Document 1.10   "Lyndon's Letter," March 1947
*Representative Johnson communicated with his constituents in a weekly letter to his district. After ten years in Congress in 1947, Johnson took on world events in the following letter.*

This is your chance!
In my weekly report to you, you will have the opportunity to take a more active part in World Affairs,—the Affairs of Texas, and to narrow it down still further—your 10th Congressional District.

These are critical days!

Neither TIME, the TIME OF EVENTS nor the ATOM BOMB will wait for shadow boxing. For this reason, I feel that the people whom I represent should let their Congressmen know how they would like him to represent them. This is the RIGHT as well as the OBLIGATION of every thinking American.

The World is getting pretty small!

Last week a Texas trained airman, Lt. Col. Robert E. Thacker flew his P082 fighter, Betty Jo, from Honolulu to New York City in 14 hours and 33 minutes, a distance of 4,978 miles. This was a new non-stop record.

It is 5,946 miles from Austin to Moscow. From Russian bases in Siberia the mileage is 4,424 miles. These sound great distances. They are—but not if we are thinking as every modern Texan—every American, ought to think.

Let's not become hog-tied!

When the Soviet Union shows a willingness to reduce its Armed Forces, its expansion maneuvering in the Far East, and when it starts making an earnest bid for cooperation with the rest of the world, then and only then, do I believe we should curtail the appropriations for our Armed forces and other vital agencies.

I am 100% for governmental economy, but not the hit or miss kind! . . .

On February 22nd, I had the honor to be a member of the official party that went [to Mount Vernon] to pay tribute to Mr. Washington. President Truman laid a wreath on behalf of the National Organization of the Veterans of Foreign Wars. When it came my turn to do the same for the Texas Veterans the hard fact of our responsibility—what is expected of us—really hit me. In the American people lies the safety of the World.

I was thinking of this when I voted against the Constitutional Amendment, limiting the Presidency to two terms!

The safest repository for proper Governmental Control lies in the people themselves. It is for you and you alone to say, just how long your Chief Executive remains your leader. My power rests in you, I could not and would not vote to see my intelligence above yours. It was those who FEAR the PEOPLE that voted for it!

In 1776, a great man looked across the Atlantic to a far distant America and thought, and then wrote, "This people is the hope of the human race: It may become the model. The Americans should be an example of political, religious, commercial and industrial liberty. But to obtain these ends for us America must secure them for herself; and must not become a mass of divided powers."

America has become the HOPE of the World!

We are looked toward, in this year 1947, anxiously and we must become the MODEL. To be worthy of this trust we must begin to think not only district-wide, state-wide, nation-wide, but WORLD-WIDE! And we must begin now! Washington, Jefferson, Lee, and our own Sam Houston, if they were alive today, would urge us to think in this way. The higher Standard of Living in other parts of the world the more prosperous we become,—the more benefit to all income brackets. It is by the sweat and courage of red-blooded Americans that we have reached a peak in Standards of Living.

DO WE WANT TO STOP HERE?

*Source:* LBJ Library.

**Document 1.11     Johnson Starts His Campaign for the U.S. Senate, May 12, 1948**

*After Johnson's 1941 loss to "Pass the Biscuits Pappy" O'Daniel for a seat in the U.S. Senate, Johnson upheld a campaign promise that if the United States entered World War II he would join the military. Johnson returned to Congress in July 1942—too late for a rematch against O'Daniel; the next opportunity to run for that seat came in 1948. In the following selection, Johnson announces his intention to run for the Senate. Unlike in the special election of 1941, in which Johnson retained his House seat after losing the Senate race, a loss in this election would have booted him out of Congress.*

TO THE PEOPLE OF TEXAS:

For eleven years I've represented the tenth Congressional District. They were good years because, like you, I'm happiest when doing a job. Together we've helped our district grow. Today there's another job to do for the state and nation. Working together, we can do it.

I am a candidate for the United States Senate. Like most Texans, I believe our Senator should be young enough to have energy for the work; experienced and level-headed enough to be heard with respect in our capitol; and with the courage and independence to make his own decisions.

The easier way would have been to ask re-election. Two years ago, 70 percent of voters approved my record. Word has reached me that men who have never supported me urged that I stand for re-election. The fact is, they fear I will win. They don't want me in the Senate. That helped me to decide.

Texans don't have much patience with people who play only cinches. You and I know that right now nothing is safe and easy. You're fed up with has-beens who want to sit things out.

In 1941, I lost this great office by 1,311 votes. Three votes changed in each county would have meant my election. I was urged to contest that result. I tried to be a good sport. Lots of folks said they'd support me the next time—but the war intervened. This is the first opportunity since 1941. I know the fair-minded people of Texas will help me win that promotion to which I came so close before.

I believe I share this philosophy with most Texans: We'll do anything within reason to get along with our fellow human beings. But we won't stand for being pushed around. That goes for nations; and that goes for pressure groups within the nation—big money, big labor, big bureaucrats, big anybody else who tries to steamroller us.

That conviction is the basis of my candidacy for the Senate. I will open my campaign in Austin on May 22; and I make you this promise: when you vote on July 24th, you're going to know one of two things. You'll know how every candidate stands on every issue; or you'll know he's scared to tell you for fear of losing your vote. I want everyone who will join me in this fight to come to the opening of this campaign.

*Source:* LBJ Library.

## Document 1.12    Helicopters and the Political Process

*Bell Aircraft Corporation intended to revolutionize commercial aviation with its "Model 47 helicopter," the first such machine to be built with a gyroscopically stabilized, two-blade rotor. To get the public interested in this new machine, Larry Bell, founder and president of the company, turned to test pilot Joe Mashman. "Joe, I want you to take a helicopter down to Texas and fly this young congressman around who wants to become a senator. . . . We're interested in helping him out because helicopters are new and if we get an important person such as a congressman showing enough confidence to fly in our aircraft, it would help us and the overall industry." In Johnson's 1948 Senate race, he and Bell both got what they wanted.*

*Mashman:* The helicopter wasn't just a means of getting him from place to place. The helicopter was quite an innovation. It would draw people. Even these days, if you land a helicopter in the center of a small community, the children want to come out and the parents have to go along with the children to keep them from getting hurt and once you get the parents there, you try to keep them there while you tell them your story. That was the basic technique used then. The thing that impressed me then was how well organized this small compact group of individuals were, starting off in the morning when we had a list of places where we were going to land. The previous evening we had gotten an up-to-date list of the people in the community who had written to the Congressman sometime or other during the past, the critical issues, the key issues, interests in the community. And that was all digested by the President and whatever information that had to be passed down to the people on the ground that were there. We had contingency plans so that if we got to the area and for some reason or other I deemed it inadvisable to land, there was a car that would follow us to an area outside of town, usually right alongside the highway where I would land the President so he could ride in the car to my scheduled landing spot. In most cases I was able to land at our scheduled spot, but in many cases, due to the lack of performance of the helicopter compounded by obstructions, wires and surrounding buildings, we were unable to take off with the President. This was compounded by the fact that we always tried to land right next to the courthouse or the center of town. The President would stay on the ground and dramatically tell the people of the impending dare devil feat. In fact that was one of the drawing cards: Before he got out of the aircraft I would inform him as to whether he was going to leave with me or not; if he wasn't going to leave with me, he would tell the people, "Now all you folks come on around here. I have a story to tell you and before I tell you the story, I want you to know that my good pilot here, Joe, tells me that it's going to be too dangerous for the two of us to take off together because of those high-tension wires,"—or whatever the reason might be—"so if you all stay here with me until we get through, we'll all wait and hope that the good Lord sees that Joe gets off safely. We'll be here helping pray for him." Or some such thing as that. (Laughter)

*Frantz:* The Lord and Lyndon Johnson.

*Mashman:* Right. We covered as many as thirty towns a day and some little towns, we'd just fly over because if we were going from one speaking town to another, we would pass a number of smaller towns on the way. In that list of activities for the day, we'd have perhaps the names of one or two of the individuals in the little town who at one time or other had written to the Congressman. As we'd fly over the town, we'd slow down and after a few weeks I'd just about memorized this jargon that said: "Hello, there, Mr. Jones. This is your friend, Lyndon Johnson. I'm sorry we can't land today, but I want you to know that I'm up here thinking of you and appreciate your kind letter and comments. I just want you to be sure and tell your friends to vote for me at election time." And then we'd go on.

*Frantz:* Mr. Jones was well hooked by then, I imagine.

*Mashman:* That's right.

*Frantz:* None of this was ever by chance. You weren't flying from, say, Weatherford to Graham and just suddenly realize that's Peaster down there or something like that.

*Mashman:* No, no. It was all planned and programmed. And then the press followed in another car or cars so we actually had a program route. However, we did have unscheduled stops. Sometimes on the way if he'd see, say, a railroad repair crew working there on the railroad tracks—there was, you know, four or five men there—we'd stop and land there and talk to them, especially if it was an area close to the highway where the press were bound to be, keeping up with us. We'd land there so the press could get a story.

*Source:* Joe Mashman, interviewed by Joe B. Frantz, March 28, 1974, LBJ Library.

## Document 1.13   Johnson's Senatorial Elections, 1941–1960

*The table shows the results of Johnson's Senate elections from his failed bid in 1941 through his victory in the election of 1960, when he concurrently ran for vice president.*

| Election | Candidates | Votes | Percentage |
| --- | --- | --- | --- |
| Special election, 1941 | W. Lee O'Daniel (D) | 175,590 | 30.5% |
| | Lyndon B. Johnson (D) | 174,284 | 30.3 |
| | Gerald C. Mann (D) | 140,807 | 24.5 |
| | Martin Dies (D) | 80,551 | 14.0 |
| Democratic primary, 1948 | Coke R. Stevenson (D) | 477,077 | 39.7 |
| | Lyndon B. Johnson (D) | 405,617 | 33.7 |
| | George Peddy (D) | 237,195 | 19.7 |
| Democratic primary runoff, 1948 | Lyndon B. Johnson (D) | 494,191 | 50.0 |
| | Coke R. Stevenson (D) | 494,104 | 50.0 |
| Senate election, 1948 | Lyndon B. Johnson (D) | 702,785 | 66.2 |
| | Jack Porter (R) | 349,665 | 32.9 |
| Democratic primary, 1954 | Lyndon B. Johnson (D) | 883,264 | 71.4 |
| | Dudley T. Dougherty (D) | 354,188 | 28.6 |
| Senate election, 1954 | Lyndon B. Johnson (D) | 539,319 | 84.7 |
| | Carlos G. Watson (R) | 94,131 | 14.8 |
| Democratic primary, 1960 | Lyndon B. Johnson (D) | | 100.0 |
| Senate election, 1960 | Lyndon B. Johnson (D) | 1,306,605 | 58.0 |
| | John G. Tower | 926,653 | 41.1 |

*Source:* Compiled from data in *Congressional Quarterly's Guide to U.S. Elections,* 4th ed. (Washington, D.C.: CQ Press, 2001), 2:1298, 1365.

## Document 1.14    Johnson's Many Daddies

*Johnson cultivated relationships with a number of powerful men several decades his senior. This pattern continued for much of his life; Johnson would develop a relationship that extended beyond politics and into the personal lives of his "daddies." Scornful contemporaries derided his "professional son" routine, but he was genuinely close to each of his mentors, the more savvy of whom knew as well as Johnson did that his interest in them sprang from personal ambition. The table lists the men with whom Johnson established a surrogate son relationship.*

| Daddy | Position | Year relationship established |
|---|---|---|
| Cecil Evans | President, Southwest Texas State Teacher's College | 1927 |
| H. M. Greene | Professor of government, Southwest Texas State Teacher's College | 1928 |
| Alvin J. Wirtz | Attorney, lobbyist, New Dealer, political adviser | 1934 |
| Samuel T. Rayburn | U.S. Representative, D-Texas, 1913–1961; Speaker of the House, 1940–1946, 1949–1956, 1955–1961 | 1935 |
| Franklin Delano Roosevelt | President of the United States, 1933–1945 | 1937 |
| Richard B. Russell Jr. | U.S. senator, D-Ga., 1932–1971 | 1949 |

*Source:* Compiled by the author.

## Document 1.15    Letter from Johnson to Sam Rayburn, May 13, 1939

*Rep. Sam Rayburn, D-Texas, was a powerful member of Congress when Johnson was first elected to the House. They immediately developed a close relationship that Rep. F. Edward Hebert, D-La., described as a "mutual love for each other" (LBJL). Rep. Hale Boggs, D-La., recalled that Rayburn had a number of close relationships with young legislators. "He told me one time that this was one of the sources of his inner strength that kept him moving, that kept his enthusiasm up—his zest for the House and for living. . . . Most of these*

*[young] members thought about life the way Mr. Rayburn did, hard work-*
*ing, pragmatic individuals" (LBJL).*

House of Representatives, Washington, D.C.
May the thirteenth, 1939

My dear Sam:

Two years ago today you walked me down the Aisle of the House of
Representatives with me and stood with me while I raised my hand and
took my oath.

Some way, somehow, I felt your agreeableness to help me get inducted
indicated at that time you wanted me to get started right and to give me
a chance.

You've been very good to me, Sam, and have treated me like a Daddy,
and before I close up tonight, I want you to know how much you meant to
me on May the thirteenth, 1937, and how grateful I am to you for your
measured words of counsel and your thoroughgoing cooperation ever since.

Sincerely,
Lyndon B. Johnson

*Source:* LBJ Library.

## Document 1.16    Experiencing the "Johnson Treatment"
*These excerpts describe the famed "Johnson Treatment," the unique personal
style that Johnson used to persuade others in face-to-face conversations. Ben
Bradlee was the managing editor of the* Washington Post *during Johnson's
second term. Robert S. Allen was a syndicated columnist.*

*Benjamin C. Bradlee:* When Johnson wanted to persuade you of something,
    when you got the "Johnson treatment," you really felt as if a St. Bernard
    had licked your face for an hour, had pawed you all over. When he was
    in the Senate, especially as majority leader, it was like going to the zoo.
    He never just shook hands with you. One hand was shaking your hand;
    the other hand was always someplace else, exploring you, examining you.
*Robert S. Allen:* Humphrey told me how Johnson gave him pep talks and
    Humphrey demonstrated saying, "He'd grab me by the lapels and say,

'Now, Hubert, I want you to do this and that and get going,'" and with that he would kick him in the shins hard. Then Humphrey added, "Look," and he pulled up his trouser leg and, sure enough, he had some scars there. He had a couple of scars on his shins where Lyndon had kicked him and said, "Get going now."

Source: Merle Miller, Lyndon: An Oral Biography (New York: Putnam, 1980), 174–175.

## Document 1.17    The McCarthy Censure

Sen. Joseph McCarthy, R-Wis., gained national attention in February 1950 by charging that the State Department had been infiltrated by communists. Communist advances in Korea and China fueled public fascination with McCarthy's crusade. With a Republican majority in the Senate, McCarthy was able to become chair of the Government Operations Committee and its Permanent Subcommittee on Investigations. He then expanded his investigation, recklessly claiming that scores of high-ranking public officials were communists.

As leader of the Senate Democrats, Johnson was urged by his colleagues to end McCarthy's attacks. Recognizing the volatility of the situation, Johnson formulated a plan and waited for the right moment to enact it. He convinced John McClellan, D-Ark., a member of McCarthy's subcommittee, to push for televising a hearing to be chaired by Karl Mundt, R-S.D., that intended to look into some of the charges levied by and against Senator McCarthy. Johnson used his broadcasting contacts to ensure that the hearings would air on a major network, the American Broadcasting Company (ABC). Following the hearings, which thoroughly embarrassed McCarthy and turned the tide of public opinion, the final element of Johnson's plan was enacted. As the oral histories of two Senate colleagues, Hubert Humphrey, D-Minn., and Earle Clements, D-Ky., describe, Johnson worked to establish a bipartisan commission that would make a full report to the Senate on McCarthy's actions.

Humphrey: Johnson never seemed to show any friendship at all for McCarthy. Proper, as a senator, I suppose a certain amount of pleasant talk, but from the very beginning I sensed that Johnson looked upon McCarthy, first of all, as a flash in the pan, and, secondly, as a kind of maneuverer and a sort of political serpent. I remember he used to say—he had a saying that "if you're going to strike a snake with a hoe, you want to be sure that you get him with the first blow." And I got to know Johnson quite well about that time with McCarthy, because he used to think that many of those of us that were on the liberal side were picking at him, only to feed his grist mills. He used to warn me, he'd say, "Now look, he just eats fellows like you. You're nourishment for him. You keep away from him." Time after time he'd say to me, "The only way we'll ever get Joe McCarthy is when he starts attacking some conservatives around here, and then we'll put an end to it."

I remember one day that I was walking in the Cloak Room with Johnson and he went on over to the bulletin board, and there was an AP story where McCarthy had attacked Bishop Oxnam, the Methodist bishop. He said, "He has made a fatal mistake. Bishop Oxnam is a personal friend of Harry Byrd's. He had made a fatal mistake. He has attacked George Marshall, and he's a personal hero of Willis Robertson. Hubert, people like you, when he attacks you and your kind and your ADA-ers and the labor leaders, and so on, that's just what he loves. And if you fellows feed into that, you're just giving him fuel for his engine. Stay away. Don't let him get at you, and don't start to take him on." Because some of us had from time to time. But he said, "He'll go too far." And when he saw that story, he said, "That's the beginning. He's in trouble, because you can't attack Harry Byrd in this Senate. You can't attack Harry Byrd's friends in this Senate, not in this Senate. Mark my words, Hubert, he's in trouble." . . .

And when the time came, Johnson knew that the one thing that would trip McCarthy was to violate the code of the Senate. I remember him telling me point blank, he said, "He can attack people all over this country, but one of these days he's going to violate the rules of this body, he's going to violate the code of the Senate, and that's when he'll get in trouble, when he picks on the conservative friends and violates the rules of the Senate." And that's what he did.

Then of course Johnson got that resolution through for the appointment of that special committee to examine into charges against Joe McCarthy.

*Clements:* Ralph Flanders, from that granite territory in the New England states, when he filed [a censure resolution condemning McCarthy for actions contrary to senatorial traditions], had a good many early allies on the Democratic side. Nothing could have been handled any better, in my judgment. I don't think anybody in the Senate could have handled that as well as Johnson did. I wouldn't be surprised if you could look back into Joe's mental reflexes today that he never thought that Johnson would vote for that resolution. Of course, it was really the passage of that resolution that I think was occasioned in great measure by the fact that Joe abused the committee to the extent he did on the floor. I doubt if that resolution would have passed until he made the many misstatements that he did and the brutal statements that he did about some of those six people that were on the McCarthy committee.

*Gillette (interviewer):* Do you think that the selection of the Democratic members of that committee, then, was also of strategic importance, getting people who were unassailable?

[Interruption]

*Clements:* When Bill Knowland and Johnson met, I was present. They agreed that the two people that ought to be on that committee were maybe the two wise lawyers on each side of the aisle: one was Walter George and the other one was Gene Millican from Colorado. Johnson got Walter George to agree to serve provided that Gene Millican would serve. I was not present when Bill Knowland told Johnson that Gene Millican wouldn't serve, but in conversations with Knowland and in conversations with Johnson, I learned why Gene Millican wouldn't serve. It was not on account of any relationship he had with Joe McCarthy, because neither he nor Walter George had been in the squabble that many had been with Joe on one side or the other. Gene Millican was reputed to be one of the great lawyers of the Senate as Walter George was recognized as probably the peer of all others in the Senate. Gene Millican told Knowland that he could not serve and gave as his reason his health. He said he probably wouldn't last out that year, that he had an illness. He was then slightly stooped, and no one else in that Senate, to my knowledge, knew that Gene Millican was that close to departing this life. Well when he wouldn't serve, Walter George wouldn't serve. If I may state this as a belief, Gene Millican was the only person over there that was the equal or near equal to him. Then Johnson made an effort to get Dick Russell to serve, and Dick Russell declined and said, no, he did not want to serve on that committee.

*Gillette:* What were his reasons, do you know?

*Clements:* I cannot tell you. Dick Russell didn't give you all the reasons every time you asked him whether he could be for this or be for that or be for something else. He just told you that he would or he wouldn't. There were many members on the Democratic side that had publicly stated on the floor of the Senate their opposition to things that Joe McCarthy was doing. Of course, if you were going to have a result from the committee or recommendations from the committee, you wanted it just like you did, from an impartial jury. You wanted them to be as impartial as they could be. You just didn't find the lawyer that fit that on the Democratic side. And it is difficult on the Republican side. There were many lawyers over there on that side that just wouldn't fit the same impartiality posture, like a juror that had some known feelings in the case. He finally got Ed Johnson from Colorado, who was not a lawyer. He'd been governor of his state and was a person that was respected for honor and integrity, and he agreed to serve. And of course, that was his first accomplishment, and he sold Ed Johnson on serving on that committee. And Ed Johnson did not want to serve. I don't think there was a member in the Senate that wanted to serve—on either side—that was unbiased in the case that their judgment would be respected. Bill Knowland came up then in a meeting that I was with them, and he got Arthur Watkins from Utah, who was a good lawyer, who was an honorable man. I can't give you any basis for why the other Republicans were named, but both of them were men of competence and men who were respected in the Senate. That was Frank Carlson, who was from Kansas, whom Johnson had served with in the House. I had served with him in the House. Carlson and I were contemporary governors of our states and came to the Senate in the same election in 1950. The next person that Johnson picked that he thought would fit the assignment was John Stennis from Mississippi. I was in his office when he talked about John Stennis, and I said, "Well I can tell you one thing about John Stennis. John Stennis is going to take a trip in which he's going to inspect all of the bases under an assignment from Senator Russell as Chairman of the Armed Services Committee, and he's going to take his son with him. His son next year will graduate from Princeton University. John told me the other day that he was going to take this trip, and he thought that it probably might be the last time that he would ever have a month with his son, because when he got out of school that he never thought he'd ever have a month with him again." He was a natural choice, because he'd been a judge of their Circuit Court in Mississippi. When Johnson had that information, what would be the deterrent to John Stennis's serving—those were things that he liked to get, you know, and the same way with his activities on legislation—he twisted his arm. He took him away from his son on that trip through Europe and prevailed upon him through telling his natural thing—typical of him—that his country needed him and the Senate needed him, and he agreed to serve.

*Gillette:* Did Senator Stennis respond readily to this argument, or was there a long—

*Clements:* No! No, I can assure you that he didn't respond readily to it. But then he was down to where he needed one more. He and I met in G-23, which was the place that had been assigned to me as a Whip, on the third floor, and he said, " 'Well, we've run out." I said, "Well, I don't think so." I said, "Do you know, there's a person here with a unique background. He has served in every level of the judgeship of his state, from police judge to the Supreme Court of his state," and I said, "He just came in the first of this year." He said, "Who's that?" I said, "Sam Ervin. The reason I know that is because his brother was in the Congress when I was, in the House when I was and when you were, and he was my next-door neighbor, and he took his life. The committee met in North Carolina, and they named his brother as the nominee in the special election. He served, but he would not stand for reelection. But he served that time in there, and I got to know him." Since I had been a county judge in my home state, we would naturally drift into discussions about that, and he was surprised that I'd be a county judge in my home state and not be a lawyer. I remember telling him that in our state, you didn't have to have any more qualifications to be a county judge than you did to be a member of the Supreme Court. Johnson said, "But he' s just got here." I said, "I don't know of anybody here that has more qualifications that they could point to as being a fair person and being a person with legal knowledge than a person who had served on every level of the court in their home state." It struck him. Everybody was kind of at loose ends, you know, who the other one would be because he talked to Russell; he talked to many others, I'm sure, in the Senate. We telephoned Sam Ervin, and he came up to the office. One of the first things after Johnson had put the push to him, you know, about what his responsibility was to his country and what it was to the Senate—the customary line that he would use in the area of persuasion. Sam Ervin as proof of his sense of fairness, of openness, when you asked him if there was any reason he couldn't serve—had he ever said anything about McCarthy—he said, "Well, I wrote a letter, I recall, in answering somebody, and," he said, "I didn't commit myself against Joe, but the letter may appear to do it." So the letter was sent for, and the letter was brought over. We read it, and it was one of those letters where the person had criticized Joe very strenuously. I don't recall the details of that letter. But the letter that Sam wrote in reply was kind of an 'iffy' letter: "if what he said was so—" He only agreed with him on that basis "if this was so," which to me did not disqualify him in the least. Johnson immediately told him that he didn't think that barred him at all. I recall asking him how many times, when he was sitting as a judge or when he had practiced law and when he was interviewing a juror for his competence, that he had asked if he could give the man a fair trial. I said, "I just want to propound that to you: could you give him a fair trial?" "Oh, yes, yes. I could give him a fair trial." When he said that to Johnson, Johnson closed that door on him right quick, you know, and said, "You're the third member." And he told him it'd be Ed Johnson, and it'd be John Stennis, and it'd be him. I guess that's the end of the story.

*Source:* Hubert H. Humphrey, interviewed by Joe B. Frantz, August 17, 1971, LBJL; Earle C. Clements, interviewed by Michael L. Gillette, October 24, 1974, LBJL.

## Document 1.18    Meeting Ordinary People

*George Reedy traveled with Vice President Johnson as a special assistant to coordinate speechwriting and press relations. In this selection, Reedy comments on one of the highlights of Johnson's otherwise frustrating vice presidency— meeting and greeting ordinary people on a visit to a foreign country.*

In a tiny village outside Agra, for example, he stopped alongside of a well from which the Indian peasants drew water by hand in a bucket at the end of a long rope. Johnson pulled up a bucketful and then turned to the crowd with an impromptu speech. Through an interpreter, he explained that when he was a small boy in Texas, his family had been supplied with water out of a similar well. Graphically, he described the efforts it took to bring up enough for the family washing. The whole thing sounded corn-ball to a city boy like me until I realized that he had the crowd's rapt attention. Sometimes, he said, the rope would slip and burn the palms of his hands. Several of the villagers grinned and rubbed their palms together. Sometimes, the well would run dry and he would have to ride a donkey ten miles to the next water source. More grins from the audience. Even in translation, they knew—and appreciated—what this man was saying.

The talk ended with a description of the organization of farmers and ranchers in his district to form a rural electric cooperative on money borrowed from the U.S. government. I doubt whether the intricacies of the REA financing made much sense to the Indian peasants. But they got a message which may well have justified the whole trip. What they heard was that this powerful man understood the problems of poor people and was part of a government that did something about those problems.

*Source:* George Reedy, *Lyndon B. Johnson: A Memoir* (New York: Andrews McMeel, 1982), 24–25.

## Document 1.19    The Great Society Suffers

*Johnson recognized his dilemma in pursuing the Vietnam War and the Great Society simultaneously. While in retirement on the LBJ ranch, he said, "The kids were right. I blew it." (Herman Wouk, "A Choice for Freedom," Parade, October 19, 1980, 6). He also gave biographer Doris Kearns Goodwin this statement.*

I knew from the start that I was bound to be crucified either way I moved. If I left the woman I really loved—the Great Society—in order to get involved with that bitch of a war on the other side of the world, then I would lose everything at home. All my programs. All my hopes to feed the hungry and shelter the homeless. All my dreams to provide education and medical care to the browns and the blacks and the lame and the poor. But if I left that war and let the Communists take over South Vietnam, then I would be seen as a coward and my nation would be seen as an appeaser and we would both find it impossible to accomplish anything for anybody anywhere on the entire globe.

*Source:* Doris Kearns Goodwin, *Lyndon Johnson and the American Dream* (New York: St. Martin's Press, 1991), 251–252.

## Document 1.20    The Humor of Lyndon Johnson

*Lyndon Johnson acquired much of his political style from his father. The famed "Johnson Treatment" that he administered to members of the Congress was nearly identical to Sam Johnson's style of getting nose to nose with colleagues in the Texas State Legislature. The president's use of folksy humor to convey messages was also a talent at which his father had excelled.*

"A BIG 'OL LION IN OUR BACK YARD"
I hope I haven't exaggerated, but I may have. We had a little boy down in our country that ran out one day. He said, "Mama, come here quick, I saw a big 'ol lion in our back yard."

And the mother went out and there was the old family dog Rover standing there and she said, "That's not a lion, that's Rover. Now, you told a story. You go up there in that room, stay an hour, turn off the lights, and get down on your knees and beg to the Lord to forgive you for telling a story. I'll come back and get you in an hour."

She came back and said, "Did you say your prayers?"

"Yes."

"Did you ask the Lord to forgive you?"

He said, "Yes."

She said, "What did the Lord say?"

He said, "Mama, the Lord said he thought it was a lion too!"

Now, I don't know whether you see all these problems that face America. The priorities, the tinder boxes, the poverty, and the filth, and the education, and the disease, and the isolationism, and the matter of nationalism, and the protectionism. I don't know whether you see these lions or not. But, I hope you do, and I hope the Lord thinks they're lions too.

DEAD DADDY VOTING
Senator Johnson used self-deprecating humor to deflate the sting of an 87-vote win in his 1948 runoff for the senate. A man, Johnson would relate, came across a Mexican-American boy crying on the sidewalk in San Antonio (or El Paso, or wherever Johnson felt like placing him in the telling).

A man saw the little boy and said, "What are you crying about, Juan?" Juan answered, "My father came to town yesterday and he didn't come to see me." The man said, "Why Juan, you know your father has been dead for two years." Juan replied, "My daddy came to town to vote for Lyndon Johnson; why didn't he come to see me?"

*Source:* "The Humor of LBJ: 25th Anniversary Edition," audio recording, LBJ Museum Store; "The Man and His Humor Are Recalled," *New York Times,* January 25, 1973.

*Johnson and the Sikorsky helicopter campaign for the U.S. Senate, June 7, 1948.*

# CHAPTER TWO

# Campaigns and Elections

S ome presidents enter the White House through a succession of appointive offices or through gaining national exposure and executive experience as governor. Lyndon Johnson's path was a slow and steady climb up the ladder of national elective office. After learning the ways of Washington as secretary to Rep. Richard Kleberg and gaining experience as Texas director of the National Youth Administration, a New Deal agency, Johnson entered and won his first electoral contest, a seat in the U.S. House of Representatives, in 1937. Representative Johnson held his seat in the House until 1948, when, in his second try, he won a place representing Texas in the U.S. Senate. (He had been able to keep his post in the House after his first, failed, bid for the Senate because that 1941 race was a special election.) Johnson easily defended his Senate seat in 1954.

It is useful to look into Johnson's early campaigns for elements of continuity, as both indications of Johnson's character and clues to the kind of campaigns he would run for the presidency. Taken as a whole, they demonstrated two themes: effort and skullduggery.

## EARLY CAMPAIGNS: EFFORT AND SKULLDUGGERY

As a campaigner, Johnson knew that he might at times face disadvantages beyond his control. He might even be outsmarted, as he was in 1941, but Johnson was never outworked. When he entered the 1937 special election for Congress, he instructed Lady Bird to lock the screen door and never let him inside the house while it was still light outside. The instructions proved to be unnecessary. In this election, as in most of his others, Johnson worked himself to the point of exhaustion and illness, punctuating the campaign with admission to the hospital. On the long drives from one campaign stop to another, the candidate would sometimes try to sleep but typically could not. So as not to waste the time, he would study—committing to memory the names, faces, and details of the lives of the voters he had just met or would hope to greet in the next small town. By the end of the campaign, he knew an enormous number of the men and women of the Tenth Congressional District (see Document 1.1). Johnson's manic approach to campaigning never disappeared.

The skullduggery of Johnson's campaigns was not out of the ordinary for his time and place, but nonetheless it deserves to be mentioned. The tactics Johnson employed to win his House and Senate races included a variety of small-time dirty tricks and some more serious misconduct as well. The dirty tricks were the ordinary stuff of heated campaigning. The most significant such trick was brilliant in its brazen absurdity.

In 1948 Johnson's main competition for the Senate was Gov. Coke Stevenson. Stevenson, a reactionary conservative, had never publicly expressed a liberal sentiment. Despite this, Representative Johnson, running as a conservative Democrat, insinuated that his opponent had made a secret deal for the support of northern labor bosses. It was an outrageous charge, but Stevenson naively believed that because it was so outlandish he could ignore it. The resulting confusion over Stevenson's stand on labor helped Johnson fight to a virtual tie in the runoff for the Senate seat.

To win that runoff, the Johnson campaign went from trickery to alleged thievery. In corrupt precincts of south Texas, Johnson's supporters cast votes for persons registered to vote who had not voted while the polls were open; among them were deceased voters who had not yet been removed from the registration list. Only a high-risk legal maneuver on Johnson's part kept the dispute from being decided in federal court. Johnson's attorneys, with Abe Fortas in the lead, decided to appeal a federal district judge's decision to hold hearings on election fraud to an appeals court judge who was almost certain to rule against Johnson. That would leave Johnson with one final recourse, an appeal to the Supreme Court. On September 28, Justice Hugo Black ruled in Johnson's favor. Before the case was closed, however, prosecutors had entered enough testimony and evidence into the record to establish clearly that the Johnson side stole the votes that sealed the election. Of course, a more comprehensive inquiry might have shown, as Johnson insinuated at the time, that the Stevenson campaign had itself been stealing votes elsewhere.

A scholarly assessment of the record, by Dale Baum and James Hailey, concluded that the key to Johnson's victory was, in any event, not the infamous Ballot Box 13 in boss-controlled Jim Wells County, but Johnson's ability to mobilize his supporters to the polls. Although only an estimated 4,000 Texans who voted for Johnson in the first election sat out the runoff, more than 100,000 Stevenson voters did not vote in the crucial runoff election (Baum and Hailey 1994, 599).

There is no evidence that either candidate was personally involved in the vote fraud of 1948. There is evidence of Johnson's involvement in raising illegal campaign contributions in his first, unsuccessful, race for Senate. In 1942 the Internal Revenue Service, while auditing the Brown and Root Construction Company, became suspicious of hundreds of thousands of dollars in unusual attorney's fees and bonuses the company had claimed as deductible business expenses. The IRS, in following the trail of these expenditures, found that the money had been funneled to the Johnson campaign.

There were two big problems here. First, Brown and Root might be charged with attempting to defraud the government of taxes. Second, the Johnson campaign had clearly received huge sums of money at a time when the Corrupt Practices Act capped permissible expenditures to $25,000. Robert Caro, who has pieced the story together more completely than anyone else, believes that the personal intervention of President Franklin Roosevelt with the IRS quashed the investigation that might have ended Johnson's career (Caro 1982, 753).

## PREPARING FOR AND WINNING NATIONAL OFFICE

Even with the help of such friends as Franklin Roosevelt, it was difficult for Johnson to make himself a candidate for national office. It was an article of faith in the South that no southerner could be elected to the nation's highest office. None had been elected since Reconstruction following the Civil War. (Woodrow Wilson was born in the South but entered politics in New Jersey.) To overcome the southern handicap, Johnson began in the 1950s to moderate his record on civil rights.

First, he refused to sign the "Southern Manifesto," a pledge by 101 rep-

resentatives and senators to resist the 1954 Supreme Court decision inte-
grating public schools (*Brown v. Board of Education*). All southern senators except Johnson and two others signed the statement. In the eyes of
Johnson's Senate colleague from Oregon, Richard Neuberger, as quoted
by Robert Dallek in *Lone Star Rising*, it was "one of the most courageous
acts of political valor" he had ever seen. More to the point, it was a finely
calculated risk. Johnson could not help but chance alienating some of his
Texas constituency if he wanted, someday, to win nationwide.

Second, once he made it to the Senate, Johnson led Congress in passing the first civil rights bill in almost one hundred years. His leadership
of this bill, the Civil Rights Act of 1957, was not sufficient evidence to
some liberals that Johnson had truly overcome his reputation as just
another southern white on racial issues. Johnson had started out in politics as a hundred-percent New Dealer, but the New Deal had been virtually silent on racial issues. In Johnson's elevation to the Senate, he
railed against his national party's "so-called antilynching" bill, which, he
said, threatened to set up a police state in the South. Moreover, although
some commentators, such as the *New York Times*, credited Johnson for
having pushed Congress to take a good first step in 1957, others, including Eleanor Roosevelt, thought the bill a sham.

Liberals remained skeptical of a Johnson conversion on race issues, but
Johnson was genuinely determined to lead the South back into the mainstream of national life, as well as to win the presidency (Dallek 1991,
519). Neither task could be accomplished without overcoming the
South's legacy of racial division.

## THE 1960 ELECTION

Johnson's first attempt to win the presidency landed him in the vice presidency. His 1960 campaign for the Democratic presidential nomination
was an odd affair. Either Johnson was not as serious about this election as
he had been about every other one he entered, or he grossly miscalcu-
lated the importance that primaries had assumed in the nominating
process (see Document 2.1). If he was serious, Johnson seems to have
believed that his status with party leaders would ensure his nomination
from among unpledged delegates. Most states in the 1960s still did not
hold primary elections. Delegates were picked instead in party caucuses
dominated by state officeholders, and party leaders would barter the votes

of these delegates at the national convention. But in the television age, primary campaigns were critical tests of a candidate's broader appeal. Public opinion polls taken in 1960 show that Johnson's appeal was regional and never came close nationally to that of the junior senator from Massachusetts, John F. Kennedy (see Documents 2.2 and 2.3). Even party insiders, the group Johnson courted, tended to favor Kennedy as the more electable candidate (see Document 2.4). Senator Kennedy proved his ability to excite popular enthusiasm by winning every primary that he entered (see Document 2.5). At the convention, Kennedy won the nomination on the first ballot (see Document 2.6).

The night of Kennedy's nomination, in a confusing series of conversations between the Johnson and Kennedy campaigns, Johnson was offered the vice presidential spot on the ticket. Robert Kennedy, the candidate's brother, thought Johnson's selection was a mistake. He sometimes suggested to friends and reporters that John Kennedy had never really wanted Johnson on the ticket; Johnson was expected to say "no thanks" to the offer of the number-two spot. But John Kennedy had good reason to want Johnson by his side. Johnson provided regional balance to the ticket, and he had the legislative leadership experience that Kennedy was short on. Johnson also was considered more conservative than Kennedy. His place on the ticket thereby moderated the party's image with conservative voters. Most important, Johnson could help deliver Texas for the ticket, and Texas by itself brought twenty-four electoral votes in 1960.

While Kennedy toured the nation and defeated Richard Nixon in the first televised presidential debates, Johnson's campaigning was concentrated in the South, where he made a whistle-stop tour. In San Antonio, Johnson introduced his running mate in a rally in front of the Alamo. No one had to pass a religious test to die at the Alamo, Johnson declaimed in front of the shrine of Texas liberty. Therefore, no good southerner should think to deny Kennedy the presidency on account of his Catholicism, an issue that drew great attention during this campaign. (Kennedy would be the first Roman Catholic elected president and the only one to hold the office to date.) As Sam Houston Johnson understood, it was precisely his brother's ability to sell the ticket in the South that made him an invaluable running mate to Kennedy (see Document 2.7).

Despite anxiety about the outcome in Texas, which led Johnson to reach new heights of abuse against his loyal staff, the Kennedy–Johnson ticket beat the Richard Nixon–Henry Cabot Lodge team with the votes of Texas and twenty-one other states, in one of the closest popular elections in American history (see Document 2.8). The Democratic advantage in Texas was fewer than 50,000 votes, attesting to the importance of the Boston-Austin alliance in securing the presidency for Kennedy. Although both houses of Congress remained Democratic, the Republicans picked up two Senate seats and twenty-one seats in the House.

## THE 1964 ELECTION

In 1964 Johnson ran for a presidential term of his own. Heading toward the 1964 presidential contest, the first item of business that Johnson and his staff had to take care of was Johnson's ritualistic consideration of withdrawal. As his longtime aide George Reedy recollected, Johnson's insecurity led him to talk habitually of quitting at critical moments in campaigns throughout his career. The storm could come at any place—at Johnson's ranch, in his office, or in a hotel suite on the campaign trail. Leading up to the Democratic National Convention of 1964, Reedy feared that Johnson would make good on his threat and stun the Democratic convention by declining the nomination for president. Reedy was frightened because Johnson's worries—expressed to him after the convention had opened in August—seemed so heartfelt: Could he unite the nation; was he the right person for the job; would the liberals ever accept him (liberals, Johnson complained, were worse than cannibals, because cannibals do not devour their own); could he keep the conservatives from destroying all his progress in an antiliberal backlash; if Bobby Kennedy followed him into the White House someday, would Johnson even be remembered by history as more than a footnote to a Kennedy dynasty? These questions haunted him (Reedy 1982, 59–61; see also Documents 2.9 and 2.10). Whether he was serious or not, the first lady, Lady Bird Johnson, played a familiar role, calming her husband and reassuring him of her devotion. She also brought Johnson down to earth with the reminder that if he withdrew his friends would be devastated and his enemies overjoyed.

Once he accepted the party's nomination at Atlantic City, the president was finally, irretrievably committed to the race. In typical Johnson style, he now sought not just victory, but a landslide, to demonstrate the unity of the nation behind his presidency. "LBJ for the USA" screamed thousands of posters and billboards produced by the campaign. Even before the temperamental, tough-talking senator Barry Goldwater emerged as the likely

Republican candidate, the Johnson campaign laid claim to the calm and reasonable middle ground. Consensus and moderation were to be the themes of the Johnson campaign. As part of his campaign strategy, Johnson would spend much of the summer of 1964 in the White House, projecting a nonpartisan presidential image.

Picking up on the Kennedy–Johnson theme of 1960, Johnson's campaign sent the message that the Democrats had got America "moving" and had the legislative record to prove it. In just a few short months, the caretaker president had led Congress to declare war on poverty and to pass a new civil rights act along with a supply-side tax cut—passed just in time to accelerate the economy before the November election. President Johnson also took credit with the voters for his April 1964 success in brokering an agreement that averted a damaging strike in the railroad industry.

In foreign policy, Johnson delayed a final decision on the depth of America's commitment to the Vietnam War until after the election. With memories of the highly unpopular Korean War fresh in people's minds, Johnson sought to reassure voters that he would not send American boys to die in another Asian war. At the same time, Johnson led Congress in passing the Gulf of Tonkin Resolution in August 1964. The resolution demonstrated broad bipartisan support for the president's handling of the Vietnam War, effectively denying Goldwater the opportunity to launch a Republican assault on Johnson for his handling of the war.

## The Opposition

On the Republican side, a fight among factions of the party erupted in 1964 with name-calling invective. The conservatives of the West, called "primitives" and "barbarians" by their critics within the party, favored the crusty Senator Goldwater of Arizona. The moderate Republicans of the Northeast (tagged by the other side as "establishmentarians" or "liberals") wanted Nelson Rockefeller of New York. The barbarians, mostly businessmen from smaller cities and towns, made an uneasy alliance with more extreme conservative activists and intellectuals. Through control of party caucuses in key states, and with a surprise victory in the California primary, Goldwater gained control of a majority of delegates in June 1964. Moderate Republicans attempted to launch a stop-Goldwater movement to win loosely committed and unpledged delegates to an alternative candidate before the convention, but the Goldwaterites, intense in their convictions, won the nomination for Goldwater and his vice presidential candidate, Rep. William Miller, on the first ballot.

Goldwater's difficult path to his party's nomination exposed voters to charges made against him by leaders of his own party. At the Republican National Convention in San Francisco, Goldwater delegates tried to jeer off the stage New York governor Nelson Rockefeller—who had called the Goldwaterites "kooks." Even after Goldwater's nomination, Sens. Kenneth Keating and Jacob Javits of New York and George Romney of Michigan joined other Republicans who refused to endorse the ticket. Their opposition made it all the easier for Johnson's campaign to castigate Goldwater as a fringe figure, representing a mere faction of a fragmented party.

The Democratic candidate's campaign exploited the Republican disharmony, focusing on harmony as one of its core messages. The nation, not just the Democratic Party, was to get behind the Johnson administration. Could Goldwater unify the nation when he could not unite his own party? Moreover, Goldwater's vote against the Civil Rights Act of 1964 was portrayed as a vote against domestic accord. Johnson meant peace; Goldwater meant fighting. Goldwater's off-the-cuff remarks following his nomination, such as his suggestion that the United States "lob one (meaning a nuclear bomb) into the men's room of the Kremlin," provided the Johnson campaign with fresh opportunities to damage the Republican's image (Jamieson 1996, 179).

## Trouble in the Democratic Campaign

Early in the campaign, even before Johnson officially became the Democratic candidate, there were a few signs of trouble in his campaign, but these proved, in hindsight, to be augurs of Democratic disaster not in 1964 but in 1968 and 1972. First, Johnson's campaign managers saw summer protests and riots in a few northeastern cities as possessing the potential to stir a backlash against government aid for blacks. Fortunately for the Democrats, the number of such "Goldwater rallies" was small in 1964 and occurred only in one part of the country—the Northeast.

A second issue that emerged in 1964, but that ultimately did little damage to Johnson, was an alleged ethics and morals gap between the Democratic Party and mainstream America. The president's image as an uncouth country boy, publicized in national media stories in the winter of 1964, had caused Johnson anguish, but few people thought such habits as tearing around his ranch at high speeds in his Lincoln convertible or pulling his dogs' ears rose to the level of moral turpitude. Two other stories, however, that also broke in early 1964 as Johnson contemplated his upcoming campaign gave him reason for concern.

In March 1964 the *Wall Street Journal* raised questions about the fortune Johnson and his wife had amassed through investments in radio and television, a highly regulated industry. President Johnson had always maintained the fiction that the Johnson-owned radio and television stations in Texas were his wife's businesses and that he was merely an appreciative spectator of her tremendous success. In reality, Lyndon was very much involved in getting the original license that started the Johnsons on their way to a considerable fortune, and he had played a role in daily operations off and on since the beginning (Caro 1990, 87–89, 92–118). Still, the *Journal*'s reporting was just that, reporting, and no official investigations of alleged improprieties were begun.

In 1964, however, formal investigations of another matter involved the president. As Senate majority leader from 1955 through 1960, Johnson had worked closely with the majority's secretary, a wheeler-dealer named Bobby Baker. Baker, Johnson once said, was the first man he saw in the morning and the last man he spoke with at night. Baker was a genius at vote counting and getting things done in the Senate, but he was not so clever at hiding the way in which he improperly cashed in his Senate influence to make millions of dollars in shady business deals. When congressional investigators reported in July 1964 that Baker was guilty of "gross improprieties," the scandal threatened to tarnish Johnson's reputation, given how close everyone in the Senate knew the two to be. But the public did not know what everyone in the Senate knew, and because many senators were closer to Baker than they wanted to admit, no one was eager to contradict the president when he said that Baker was no protége of his.

The biggest story from 1964 that might have, but did not, derail Johnson's reelection prospects broke at an even more sensitive time, during the general election campaign following the party's summer conventions. In October, Walter Jenkins, a top White House and campaign aide who had been with Johnson for years, was arrested for homosexual conduct in a public men's room near the White House. Johnson was certain that Jenkins had been set up by Republican operatives. Whether he was the target of a sting operation or not, Johnson believed that Jenkins must have worked himself into some sort of homosexual sickness and should not be held strictly accountable for his actions. (The American Psychiatric Association at that time viewed homosexuality as an illness.)

Goldwater's advisers urged their candidate to exploit the arrest as a metaphor for the allegedly sick nature of Johnson's liberal agenda. But Goldwater, despite making some locker-room jests about the incident, declined to exploit the scandal to its fullest potential.

## How Johnson Won

Johnson's advertisements in the campaign struck hard and negatively at Goldwater. Jack Valenti, a Johnson all-purpose aide and former advertising executive from Houston, devised the winning strategy: "Our main strength lies not so much in the *for* Johnson but in the *against* Goldwater. Therefore, we ought to treat Goldwater not as an equal, but as a radical, a preposterous candidate who would ruin this country and our future" (Dallek 1998, 169). In keeping with this approach, Johnson declined to debate Goldwater, and the president's campaign staff put together several devastating negative television advertisements.

In the "Daisy" spot, which aired only once, on September 7, a little girl stands in a field of daisies, picking petals and counting (actually, miscounting) to ten. Her count is drowned out by a man's voice, counting down. As the count reaches zero, the little girl looks up, startled. The camera zooms in on her eye, which dissolves into the mushroom cloud of an atomic blast. Johnson's own voice adds the postscript: "These are the stakes—to make a world in which all of God's children can live, or to go into the dark. We must love each other, or we must die." After the advertisement ran, it was replayed endlessly—for free—by the nightly news (see Documents 2.11 and 2.12).

Shortly after it aired, Johnson sat in the Oval Office and listened with mock innocence as a group of dinner companions complained to him about the ad. The president called in Bill Moyers, who coordinated advertising for the campaign, and dressed him down in front of his visitors for having authorized the spot. Walking his presumably chastened aide from the room, Johnson lowered his voice and asked Moyers whether maybe the campaign should air it again. Moyers, who had understood the scene and played along, assured the president that, with all the free airtime the ad had generated, once was enough.

Other Johnson campaign spots blasted Goldwater for opposing a nuclear test ban treaty. Once upon a time, an announcer told viewers in this ad, while the screen showed a different little girl licking an ice cream cone, atmospheric testing of nuclear weapons had poisoned the environment. The test ban treaty had begun to lift these dangers, "But now, there is a man who . . . doesn't like this treaty."

Bumper stickers and posters contributed to a barrage of anti-Goldwater messages. A common tactic was to reverse a Goldwater slogan. "In your heart, you know he's right" became "In your heart, you know he might," or "In your gut, you know he's nuts." According to Goldwater's own pollster, Thomas Benham, writing for *Political Opinion Quarterly* after the defeat, by the end of the campaign fully one-half of voters thought of Goldwater as a man who "would act without thinking." Goldwater was perceived as an extremist, whereas Johnson had firm hold of the middle ground in the public's estimation of where the candidates stood (see Document 2.13).

President Johnson headed up his elaborate campaign operation of 1964 but did not want anyone to notice this fact. As Theodore White wrote, "At the White House, a pious innocence ruled. From the lowliest White House courtier to the President himself, a question on politics drew a reply of hurt and embarrassment, as if one were guilty of tasteless vulgarity" (White 1965, 255).

Hubert Humphrey, the vice president and vice presidential nominee, traveled extensively and exhorted the liberal base to remain committed to Johnson. Humphrey was deployed heavily in the Midwest, to counter Goldwater's only possible regional path to victory, which would combine that region with the South and West.

In the White House, Walter Jenkins, until his arrest, was a key manager in the campaign. Also helping organize activities were Jack Valenti, George Reedy, and Bill Moyers. These men, along with a dozen others, formed a "Committee of Sixteen," which met in secret during the campaign to determine strategy and assess needs. The process was chaotic but highly effective.

In October 1964 Johnson stepped out of the role of White House captive, too busy to campaign, and authorized a late splurge of spending. He also made some effective public appearances at this time. As Johnson's former aide John Roche told this author in a 1987 interview, "In October of '64, Johnson decided that the original scenario for the election, which was that he, Johnson, was going to go to Mt. Sinai and communicate with God while Humphrey ran against Goldwater, was not going to get more than 90 percent of the votes, so he threw himself into the campaign" (Roche 1987, n.p.).

Beyond widening his margin of victory, Johnson's personal appearances were designed to give the voters something to vote for rather than merely someone to vote against. Sometimes this meant taking a risk on the campaign trail. A high point in the new, active campaign came in New Orleans. At a fund-raiser, Johnson ignored his advisers, who wished him not to speak of civil rights in the South, and explained the linkage he saw between economic prosperity and racial equality. "If we are to heal our history and make this nation whole, prosperity must know no Mason-Dixon line and opportunity must know no color line," the president remarked. Departing from his text, Johnson told a story about an aging southern politician. "I wish I felt a little better," this man supposedly said one time. "I would like to go back home and make them one more Democratic speech. The poor old State [Mississippi], they haven't heard a Democratic speech in thirty years. All they ever hear at election time is 'nigra, nigra, nigra'" (Miller 1980, 398; see Document 2.14).

## THE THIRTY-SIXTH PRESIDENT

The 1964 campaign resulted in an overwhelming victory for Johnson and strong majorities in the newly elected Congress. The Johnson–Humphrey victory was record breaking in many respects. The Democrats recorded the largest vote, the greatest popular vote margin, and the biggest percentage win ever to that point in U.S. history. Johnson's electoral college margin was second only to that won by Franklin Roosevelt in 1936 (see Document 2.15). As was Johnson's habit, he interpreted the outcome in highly personal terms. Staying up all night to savor the victory, the president accepted congratulations from his friends and hosted a barbeque the next day at the LBJ ranch. "It was a night I shall never forget," he told his biographer, Doris Kearns Goodwin. "Millions upon millions of people, each one marking my name on their ballot, each one wanting me as the President. . . . For the first time in all my life I truly felt loved by the American people" (Goodwin 1991, 209).

In his inaugural address (Document 2.16), President Johnson reiterated themes from the campaign and elaborated a traditional theme of American civil religion. The American people, he said, had made a covenant "with this land." The American covenant comprised the elements of justice, liberty, and union. To renew this covenant in the 1960s required the American people to get behind their president with "toil and tears" to move toward the Great Society. "Is our world gone?" Johnson asked. "We say farewell. Is a new world coming? We welcome it—and we will bend it to the hopes of man."

## THE 1968 AND 1972 ELECTIONS

At the beginning of 1968, the Johnson presidency was in trouble. Public opinion in support of the war in Vietnam was crumbling, and the president's reelection prospects were highly uncertain (see Document 2.17). The administration had promised in the fall of 1967 that the end of the war was near; now no one could say how long the fighting would continue. Between 1965 and 1968 President Johnson had actually kept an unusually large number of his campaign promises (see Document 2.18), but he had often exaggerated and had not always told the complete truth. For these reasons, he suffered from a damaging lack of credibility. Even in domestic policy, the president had reason in 1968 to feel besieged. Congress was pressing for a choice between guns and butter, and a middle-class backlash was looming against the Great Society. If Johnson ran for and won reelection, what could he look forward to (see Document 2.19)? In the New Hampshire primary, March 12, 1968, the first of the season, Eugene McCarthy received 42 percent of the vote, to the president's 49 percent. McCarthy's showing exceeded expectations and demonstrated Johnson's vulnerability.

At the close of a speech on the Vietnam War, on March 31, 1968, President Johnson surprised the nation by declaring that he would not stand for reelection (see Document 6.1). His own party's internal divisions on the war and Republican candidate Richard Nixon's more hardline position left Johnson on the sidelines for much of the campaign. He may have hoped for a draft at the August 1968 Democratic convention, but instead the convention chose his vice president, Hubert Humphrey, to the backdrop of convention-floor confrontations over the Vietnam War, televised across the nation. On the streets of Chicago, antiwar protestors clashed violently with police. The president began to campaign vigorously for Humphrey only after Johnson became convinced that the Republican nominee, Richard Nixon, was sabotaging the prospects for a peace accord in the war in Vietnam.

The results were dispiriting for the Democrats. In an election almost as close as that of 1960, which Nixon had lost, this time he won, with 31,710,470 votes to Humphrey's 30,898,055. The candidate of the American Independent Party, George Wallace of Alabama, had campaigned on a pledge to overturn civil rights and jail radical agitators. His 9,446,167 votes represented the largest number to that date received by a third party candidate.

As a postscript to Johnson's history with campaigns and elections, 1972 bears a brief mention. In that election, the incumbent president Nixon, who was running for reelection, and former president Johnson traded threats against each other until intermediaries worked out a truce.

In 1972 Johnson was disappointed in the antiwar drift of his party and disgusted by the Democrats' quixotic infatuation with South Dakota senator George McGovern. McGovern was the Democrats' Goldwater, a man of personal integrity beloved by the more extreme members of his party but with no chance of appealing to the mass of moderate voters. Nominated by his party in the summer of 1972, McGovern was derided by the news media for his campaign pledge to issue a government check for $1,000 to every American. Republicans blasted away at McGovern's image as soft on extremism. He was, said his opponents, the candidate of the "three A's"—amnesty (for draft evaders), acid (LSD, a hallucinogen popular among hippies), and abortion. Publicly, Johnson stood by his party and its nominee, but privately, he supported Nixon's successful bid for reelection.

Johnson's support for Nixon in 1972 even survived a blackmail attempt. When Nixon got into trouble as a result of the Watergate break-in, which occurred June 17, 1972, shortly before the Democratic and Republican nominating conventions, the president tried to pressure Johnson to use his influence with senior Democrats to soft-pedal their investigation into the apparent burglary. To turn up the heat on Johnson, Nixon threatened to expose Johnson's alleged wiretapping of the Republican presidential and vice presidential candidates' campaign planes in 1968. (It is unclear whether the bugging actually took place. Wiretaps had been considered as a means of investigating Nixon's alleged efforts to foil Vietnam peace talks.)

As Nixon's chief of staff, Bob Haldeman, recorded in his published diary, Johnson, through his friend and former FBI liaison, Deke DeLoach, let Nixon know that Johnson would strike back by disclosing Nixon's attempts to scuttle the peace talks and other classified material (Haldeman 1994, 567). Most historians believe that those other materials related to Nixon's illegal receipt of large cash campaign contributions from the Greek military dictatorship in 1968, money that represented the Nixon administration's support for Greece's 1967 military coup.

Testifying to the cool, if cynical, professionalism of both presidents, Nixon and Johnson continued to enjoy a cordial relationship throughout the campaign and for the remainder of Johnson's life. This was, apparently, "just politics."

BIBLIOGRAPHY

On the prepresidential races of Lyndon Johnson, see Robert Dallek, *Lone Star Rising: Lyndon Johnson and His Times, 1908–1960* (New York: Oxford University Press, 1991) and *Flawed Giant: Lyndon Johnson and His Times, 1960–1973* (New York: Oxford University Press, 1998); and Robert Caro, *The Years of Lyndon Johnson: The Path to Power* (New York: Knopf, 1982) and *The Years of Lyndon Johnson: Means of Ascent* (New York: Knopf, 1990). On the 1948 Senate race, see also Dale Baum and James L. Hailey, "Lyndon Johnson's Victory in the 1948 Texas Senate Race: A Reappraisal," *Political Science Quarterly* 109 (fall 1994): 574–595.

One of the best accounts of the 1964 race is Theodore H. White, *The Making of the President, 1964* (New York: Atheneum, 1965). See also Rowland Evans and Robert Novak, *Lyndon B. Johnson: The Exercise of Power* (New York: New American Library, 1966). Kathleen Hall Jamieson, *Packaging the Presidency: A History and Criticism of Presidential Campaign Advertising*, 3d ed. (New York: Oxford University Press, 1996), looks at the Johnson–Goldwater contest in the context of the development of the modern, media-saturated presidential election.

Barry M. Goldwater, *With No Apologies* (New York: Morrow, 1980), provides the perspective of Johnson's opponent in the 1964 race.

Johnson's campaign book, Lyndon B. Johnson, *A Time for Action* (New York: Atheneum, 1964), compiles speeches by the candidate and shows how the president's campaign wished its man to be perceived.

On campaign advertising, see Edwin Diamond and Stephen Bates, *The Spot: The Rise of Political Advertising on Television* (Cambridge: MIT Press, 1984).

The inaugural festivities are covered in detail, along with useful historical essays, in *Threshold of Tomorrow: The Great Society, the Inauguration of Lyndon Baines Johnson, 36th President of the United States, and Hubert Horatio Humphrey, 38th Vice President of the United States, January 20, 1965* (Washington, D.C.: Program and Book Committee of the 1965 Presidential Inaugural Committee, 1965).

President Johnson's surprise announcement not to run in 1968 is discussed by Dallek and Caro, as well as by Johnson himself in *The Vantage Point: Perspectives on the Presidency, 1963–1969* (New York: Holt, Rinehart, and Winston, 1971). In "Drafting Lyndon Johnson: The President's Secret Role in the 1968 Democratic Convention," *Presidential Studies Quarterly* 30 (December 2000): 688–709, Justin A. Nelson argues that the president unsuccessfully conspired to engineer a draft-Johnson movement at the convention.

Other works cited in this chapter include Doris Kearns Goodwin, *Lyndon Johnson and the American Dream* (New York: St. Martin's Press, 1991); H. R. Haldeman, *The Haldeman Diaries: Inside the Nixon White House* (New York: Putnam, 1994); Merle Miller, *Lyndon: An Oral Biography* (New York: Putnam, 1980); George Reedy, *Lyndon B. Johnson: A Memoir* (New York: Andrews McMeel, 1982). For an earlier book, Thomas Langston, *Ideologues and Presidents* (Baltimore: Johns Hopkins University Press, 1992), the author interviewed a number of people who worked for Lyndon Johnson, including former White House special assistant John Roche (taped interview, Medford, Mass., June 19, 1987).

## Document 2.1    Kennedy's Strategy for Winning the Presidency

*Sam Houston Johnson, Lyndon's younger and only brother, took an active role in Lyndon's political career. In this selection, Sam points out that John F. Kennedy's strategy for winning the Democratic presidential nomination was superior to Johnson's.*

John F. Kennedy had already bagged the 1960 Democratic nomination for President at least a month before the convention. With a highly financed new-style machine that was operated with brutal efficiency by brother Bobby, he swept through primary after primary while Lyndon sat in Washington, still hoping his old alliances in the House and Senate would grab the prize for him in a tight convention.

He thought, for example, that Senator Tom Dodd would line up the Connecticut delegation. So did Tom. Neither of them knew that John Bailey, the state chairman, had put together a slate favoring Kennedy.

Several other senators and congressmen had given my brother the same innocent assurances: "Don't you worry about the people in my state, Lyndon—I'll have 'em for you when the time comes."

Bolstered by such ill-founded promises, Lyndon stayed away from the primary races, never entered a single one. He knew, as does everyone, that it's possible to win all the open primaries and still lose the nomination because most of the delegates are chosen in closed state conventions, usually under the tight control of party bosses.

Obviously, Jack and Bobby Kennedy knew the same damned thing. They weren't banking solely on those primary elections; they had their people all over the country, button-holing the party brass and thousands of delegates and potential delegates to those private conventions. But they also knew that a solid string of victories in those states that held open primaries would undoubtedly affect the attitudes of delegates to the closed conventions. After all, electability has to be a most important consideration in picking a candidate. So the Kennedys spent millions to prove JFK was electable.

*Source:* Sam Houston Johnson, *My Brother Lyndon* (New York: Cowles, 1970), 103–104.

## Document 2.2     Public Opinion, March 27, 1960

*Gallup pollsters asked likely Democratic voters to name their favorite candidate several times during the 1960 presidential race. Johnson's appeal peaked early, in a March 27, 1960, poll. As Kennedy entered and won primaries, Johnson's support eroded.*

| Candidate | Percentage favoring, March 27, 1960[a] | Percentage favoring, May 27, 1960[b] |
|---|---|---|
| John F. Kennedy | 34% | 41% |
| Adlai Stevenson | 23 | 21 |
| Lyndon Johnson | 15 | 11 |
| Stuart Symington | 6 | 7 |
| Hubert Humphrey | 5 | 7 |
| Edmund Brown | 3 | 0 |
| Other | 6 | 9 |
| None | 8 | 4 |

[a] Interviewing dates: March 2–March 7, 1960.
[b] Interviewing dates: April 28–May 3, 1960.

*Source: The Gallup Poll: Public Opinion 1935–1971, Volume Three: 1959–1971* (New York: Random House, 1971), 1660, 1669.

# Document 2.3    Johnson's Ratings in the South, March 16, 1960

*Only in the South did Johnson's appeal surpass Kennedy's. Johnson recorded his highest level of election-year south-ern support on March 16. Even Johnson's lowest level of southern support, from April 22, 1960, exceeded Kennedy's support.*

| Candidate | Percentage in South favoring (March 16, 1960)[a] | Percentage outside South favoring (March 16, 1960)[a] | Percentage in South favoring (April 22, 1960)[b] | Percentage outside South favoring (April 22, 1960)[b] |
|---|---|---|---|---|
| Lyndon Johnson | 35% | 5% | 30% | 4% |
| John F. Kennedy | 20 | 37 | 27 | 43 |
| Adlai Stevenson | 18 | 30 | 13 | 24 |
| Estes Kefauver | 6 | 6 | 0 | 0 |
| Stuart Symington | 4 | 6 | 5 | 7 |
| Hubert Humphrey | 4 | 5 | 6 | 7 |
| Other | 3 | 7 | 8 | 8 |
| None | 10 | 4 | 11 | 7 |

[a] Interviewing dates: March 2–March 7, 1960.
[b] Interviewing dates: April 28–May 3, 1960.

*Source: The Gallup Poll: Public Opinion 1935–1971, Volume Three: 1959–1971* (New York: Random House, 1971), 1658, 1664.

## Document 2.4     Presidential Choices of Democratic County Chairmen, June 22, 1960

*Early in the summer of 1960, it was clear that Johnson's casual assumption that party insiders would prefer him to the less experienced Senator Kennedy was mistaken. In a poll taken on June 22, 1960, Democratic county chairmen were asked: "As of today, which one of these men do you personally prefer as the Democratic candidate for President in 1960?" Two days later, on June 24, 1960, Democratic county chairmen were asked: "Regardless of whom you personally prefer, what is your best guess at this time as to who actually will get the Democratic nomination for President in 1960?"*

| Candidate | Percentage who personally prefer candidate | Percentage who think candidate will be nominee |
| --- | --- | --- |
| John F. Kennedy | 34% | 51% |
| Lyndon Johnson | 28 | 18 |
| Stuart Symington | 21 | 14 |
| Adlai Stevenson | 12 | 11 |
| Other | 4 | 1 |
| None | 1 | 5 |

*Source: The Gallup Poll: Public Opinion 1935–1971, Volume Three: 1959–1971 (New York: Random House, 1971), 1674.*

## Document 2.5     Democratic Presidential Primary Results, 1960

*Senator Kennedy swept every primary he entered.*

SCHEDULE OF PRIMARIES

March 8—New Hampshire: Kennedy wins 85.2 percent of the vote.
April 5—Wisconsin: Kennedy wins 56.5 percent.
April 12—Illinois: Kennedy wins 64.6 percent.
April 19—New Jersey: Unpledged delegates
April 26—Massachusetts: Kennedy wins 92.4 percent.
April 26—Pennsylvania: Kennedy wins 71.3 percent.

*continued*

**Document 2.5** *continued*

May 3—District of Columbia: Hubert Humphrey wins 57.4 percent.
  (Kennedy did not enter.)

May 3—Indiana: Kennedy wins 81.0 percent.

May 3—Ohio: Michael V. DiSalle wins 100.0 percent.
  (Kennedy did not enter.)

May 10—Nebraska: Kennedy wins 88.7 percent.

May 10—West Virginia: Kennedy wins 60.8 percent.

May 17—Maryland: Kennedy wins 70.3 percent.

May 20—Oregon: Kennedy wins 51.0 percent.

May 24—Florida: George A. Smathers wins 100.0 percent.
  (Kennedy did not enter.)

June 7—California: Edmund G. Brown wins 67.7 percent.
  (Kennedy did not enter.)

June 7—South Dakota: Humphrey wins 100.0 percent.
  (Kennedy did not enter.)

| Candidate | Primary vote totals | Percentage |
|---|---|---|
| John F. Kennedy | 1,847,259 | 32.5% |
| Edmund Brown | 1,354,031 | 23.8 |
| George McLain | 646,387 | 11.4 |
| Hubert Humphrey | 590,410 | 10.4 |
| George Smathers | 322,235 | 5.7 |
| Michael DiSalle | 315,312 | 5.5 |
| unpledged | 241,958 | 4.3 |
| Wayne Morse | 147,262 | 2.6 |
| Adlai Stevenson | 51,665 | 0.9 |
| Stuart Symington | 29,557 | 0.5 |
| Richard Nixon | 15,782 | 0.3 |
| Lyndon Johnson | 15,691 | 0.3 |
| Other | 110,192 | 1.9 |

*Source: Congressional Quarterly's Guide to U.S. Elections,* 4th ed. (Washington, D.C.: CQ Press, 2001), 1:346–347.

## Document 2.6   Democratic Party Convention Ballots, 1960

*The 1960 Democratic National Convention took place in Los Angeles, California. Senator Kennedy won the presidential nomination on the first ballot.*

| Candidate | Votes |
| --- | --- |
| John F. Kennedy, Massachusetts | 806 |
| Lyndon B. Johnson, Texas | 409 |
| (William) Stuart Symington, Missouri | 86 |
| Adlai E. Stevenson, Illinois | 79.5 |
| Robert B. Meyner, New Jersey | 43 |
| Hubert H. Humphrey, Minnesota | 42.5 |
| George A. Smathers, Florida | 30 |
| Ross Barnett, Mississippi | 23 |
| Herschel C. Loveless, Iowa | 1.5 |
| Edmund G. Brown, California | 0.5 |
| Orval E. Faubus, Arkansas | 0.5 |
| Albert D. Rossellini, Washington | 0.5 |
| Total votes | 1,521 |
| Number necessary for nomination | 761 |

*Source: Congressional Quarterly's Guide to U.S. Elections,* 4th ed. (Washington, D.C.: CQ Press, 2001), 1:620.

### Document 2.7    Accepting the Number-Two Spot

*Johnson's brother, Sam Houston, reveals some of the emotion involved in Johnson's decision to accept the number-two spot on the ticket.*

Like any other Presidential nominee, Kennedy could choose anyone he wished as a running mate. Lyndon certainly didn't expect to be chosen. He had rubbed a sensitive nerve when he reminded certain liberals that Kennedy had not voted to censure Senator Joe McCarthy, and the Kennedys weren't known as easy forgivers—certainly not Bobby. Neither is Lyndon, for that matter. Few politicians are. Yet, despite his brother's strong objections (which were well known), John Kennedy obviously realized he needed Lyndon Johnson. As a Catholic attempting to overcome an historical bias against people of his faith, he particularly needed someone to boost him in the Bible Belt of the South and Southwest.

When he was first approached, my brother was naturally reluctant. Why should he give up being majority leader to accept the frustrating do-nothing job of Vice-President? Sam Rayburn certainly didn't think he should. Nor did any of the powerful Southern senators like Dick Russell.

Finally, John Kennedy personally called on Rayburn to persuade my brother to accept, basing his appeal on the quite logical ground that "Lyndon would be the most qualified man for the Presidency if anything should happen to me."

Lyndon was still reluctant. He wanted to be damned sure, he later told me back at the ranch, that Kennedy really wanted him over the long haul and not just for the fall election. Then, much to the dismay of Brother Bobby, certain labor bosses like Walter Reuther, and a few Southern congressmen who preferred Lyndon in the Senate, my brother accepted the nomination.

*Source:* Sam Houston Johnson, *My Brother Lyndon* (New York: Cowles, 1970), 106–108.

## Document 2.8     1960 Election Results

*In one of the closest presidential elections in U.S. history, John F. Kennedy and Lyndon Johnson bested Richard Nixon and Henry Cabot Lodge. However, President Kennedy had difficulty claiming a mandate following such a close election, and his difficulties were magnified by his party's setback in other elections that year.*

|  | Popular vote | Electoral vote |
|---|---|---|
| John F. Kennedy (D) | 34,221,349 (49.71%) | 303 |
| Richard M. Nixon (R) | 34,108,647 (49.55%) | 219 |

|  | House | | | Senate | | | Governors | | |
|---|---|---|---|---|---|---|---|---|---|
|  | Old House | Gains/ losses | New House | Old Senate | Gains/ losses | New Senate | Old lineup | Gains/ losses | New lineup |
| Democrats | 283 | –20 | 263 | 64 | 0 | 64 | 35 | –1 | 34 |
| Republicans | 153 | +21 | 174 | 34 | +2 | 36 | 14 | +2 | 16 |

*Source:* Svend Petersen, *A Statistical History of the American Presidential Election with Supplementary Tables Covering 1968–1980* (Westport, Conn.: Greenwood, 1981), 113, 115; Lyn Ragsdale, *Vital Statistics on the Presidency: Washington to Clinton,* Rev. ed. (Washington, D.C.: CQ Press, 1998), 378–379; and *Congress and the Nation, 1945–1964: A Review of Government and Politics in the Postwar Years* (Washington, D.C.: Congressional Quarterly, 1965), 32.

**Document 2.9   Telephone Conversation between Johnson and George Reedy, August 25, 1964**

*Johnson was sufficiently insecure in the summer of 1964 to contemplate refusing the nomination of the Democratic National Convention in Atlantic City. In the conversation below from a White House recording, the president explains his reasoning to his close aide, George Reedy.*

*Pres.:* I am just writing out a little statement that I think I am going to make—either at a press conference here or go up to Atlantic City this afternoon to make, but I don't think we can tell them [the press] about it now. . . .

Here is what I think I am going to say to them—whatever number of months it is—forty months ago I was selected to be the Democratic Vice President. Because I felt I could best serve my country and my Party I left the Majority Leadership in the Senate to seek the Vice President's post, believing I could unify the country and thus better serve it. In the time given me I did my best. On that fateful November day last year I accepted the responsibility of the Presidency asking God's guidance and the help of all our people. In these nine months I have carried out as effectively as I could. Our country faces grave dangers. These dangers must be faced and met by a united people under a leader they do not doubt. After 33 years in political life most men acquire enemies, their ships accumulate barnacles, a time to acquire leadership about which there is no doubt—a voice that men of all color and sections can follow. I have learned after trying very hard that I am not that voice—nor that leader. Therefore—then I am going to say—therefore I suggest that representatives from all states of this Union selected for the purpose of picking a Democratic nominee for President and Vice President proceed to do their duty and that no consideration be given to me because I am absolutely not available. I think then we can just pick the two they want. We will then take the nominee and do the best we can to help him until January and then if he is elected why that is fine. I think he will be and he can have a new and fresh color without any of the old scars and I don't want the power of the bomb and I just don't want these decisions I am being required to make and I don't want the conniving that is required, I don't want the disloyalty that is around, I don't want the bungling and the inefficiencies of our people and all of them talk too much. . . .

Now is the time. I don't know of any better time. Apparently they've [his White House aides] got nothing else to do [besides "talk too much" to the press] and I am absolutely positive that I cannot lead the North and the South and I don't want to lead the nation without my own state, without my own section. I am very convinced the Negroes will not listen to me. They are not going to follow a white Southerner and I think the stakes are too big to try to compromise. . . .

I just want to be away from it and I know that a man ought to have the hide of a rhinoceros to be in this job but I don't have the hide of a rhinoceros and I am not seeking happiness. I am just seeking a little comfort once in a while—get away from it. I think I have earned it after 33 years and I don't see any reason why I must die in it.

*Reedy:* I think you have earned it too, Sir. I don't think it is the question of having the hide of a rhinoceros. It is the question of kind of rising above these things.

*Pres:* Well, I can't do that. I can't do that. I have a desire to unite people and the South is against me and the North is against me and the Negroes are against me and the press really doesn't have any affection for me. They require an understanding and I am unable to give it to them. . . .

I am not debating it. I know that. I know another Johnson [Andrew Johnson from Tennessee] sat in this same place and suffered more anguish than I am suffering, but I don't see any reason why I need to and I think it is a pretty peaceful period and I think they [the Atlantic City delegates] are there and they can work it out and I know that I am not the best in the country and I have faith in the system that they can select him so—they may not know I am not the best. If you have any thoughts, any way you can improve this. I am not going to make it very long. I am just about ready to sign it off, I will be glad to have them.

*Reedy:* I think your statement is as good as it can be made, Sir.

*Pres.:* Thank you, goodbye.

*Reedy:* Goodbye, Sir.

*Source:* LBJ Library.

## Document 2.10    Telephone Conversation between Johnson and Walter Jenkins, August 25, 1964

*Shortly after talking to George Reedy, the president spoke with another of his longtime aides, Walter Jenkins.*

*Pres.:* Here at the crowning point in my life when I need people's help, I haven't even got the loyalty here. Ken O'Donnell or Larry O'Brien. My Attorney General or anything like that so I just think—I don't see any reason why I ought to seek the right to endure anguish that I do endure. I want that right. People I think have a mistaken judgment. They think I want great power. What I want is great solace, a little love. That is all I want. . . .

I don't want to have to fight to carry Texas. I just don't want Texas to have to say yes to me any more. I have asked them the last time I want to ask them, and if you don't know how that feels just go out there and start asking someone to please give you a quarter for a cup of coffee. . . .

I do not believe, Walter, that I can physically and mentally—Goldwater has had a couple of nervous breakdowns and I don't want to be in this place like Wilson [President Woodrow Wilson suffered a stroke while in office] and I do not believe that I can physically and mentally carry the responsibilities of the bomb and the world and the Negroes and the South and so on and so forth. Now there are younger men and better prepared men and better trained men and Harvard educated men and I know my own limitations.

*Source:* LBJ Library

## Document 2.11    The Daisy Commercial

*The Daisy commercial aired only once, on Monday Night at the Movies, but became the most infamous advertisement of the 1964 election. A description of the spot, designed by Tony Schwartz of the Doyle Dane Bernback agency, appears below. And below that is a memo from Bill Moyers to Johnson, written September 13, 1964, pointing out that the commercial successfully painted Barry Goldwater as a reckless extremist.*

*Girl (counting leaves on a daisy):* 1, 2, 3, 4, 5, 7, 6, 6, 8, 9

*Man's voice (as camera zooms in on girl's eye):* 10, 9, 8, 7, 6, 5, 4, 3, 2, 1, 0
(bomb blast)

*Lyndon Johnson:* These are the stakes: to make a world in which all of God's children can live, or to go into the darkness. We must either love each other, or we must die.

*Man's voice:* Vote for President Johnson on November 3rd. The stakes are too high for you to stay home.


Mr. President:

While most of our radio-television campaign is to project you and your record, we decided—as you may recall—to run a few of the earlier spots just to "touch up" Goldwater a bit and remind people that he is not as moderate as his recent speeches want them to believe he is. The idea was not to let him get away with building a moderate image and to put him on the defensive before the campaign is very old.

*I think we succeeded in our first spot*—the one on the control of nuclear weapons.

It caused his people to start defending him right away. Yesterday Burch said: "This ad implies that Senator Goldwater is a reckless man and Lyndon Johnson is a careful man." Well, that's exactly what we wanted to imply. *And we also hoped someone around Goldwater would say it, not us.* They did. Yesterday was spent in trying to show that Goldwater *isn't* reckless.

Furthermore, while we paid for the ad only on NBC last Monday night, ABC and CBS both ran it on their news shows Friday. So we got it shown on all three networks for the price of one.

This particular ad was designed to run only one time. We have a few more Goldwater ads, none as hard-hitting as that one was, and then we go to the pro-Johnson, pro-Peace, Prosperity, Preparedness spots.

Bill Moyers

*Source:* Daisy Ad reference file, LBJ Library.

**Document 2.12     Correspondence between Sen. Everett Dirksen and the National Association of Broadcasters**

*Everett McKinley Dirksen, R-Ill., was Senate minority leader during Johnson's entire presidency. As a leader of the Republican Party, Dirksen defended presidential candidate Barry Goldwater from the Daisy ad, which painted Goldwater as a reckless extremist. In the correspondence below, Senator Dirksen tried to persuade the broadcast industry that the advertisement violated traditional standards. He addressed his grievance to the executive vice president of the National Association of Broadcasters, a trade association that sets broadcast guidelines and lobbies Congress on behalf of broadcasters.*

FROM EVERETT M. DIRKSEN TO VINCENT T. WASILEWSKI, SEPTEMBER 12, 1964

Dear Mr. Wasilewski:

No doubt you have seen the commercial sponsored by the Johnson for President campaign in which a little girl is interrupted from her daisy picking by an atomic bomb.

As a matter of decency and fairness this commercial seems to be in bad taste. I suggest this is in violation of your widely heralded Code of Ethics which is referred to by your stations with considerable frequency.

In light of this commercial, I would hope you would read again the Code of Ethics and ask yourself whether you agree that this is unfit for children to see and takes the level of political campaigning to a depth never before approached in the history of television.

It would be appreciated if you would see that copies of this protest reach your Board Members and that your Association be made officially and formally aware of its existence.

Sincerely,
Everett McKinley Dirksen

From Vincent T. Wasilewski to Everett M. Dirksen,
September 15, 1964

Dear Senator Dirksen:

This is in response to your letter of September 12, protesting a television commercial "sponsored by the Johnson for President campaign on the basis of taste."

While it is true that the NAB Television Code contains provisions with respect to taste in advertising, we have never considered the application of these provisions to political announcements. Because of the unique character of political advertising and, indeed, political campaigns, the imposition of Code restraints involves issues not present in other forms of television advertising.

Your letter is being forwarded to the Code Authority, which has the responsibility for administration of the Radio and Television Codes and for the recommendation of policy to the respective Radio and Television Code Boards. I am certain that this matter will receive very careful attention and review. However, I am sure you will agree that any decision in a matter of this kind can best be made at almost any time rather than the present, when we are in the middle of an intense, emotion-filled political campaign.

We appreciate your bringing the matter to our attention, and we will keep you advised of any action that may be taken.

In accordance with your request, I am sending copies of your letter and this reply to the NAB Board of Directors as well as our entire membership.

Sincerely,
Vincent T. Wasilewski

*Source:* Daisy Ad reference file, LBJ Library.

## Document 2.13     Public Opinion Poll, September 25, 1964

*Johnson's campaign to paint Barry Goldwater in a negative light was extremely effective. The Gallup poll published on September 25, 1964, reveals the public's perception of both candidates. The percentages indicate the portion of respondents who agreed with the stated description of the candidate.*

Which words on this card would you use to describe Lyndon Johnson and Barry Goldwater?

| LYNDON JOHNSON | | BARRY GOLDWATER | |
|---|---|---|---|
| Description | Percentage agree | Description | Percentage agree |
| Well-qualified | 63% | Intelligent | 33% |
| Experienced | 62 | Forceful, dynamic | 31 |
| Intelligent | 56 | Poor judgment | 2 |
| Good judgment | 46 | Not well-qualified | 25 |
| Honest | 42 | Honest | 24 |
| Forceful, dynamic | 36 | Reckless | 24 |
| Progressive | 35 | Well-qualified | 24 |
| Statesman | 29 | Just a politician | 24 |
| Attractive personality | 23 | Not for little man | 21 |
| Intellectual | 18 | Attractive personality | 19 |
| Just a politician | 18 | Experienced | 18 |
| Big spender | 13 | Statesman | 17 |
| Not for little man | 6 | Behind the times | 16 |
| Poor judgment | 5 | Progressive | 15 |
| Not well-qualified | 5 | Not sound | 15 |
| Not sound | 3 | Good judgment | 13 |
| Corrupt | 3 | Intellectual | 12 |
| Reckless | 2 | Big Spender | 5 |
| Behind the times | 2 | Corrupt | 4 |

*Source: The Gallup Poll: Public Opinion 1935–1971, Volume Three: 1959–1971* (New York: Random House, 1971), 1902–1903.

## Document 2.14    Campaign Speech, October 9, 1964

*On a campaign trip to New Orleans, Johnson spoke extemporaneously on civil rights and how racism had crippled the South's prospects for economic progress. The excerpt that follows is from the president's remarks at a $100-per-plate fund-raising dinner at the Jung Hotel.*

Whatever your views are, we have a Constitution, and we have a Bill of Rights, and we have the law of the land [the 1964 Civil Rights Bill], and two-thirds of the Democrats in the Senate voted for it and three-fourths of the Republicans. I signed it, and I am going to enforce it, and I think that any man that is worthy of the high office of president is going to do the same.

I remember Sam Rayburn telling me about a certain southern senator who came to him, and talked about how the South had always been at the mercy of outside economic interests. They exploited us. They had worked our women for five cents an hour, they had worked our men for a dollar a day, they had exploited our soil, they had taken everything out of the ground they could, and they have shipped it to other sections.

The senator said, "What a great future the South could have if we could just meet our economic problems, if we could just take a look at the resources of the South and develop them."

Wistfully, the old senator told Rayburn, "Sammy, I just wish I felt a little better. I would like to go back to ole ———," and I won't call the name of the state; it wasn't Louisiana, and it wasn't Texas—"I would like to go back down there and make them one more Democratic speech. The poor old state, they haven't heard a Democratic speech in thirty years. All they ever hear at election time is 'nigra, nigra, nigra.'"

*Source:* Merle Miller, *Lyndon: An Oral Biography* (New York: Putnam, 1980), 398.

## Document 2.15    1964 Election Results

*The 1964 election result for president was everything that Johnson might have wished for. The Democratic Party made big gains in the House of Representatives as well.*

|  | Popular vote | Electoral vote |
|---|---|---|
| Lyndon B. Johnson (D) | 43,129,598 (61.06%) | 486 |
| Barry Goldwater (R) | 27,175,770 (38.48%) | 52 |

|  | House | | | Senate | | | Governors | | |
|---|---|---|---|---|---|---|---|---|---|
|  | Old House | Gains/ losses | New House | Old Senate | Gains/ losses | New Senate | Old lineup | Gains/ losses | New lineup |
| Democrats | 258 | +37 | 295 | 67 | +1 | 68 | 34 | –1 | 33 |
| Republicans | 177 | –37 | 140 | 33 | –1 | 32 | 16 | +1 | 17 |

*Source:* Svend Petersen, *A Statistical History of the American Presidential Election with Supplementary Tables Covering 1968–1980* (Westport, Conn.: Greenwood, 1981), 249–250; Lyn Ragsdale, *Vital Statistics on the Presidency: Washington to Clinton,* Rev. ed. (Washington, D.C.: CQ Press, 1998), 378–379; and *Congress and the Nation, 1945–1964: A Review of Government and Politics in the Postwar Years* (Washington, D.C.: Congressional Quarterly, 1965), 59.

## Document 2.16    Inaugural Address, 1965

*On January 20, 1965, Johnson placed his hand on a bible held by Lady Bird and took the oath of office for the second time. After the swearing-in ceremony, Johnson delivered the following twenty-two minute inaugural address.*

My fellow countrymen:

On this occasion the oath I have taken before you and before God is not mine alone, but ours together. We are one nation and one people. Our fate as a nation and our future as a people rest not upon one citizen but upon all citizens.

That is the majesty and the meaning of this moment.

For every generation there is a destiny. For some, history decides. For this generation the choice must be our own.

Even now, a rocket moves toward Mars. It reminds us that the world will not be the same for our children, or even for ourselves in a short span of years. The next man to stand here will look out on a scene that is different from our own.

Ours is a time of change—rapid and fantastic change—bearing the secrets of nature, multiplying the nations, placing in uncertain hands new weapons for mastery and destruction, shaking old values and uprooting old ways.

Our destiny in the midst of change will rest on the unchanged character of our people and on their faith.

## THE AMERICAN COVENANT

They came here—the exile and the stranger, brave but frightened—to find a place where a man could be his own man. They made a covenant with this land. Conceived in justice, written in liberty, bound in union, it was meant one day to inspire the hopes of all mankind. And it binds us still. If we keep its terms we shall flourish.

## JUSTICE AND CHANGE

First, justice was the promise that all who made the journey would share in the fruits of the land.

In a land of great wealth, families must not live in hopeless poverty. In a land rich in harvest, children just must not go hungry. In a land of healing miracles, neighbors must not suffer and die untended. In a great land of learning and scholars, young people must be taught to read and write.

For more than 30 years that I have served this Nation I have believed that this injustice to our people, this waste of our resources, was our real enemy. For 30 years or more, with the resources I have had, I have vigilantly fought against it. I have learned and I know that it will not surrender easily.

But change has given us new weapons. Before this generation of Americans is finished, this enemy will not only retreat, it will be conquered.

Justice requires us to remember: when any citizen denies his fellow, saying: "His color is not mine or his beliefs are strange and different," in that moment he betrays America, though his forebears created this Nation.

## LIBERTY AND CHANGE
Liberty was the second article of our covenant. It was self-government. It was our Bill of Rights. But it was more. America would be a place where each man could be proud to be himself: stretching his talents, rejoicing in his work, important in the life of his neighbors and his nation.

This has become more difficult in a world where change and growth seem to tower beyond the control and even the judgment of men. We must work to provide the knowledge and the surroundings which can enlarge the possibilities of every citizen.

## THE WORLD AND CHANGE
The American covenant called on us to help show the way for the liberation of man. And that is today our goal. Thus, if as a nation, there is much outside our control, as a people no stranger is outside our hope.

Change has brought new meaning to that old mission. We can never again stand aside, prideful in isolation. Terrific dangers and troubles that we once called "foreign" now constantly live among us. If American lives must end, and American treasure be spilled, in countries that we barely know, then that is the price that change has demanded of conviction and of our enduring covenant.

Think of our world as it looks from that rocket that is heading toward Mars. It is like a child's globe, hanging in space, the continents stuck to its side like colored maps. We are all fellow passengers on a dot of earth. And each of us, in the span of time, has really only a moment among our companions.

How incredible it is that in this fragile existence we should hate and destroy one another. There are possibilities enough for all who will abandon mastery over others to pursue mastery over nature. There is world enough for all to seek their happiness in their own way.

Our Nation's course is abundantly clear. We aspire to nothing that belongs to others. We seek no dominion over our fellow man, but man's dominion over tyranny and misery.

But more is required. Men want to be part of a common enterprise, a cause greater than themselves. And each of us must find a way to advance the purpose of the Nation, thus finding new purpose for ourselves. Without this, we will simply become a nation of strangers.

UNION AND CHANGE

The third article is union. To those who were small and few against the wilderness, the success of liberty demanded the strength of union. Two centuries of change have made this true again.

No longer need capitalist and worker, farmer and clerk, city and countryside, struggle to divide our bounty. By working shoulder to shoulder together we can increase the bounty of all. We have discovered that every child who learns, and every man who finds work, and every sick body that is made whole—like a candle added to an altar—brightens the hope of all the faithful.

So let us reject any among us who seek to reopen old wounds and rekindle old hatreds. They stand in the way of a seeking nation.

Let us now join reason to faith and action to experience, to transform our unity of interest into a unity of purpose. For the hour and the day and the time are here to achieve progress without strife, to achieve change without hatred; not without difference of opinion but without the deep and abiding divisions which scar the union for generations.

THE AMERICAN BELIEF

Under this covenant of justice, liberty, and union we have become a nation—prosperous, great, and mighty. And we have kept our freedom. But we have no promise from God that our greatness will endure. We have been allowed by Him to seek greatness with the sweat of our hands and the strength of our spirit.

I do not believe that the Great Society is the ordered, changeless, and sterile battalion of the ants. It is the excitement of becoming—always becoming, trying, probing, falling, resting, and trying again—but always trying and always gaining.

In each generation, with toil and tears, we have had to earn our heritage again. If we fail now then we will have forgotten in abundance what we learned in hardship: that democracy rests on faith, that freedom asks more than it gives, and the judgment of God is harshest on those who are most favored.

If we succeed it will not be because of what we have, but it will be because of what we are; not because of what we own, but rather because of what we believe.

For we are a nation of believers. Underneath the clamor of building and the rush of our day's pursuits, we are believers in justice and liberty and in our own union. We believe that every man must some day be free. And we believe in ourselves.

And that is the mistake that our enemies have always made. In my lifetime, in depression and in war they have awaited our defeat. Each time, from the secret places of the American heart, came forth the faith that they could not see or that they could not even imagine. And it brought us victory. And it will again.

For this is what America is all about. It is the uncrossed desert and the unclimbed ridge. It is the star that is not reached and the harvest that is sleeping in the unplowed ground. Is our old world gone? We say farewell. Is a new world coming? We welcome it, and we will bend it to the hopes of man.

And to these trusted public servants and to my family, and those close friends of mine who have followed me down a long winding road, and to all the people of this Union and the world, I will repeat today what I said on that sorrowful day in November last year: I will lead and I will do the best I can.

But you, you must look within your own hearts to the old promises and to the old dreams. They will lead you best of all.

For myself, I ask only in the words of an ancient leader: "Give me now wisdom and knowledge, that I may go out and come in before this people: for who can judge this thy people, that is so great?"

*Source: Public Papers of the Presidents of the United States: Lyndon B. Johnson, 1965* (Washington, D.C.: U.S. Government Printing Office, 1966), 1:71–74.

---

## Document 2.17    The Thirteen Keys to the Presidency

*Ken DeCell and Allan J. Lichtman argue in* The Thirteen Keys to the Presidency *that victory in presidential elections can be predicted by answering thirteen simple questions (the "keys") about the leading candidates. The keys, they explain, "are stated as conditions that favor the re-election of the incumbent party. When five or fewer statements are false, the incumbent party wins. When six or more are false, the challenging party wins" (7). In their handling of the data, the keys correctly predicted every presidential election outcome since 1960.*

*In the table on the next page, Hubert Humphrey was awarded eight discrepant keys. In other words, on key issues relating to the candidates and the election climate that year, Humphrey's candidacy was at a disadvantage on eight of thirteen items. If Johnson had run instead of leaving things to his vice president, his candidacy would have been "better" than Humphrey's in only one of the key ways: he would have had the advantage of being not just the representative of the incumbent party but the incumbent president. That means Johnson would have been at a disadvantage on seven of thirteen items. From the perspective of this controversial but intriguing book, then, a loss for Johnson, had he not withdrawn from the race, could have been predicted.*

**Key 1 (Party Mandate):** After the midterm election, the incumbent party holds more seats in the U.S. House of Representatives than it did after the previous midterm election.

**Key 2 (Contest):** There is no serious contest for the incumbent-party nomination.

**Key 3 (Incumbency):** The incumbent-party candidate is the sitting president.

**Key 4 (Third party):** There is no significant third party or independent candidate.

**Key 5 (Short-term economy):** The economy is not in recession during the election campaign.

**Key 6 (Long-term economy):** Real per-capita economic growth during the term equals or exceeds mean growth during the previous two terms.

**Key 7 (Policy change):** The incumbent administration effects major changes in national policy.

**Key 8 (Social unrest):** There is no sustained social unrest during the term.

**Key 9 (Scandal):** The incumbent administration is untainted by major scandal.

**Key 10 (Foreign/military failure):** The incumbent administration suffers no major failure in foreign or military affairs.

**Key 11 (Foreign/military success):** The incumbent administration achieves a major success in foreign or military affairs.

**Key 12 (Incumbent charisma):** The incumbent-party candidate is charismatic or a national hero.

**Key 13 (Challenger charisma):** The challenging-party candidate is not charismatic or a national hero.

| | 1960 | 1964 | 1968 | 1968 (if Johnson ran) |
|---|---|---|---|---|
| Incumbent-party candidate | Richard Nixon (Republican) | Lyndon Johnson (Democrat) | Hubert Humphrey (Democrat) | Lyndon Johnson (Democrat) |
| Challenging-party candidate | John Kennedy (Democrat) | Barry Goldwater (Republican) | Richard Nixon (Republican) | Richard Nixon (Republican) |
| Discrepant keys | 9 — Incumbent loss predicted | 3 — Incumbent victory predicted | 8 — Incumbent loss predicted | 7 — Incumbent loss predicted |
| Result | Kennedy won | Johnson won | Nixon won | Johnson loses? |
| Keys: | | | | |
| 1 Mandate | F | F | F | F |
| 2 Contest | T | T | F | F |
| 3 Incumbency | F | T | F | T |
| 4 Third Party | T | T | F | F |
| 5 Short-term economy | F | T | T | T |
| 6 Long-term economy | F | T | T | T |
| 7 Policy change | F | T | T | T |
| 8 Social unrest | T | T | F | F |
| 9 Scandal | T | T | T | T |
| 10 Foreign/military failure | F | F | F | F |
| 11 Foreign/military success | F | T | F | F |
| 12 Incumbent charisma | F | F | F | F |
| 13 Challenger charisma | F | T | T | T |

*Source:* Ken DeCell and Allan J. Lichtman, *The Thirteen Keys to the Presidency* (Lanham, Md.: Madison, 1990), 310, 323, 334.

## Document 2.18    Fulfilling Campaign Promises

*Jeff Fishel tracked the number of campaign promises made by presidential candidates and the winning candidates' effectiveness in fulfilling their promises. The table below indicates the number of campaign promises that are dependent on both presidential and congressional action (P/CD = presidential/congressional dependent). Johnson's talent to get legislation passed through Congress is evidenced by the high success rate he enjoyed on promises that required Congress's involvement.*

| Legislative flow | Kennedy (1961–1963) | Johnson (1965–1968) | Nixon (1969–1972) |
|---|---|---|---|
| P/CD promises | 59 of 91 (61%) | 28 of 40 (70%) | 64 of 115 (56%) |
| P/CD proposed legislation passed | 48 of 59 (81%) | 25 of 28 (89%) | 39 of 64 (61%) |
| P/CD promises passed | 48 of 91 (53%) | 25 of 40 (62%) | 39 of 115 (34%) |

*Source:* Jeff Fishel, *Presidents and Promises: From Campaign Pledge to Presidential Performance* (Washington, D.C.: CQ Press, 1985), 38–39, 42.

## Document 2.19    Shall Not Seek Another Term

*On March 10, 1968, Lady Bird reflected on her husband's decision not to seek a second full term.*

Lyndon sent word for me to come in. . . . Earlier, I had asked him: "Suppose someone else were elected President, what could 'Mr. X' do that you could not do?" He said, "He could unite the country and start getting some things done. That would last about a year, maybe two years." I think that is what weighs heaviest on Lyndon's mind. Can he unite the country, or is there simply too much built-up antagonism, division, a general malaise, which may have the Presidency—or this President—irrevocably as its focal point?

*Source:* Lady Bird Johnson, *A White House Diary* (New York: Holt, Rinehart, and Winston, 1970), 638.

*President Johnson gives his first address to Congress after the assassination of John F. Kennedy, November 27, 1963.*

# CHAPTER THREE

# Administration Policies

L yndon Johnson's extraordinary ambition defined his presidency. He wanted to pass more legislation than his idol, Franklin Roosevelt. He wanted to lead America beyond affluence and transform it into the Great Society. He wanted to win a war in Vietnam (discussed in Chapter 4) and maintain America's advantage in the cold war. And he wanted all these things in a hurry. In Congress, Johnson had routinely cautioned overeager colleagues not to expect "heaven before breakfast." As president, Johnson recognized that the circumstances of his succession to the presidency, following President Kennedy's assassination, gave him a remarkable opportunity to throw caution aside, at least for a while, before his flurry of policymaking made him enough enemies to slow him down.

The members of Johnson's cabinet acknowledged the administration's domestic activism in their choice of a gift for their chief upon his retirement: a scroll listing the bills President Johnson signed into law. In foreign affairs as well, Johnson had a busy presidency, even leaving aside the war in Vietnam. American power was near its peak in world affairs in the 1960s, and the United States responded in the Johnson years to events and opportunities throughout the world.

## THE KENNEDY LEGACY

President Johnson's first order of business was to transform his predecessor's death into a political martyrdom. Johnson publicly interpreted Kennedy's assassination as a symbolic assault on the cause of peace and freedom and America's place in the world. Before the assassination, the atmosphere in Dallas had been poisoned by statements of hatred and reaction against Kennedy and his programs. It was as if hatred and reaction, rather than merely the bullets of an assassin, had felled the president. So that Kennedy's death would not have been in vain, the new president told a joint session of Congress that it had no choice but to take rapid action on the central items of the New Frontier, the Kennedy administration's domestic program. These items included a sizable tax cut to stimulate the economy, a civil rights act to prohibit discrimination in public accommodations, and federal aid for education.

In his 1964 State of the Union address, Johnson added to this list an "unconditional war on poverty" in America, based on initiatives that Kennedy's staff had been working on at the time of his death. In an oft-told tale, Walter Heller, chairman of the Council of Economic Advisers, briefed the new president shortly after the assassination on an antipoverty program he had been assembling for President Kennedy. Johnson gave the go-ahead to continue the effort, announcing in the process that it was precisely the sort of program that he was most interested in and that, frankly, Kennedy had been too conservative on such issues to suit Johnson's taste for aggressive liberal action.

## The Tax Cut

Johnson's *Economic Report of the President, 1965* stated that the goal of his economic policy was "to create a prosperous America" (Johnson 1965, 8). The federal government, in other words, would accept responsibility for the overall health of the nation's economy. This was a victory for the "new economics" or the "new activism" embraced by professional economists in the 1960s. At the foundation of this approach was a belief that positive federal action was needed to maintain or create economic demand. To manage demand for goods and services, the government could take two approaches. It could employ fiscal policy, using taxation levels or direct spending to influence demand. Reducing taxes, for instance, would increase the money available for spending and an increase in spending would boost the economy. The second route could be through monetary policy, whereby changes in interest rates, in the "price" of money, would indirectly affect how much businesses and individuals had available to spend on goods and services. The *New York Times* sang the praises of the

Kennedy-Johnson administration's preference for tax cuts to stimulate demand. In a four-month review of the tax reduction, the newspaper concluded, "It seems fairly clear at this juncture that the reduction had the effect hoped for" (Metz 1964, sec. 3, p. 1).

The specific proposal that President Kennedy had introduced in Congress was to reduce federal taxes, both personal and corporate, by $11 billion. The problem was that conservatives and liberals had been fighting over the bill in the Senate for almost a year. Republicans and conservative Democrats feared that tax cuts might create deficits, which would exert a drag on the economy. (The Republican Party of the 1960s was typically against tax cuts, just the opposite of more recent times.) Liberals approved of the new economics, but they were divided on which of the two approaches to use. Some wanted the government not to cut taxes but to spend more and in the process to expand government programs and services.

President Johnson took the side of the more pragmatic liberals, favoring tax cuts over government spending. Johnson's success at shaping the public's impression of him as a cautious steward of tax dollars could be seen in the way that newspaper cartoonists mocked the president's penny-pinching ways, such as his passion for turning off lights in the White House. He also employed his considerable persuasive powers on key members of Congress. In particular, the president worked hard to win the support of Senate Finance Committee chairman Harry Byrd. After a private session with the president in the White House, Senator Byrd insisted that he would have to vote against the bill to please his constituents, but he promised to work behind the scenes for the bill's passage.

The outcome of Johnson's efforts was a bill-signing ceremony on February 26, 1964, and a historic adjustment of the tax code, returning the economy, at last, to something closer to "peacetime" levels of taxation, after the high taxes of World War II and the early years of the cold war. The effects of the tax cut continue to be debated to this day. On the positive side, the lower tax rates seem to have stimulated economic activity (see Document 3.1). On the negative side, the president directed the nation back into war, after leading Congress to overturn wartime taxes; this added to economic growth, but the increase in demand ultimately increased inflation.

Whereas the economic results were mixed, the political success was overwhelming. The negative economic effects took time to materialize.

The political benefits were immediate. This was, after all, a centerpiece of the fallen president's stalled agenda. Its passage proved the new president's legislative leadership. When *Time* magazine named Johnson "Man of the Year" for 1964, it cited the tax cut as the prime example of how the new president had "worked constantly" in 1964 "to win business confidence for his Democratic Administration without losing labor's" ("Man" 1965, 14). Many years later, the fame of the Kennedy-Johnson tax cut was acknowledged by even conservative economists such as Herbert Stein, who termed its passage a "smashing victory" for Lyndon Johnson (Stein 1992, C1). The new president did not gloat over his victory, however, because it was only the beginning of what he intended to accomplish. Instead, he was careful at the bill-signing ceremony, and in talking to reporters afterward, to share credit with conservatives and Republicans so that he could use this success to build momentum for his next major move, which was civil rights legislation.

## Civil Rights

Johnson emphasized civil rights in his first major address as president (see Document 3.2). There could be, he said, "no more fitting eulogy" for President Kennedy than passing the stalled civil rights bill. After publicly conferring with leaders of the civil rights movement in the Oval Office, the president put old friends in Congress on notice that this time, unlike in 1957, when Senate majority leader Johnson engineered passage of a historic but toothless civil rights bill (see Chapter 1), there would be no compromising. The president personally warned Richard Russell, his former mentor in the Senate, that he had best get out of the way of this legislation because Johnson was going to beat him, and he did not want to embarrass his old friend.

In lobbying for the civil rights bill, Johnson repeatedly told the story of his cook, Zephyr Wright, and the indignities and slights she had suffered as she traveled from Washington to Texas and back again, ferrying the vice president's car through an inhospitable South. Johnson's greatest challenge again was in the Senate. He lobbied senators behind the scenes and in public statements, while letting members of Congress take tactical responsibility and credit for moving the legislation forward.

Everett Dirksen, a Republican senator from Illinois, at first opposed the civil rights bill. President Johnson assigned Vice President Hubert Humphrey to soften Dirksen up before calling the senator to the Oval

Office to meet with him personally. In the pivotal meeting, Johnson appealed to Dirksen's sense of national responsibility as well as his vanity. This was an opportunity, Johnson told him, to lead on a vital issue. Johnson also helped Dirksen see the potential advantage in the situation to the Republican Party. Moderate voters, Johnson reminded his old Senate colleague, were wondering if the Republicans were statesmen or obstructionists. Helping this bill pass would demonstrate Republican responsibility. After seventy-five days of filibuster on the Senate floor, Senator Dirksen rose to announce his support for the bill. With Dirksen's support, the historic vote for cloture—shutting down the filibuster—came on June 10, 1964. Before a national television audience, President Johnson signed the bill into law on July 2.

The civil rights bill would never have passed without Republican support, but it was a Democratic initiative and the president knew that it was politically risky. If anti-integrationists deserted the Democratic Party, it could realign the South and benefit the Republicans. That night, White House aide Bill Moyers asked the president why he appeared so glum following such a victory. Because, the president said, "I think we just delivered the Senate to the Republican Party for a long time to come" (Moyers 1988, C5).

The Civil Rights Act of 1964 put an end to the "Jim Crow" rules of the South, which for decades had mandated that blacks be kept separate from whites in using public transit, hotels, restaurants, movie theatres, phone booths, water fountains, and virtually every other public place. These local and state laws had inflicted daily humiliation upon black residents of the South and were the target of some of the most memorable demonstrations in the civil rights struggle. Rosa Parks's refusal to move to the back of a bus in Montgomery, Alabama, in December 1955, had spurred a citywide bus boycott and brought Martin Luther King Jr. to national prominence. Because segregation in public accommodations had for years been identified by the leaders of the civil rights movement as a vital issue, the 1964 Civil Rights Act was a landmark in governmental action on civil rights.

## WAR ON POVERTY

In this legislative onslaught, the War on Poverty came next. It was a subject dear to the president's heart. Johnson had worked all his adult life on policies that expanded opportunities. As the director of the Texas National

Youth Administration and as a member of the House of Representatives during the New Deal, he had enthusiastically preached the gospel of government as a helping hand.

Mainstream economists in the 1960s added their support to the War on Poverty as well. Johnson's Council of Economic Advisers endorsed Johnson's plan, not just for the benefits to be realized by the poor but because diminishing poverty would increase America's overall economic might. In a welfare state, after all, not only do the unemployed pay no taxes, but they also consume tax dollars that might otherwise go to more productive uses. By putting more Americans to work, the antipoverty program would increase the size of the economy, allowing Americans to produce more goods and buy more weaponry, thereby staying ahead in the cold war.

Despite this combination of emotional and intellectual support, waging war on poverty was potentially costly in political terms. The poor themselves were a weak political constituency. Not only did poor people lack the resources to promote their needs as a "special interest," but electoral turnout among the poor is also typically lower than among those who are better off. Moreover, Johnson knew that if the economy were to slow, middle-class voters might come to resent government attention to the problems of the poor. To minimize these risks, the administration took an inclusive approach in writing antipoverty laws. The War on Poverty was really a number of separate programs—the Job Corps, Volunteers in Service to America, adult and remedial education, rural assistance, Upward Bound, Head Start, and Community Action Programs—which potentially would reach into every corner of America and bring benefits to every electoral district. To force coherence onto this congeries of programs, the administration would create a new office to wage this "war," the Office of Economic Opportunity.

To build support for his antipoverty programs, President Johnson sought to keep the financial costs of his new initiatives low. First of all, the War on Poverty would not include any obvious transfer of income. Johnson did not mean to alleviate poverty simply by giving the poor a portion of the wealth of the nonpoor. Rather, he meant to achieve his goals by spreading opportunity so that the poor could create their own wealth. Second, funding was to be relatively modest at first, while the government studied its own programs and decided which should be expanded and which cut back.

To ease passage of the Economic Opportunity Act, President Johnson and his congressional liaison office recruited a conservative Georgia Democrat, Phillip Landrum, to sponsor the bill. Republicans, in desperation, sought to create division among the bill's sponsors by amending the bill to extend benefits to parochial school children. Johnson saw through the ruse. "Damn it," he remarked to the Speaker of the House in a recorded telephone conversation on May 13, 1964, "don't you realize the Republicans are promotin' all this stuff?" (LBJL).

The Republicans failed to stop the bill's progress, and on August 20, 1964, Johnson signed legislation creating the Office of Economic Opportunity and assigning to it responsibility for implementing the government's new antipoverty programs. The president may indeed, as Moyers has said, not have known exactly what this complex bill contained, but his motivation was clear: to make the poor forever *visible* in America (Moyers 1988, C5). This motivation was in keeping with the prevailing liberal wisdom of the 1960s, which held that poverty in the midst of affluence was not only an affront to national values but avoidable through the right combination of government programs.

One component of the War on Poverty—the Community Action Program (CAP)—created a host of problems for the Johnson administration. This initiative was to fulfill the law's requirement for the "maximum feasible participation" of the poor in the design and implementation of antipoverty programs in their neighborhoods. Poverty experts of the time believed that poverty was rooted as much in powerlessness as in a lack of money, and, through their local CAPs, the poor were expected to develop confidence as citizens and learn how to wield group power. In this way, they could claim for themselves some of the benefits traditionally won in American politics by organized interests.

The CAP program made for potentially shrewd but divisive politics because it was interpreted as an effort to link the president directly with poor people, especially poor blacks in major cities, bypassing mayors, the traditional power brokers in urban politics. Although blacks did not vote in as large percentages as nonblacks, in majority-black districts or in cities where the nonblack vote was divided, whoever could win the support of black voters had a definite hold on power. With a direct link between the White House and the urban poor, big-city mayors would enjoy less influence over Democratic presidents. Johnson and future Democratic presidents would not need the mayors to mobilize black voters. The programs of the federal government would instead bind black voters to the national party.

Unfortunately for the president, maximum feasible participation led to what Sen. Daniel Patrick Moynihan termed "maximum feasible misunderstanding," the title of his searching critique of the program. In some cities, such as Oakland, California, CAPs became dominated by radicals, whose rhetoric and activism alienated moderates. In many cities, the local political establishment sought to assume control over or discredit the new organizations, seeing them as a political threat. Yet President Johnson would not back off from his War on Poverty. In retirement, he expressed his conviction that the congressional "wolves who never wanted us to be successful in the first place would be down upon us at once" if the president acknowledged any failures in the program (Goodwin 1991, 291).

Johnson may have been right, but he was not right without a cost. The president's refusal to criticize any component of his antipoverty program created a credibility gap on domestic policy as the problems in his program became apparent to even sympathetic observers (Goodwin 1991, 292–293). Moreover, the successes of the administration's overall efforts to reduce poverty were obscured by the president's "see no evil" attitude and by his promise not just to diminish but to erase poverty.

Many of the specific antipoverty programs that the Johnson administration began, most notably Head Start, grew into highly successful programs with bipartisan support. But the idea of putting all antipoverty programs under one umbrella organization and the dream of eliminating rather than ameliorating poverty in the United States were casualties of the turmoil of the 1960s. No president since Lyndon Johnson has had the audacity to speak so grandly of making "war" on the conditions of life among the nation's poor. And although the composition of the poor has changed—with many elderly lifted out of poverty by the health care policies passed under the Great Society—the overall rate of Americans living in poverty, around 15 percent, has remained stubbornly resistant to government innovations.

## THE GREAT SOCIETY

Incredibly, eliminating poverty was supposed to be the easy item on the Johnson administration's domestic policy agenda. The goal of the Great Society was to move beyond economic policy and to build upon the potentials of the "postaffluent" society. The president announced the goal of creating a Great Society on May 22, 1964, in his commencement address at the University of Michigan (see Document 3.3). This speech, drafted by Richard Goodwin, with two sentences from a rough draft by author John Steinbeck, preserved at the president's insistence, proclaimed the president's goals in lofty terms. "For half a century we called upon unbounded invention and untiring industry to create an order of plenty for all of our people," the president proclaimed. "The challenge of the next half century is whether we have the wisdom to use that wealth to enrich and elevate our national life." "We have the opportunity to move . . . upward to the Great Society . . . a place where men are more concerned with the quality of their goals than the quantity of their goods." The term "Great Society" was picked up by the *New Republic* and the *Washington Post*, and it became the centerpiece of the Johnson domestic agenda.

To build the Great Society, the government would expand educational opportunities, rebuild America's cities, modernize the nation's transportation system, and preserve the nation's natural beauty. All these items were the subjects of task forces empanelled by the president to work in secret during the 1964 campaign, with small staffs and liaison officers from the Bureau of the Budget. After the election, President Johnson met at his ranch with aides to review task force initiatives, distilled in thick black binders.

## Federal Aid to Education

The highest priority was to be given to education. For Lyndon Johnson, aid to education served as a bridge between the leftover agenda of the Kennedy years and the Great Society agenda that he wanted as his legacy. The House Rules Committee and its chairman, Howard Smith, had killed President Kennedy's education initiatives. "No rules for schools" was the unofficial motto of Smith's committee. Normal House procedure declared that without a rule setting the terms of debate legislation could not move to the floor of the House. After the 1964 election, the White House worked with sympathetic House members to weaken Smith's hold on legislation.

The Democratic Caucus could, naturally, have changed the rules that the Rules Committee lived by at any time. The members of the party had not assaulted the Rules Committee in the past, though, because most members valued the job it did in protecting them against having to debate highly controversial legislation that could rupture the national Democratic Party. The 1964 elections, however, had brought to the House a large number of liberal Democrats more interested in reform than in party unity. In a vote of the Democratic Caucus in the House the majority party decreed a twenty-one-day rule. If, after twenty-one days, the House Rules Committee had still not granted a rule to a bill, the Speaker of the House could bring the bill to the House's attention by his own authority.

Johnson's 1964 task force on education, led by John Gardner, president of the Carnegie Foundation, suggested allocating federal funds for education on a to-pupil, rather than to-school basis. This would ease the central controversy over federal aid to education: sending government money to parochial schools. The government's money might flow to parochial schools under this plan, but the bill's supporters might protest that this was not the intent; the money simply followed the student to the school of his or her choice. The proposal that Johnson sent to the House called for $1 billion in aid, with grants focused on instructional and library needs. No federal money would directly support religious instruction, and though the neediest schools would receive the most money, almost 90 percent of American counties contained schools that would be eligible for some level of help.

The House passed the bill with difficulty, and the Senate, at the president's urging, avoided a possibly disastrous conference committee by voting upon the House's version of the bill as its own. The bill was signed on April 11, 1965, in a ceremony at Johnson's own primary school, with Katie Deadrich Cooney, his first teacher, at his side. Also on hand were former students from his tenure as a schoolteacher in Cotulla and Houston (see Document 3.4). Title I of the act, providing federal assistance for education of the disadvantaged, would grow tremendously over the years. By the mid-1990s the Department of Education was overseeing the spending of $1 billion in federal funds for more than six million educationally disadvantaged pupils each year. From passage of the bill to 1972, national government spending on secondary education rose rapidly as a percentage of the nation's gross domestic product (GDP). Even after significant retrenchment in federal education spending in the 1970s and 1980s, in no year did federal spending on education as a percentage of GDP fall to levels as low as those prior to 1966.

In November 1965 Congress also passed a Higher Education Act to provide money for libraries and for historically black colleges and universities, in addition to a vast expansion of the federal work-study program. By 1970 one-quarter of American college students received funds from the Higher Education Act.

Other Great Society legislation passed by the Eighty-ninth Congress, elected with Johnson in 1964, included initiatives in health, civil rights, immigration, housing, transportation and the environment (see Document 3.5).

## Health Care

The Democratic Party had been working toward the passage of a universal health care plan since the Truman administration. Opponents included the medical profession, represented by the powerful interest group, the American Medical Association. To break the stalemate in Congress over health reform, Johnson needed the support of Wilbur Mills, who headed the House Ways and Means Committee. Mills staunchly opposed federal health insurance, considering it a budget-buster. Johnson pressured Mills and other reluctant Democrats by inviting them to the White House on short notice. When they arrived, they found themselves sitting with the president to receive his plea to support Medicare, with television cameras recording their response. Similar tactics were employed to win the grudging acquiescence of the AMA. The result was Medicare and Medicaid, the former providing health benefits to the elderly and the latter providing health care to the poor.

Medicare and Medicaid, along with Social Security, are the pillars of the modern American welfare state. Over the next several decades, these health care bills brought about a significant change in the lives of older Americans. The poverty rate for persons age sixty-five and over dropped significantly, indeed below that for all other age groups. The fiscal consequences of Medicare, Medicaid, and Social Security are a serious concern for policymakers at the start of the twenty-first century, but all three programs—two from the Great Society and one from the New Deal—have widespread support from the American public and are virtually certain to continue in some form as a permanent legacy of the growth of government responsibility under Johnson and his mentor, Franklin Roosevelt.

## Voting Rights

The voting rights of African Americans were acknowledged in the Voting Rights Act of 1965. The civil rights movement had been working to publicize the denial of voting rights in the South for some years. Their efforts received the unwitting assistance of a repressive police force that turned against peaceful demonstrators in Selma, Alabama, in front of photographers and reporters, an event many would refer to as "Bloody Sunday."

President Johnson responded for the government before a national television audience in an address to Congress (see Document 3.6). Taking the chant of the civil rights movement as his own, the president promised "We shall overcome." There could be "no issue" involved in the cause of guaranteeing voting rights, the president said. It was a simple matter of protecting "human rights" and upholding the Constitution. The resulting law sent federal voting examiners to the South and led to a dramatic and rapid increase in black voter participation (see Document 3.7).

## Immigration

Immigration quotas had been introduced after World War I, in response to a change in the nation's ethnic demography brought about by several decades of rapid immigration from eastern Europe and fears that foreign-born radicals were instigating violence against the government. By the 1960s the inconsistency between the nation's restrictive immigration law and its cold war campaign to win the hearts and minds of the world's poor made the old law an embarrassment. The immigration law of the Great Society replaced national origins with skills and family ties as standards for determining an applicant's fitness for immigration. As a consequence of these changes in immigration law, the United States would experience a new wave of immigration that continued through the 1990s. In this latest increase in immigration, racial restrictions would not determine who was admitted and who was barred from entry. As a consequence, immigration from Latin America and Asia soon overtook immigration from Europe.

## Expansion of the Cabinet

In addition, Johnson expanded the cabinet to include the Department of Housing and Urban Development (HUD) in 1965 and the Department of Transportation the next year. The president named Robert Weaver to head the new cabinet-level housing agency, making Weaver the first African American to serve in a president's cabinet. In addition to demonstrating the president's interest in housing and transportation as important policy areas, the expansion of the cabinet reflected Johnson's belief in government activism and the responsibility of the national government to improve the lives of the people.

The Department of Housing and Urban Development pulled together a variety of loan guarantee and construction subsidy programs dating back to the end of World War II. The new department would oversee these programs and govern the nation's federally subsidized housing stock (the "projects"). Johnson had high hopes that the new department would invigorate the housing market but expressed disappointment in his memoirs about the effectiveness of the agency. "The moneychangers," he wrote, "have priced housing out of the market." (Johnson 1971, 331). Still, HUD's legacies are considerable, in both housing and urban development. HUD went on to make billions of dollars of loan guarantees and low-interest loans, and in the 1980s and 1990s the agency was a center of government experimentation, as Republican and Democratic HUD secretaries sought new approaches to the empowerment of poor urban residents.

The Transportation Department was also created primarily to bring together in one place work that was already being undertaken elsewhere in the government. Every president since Dwight Eisenhower, who persuaded Congress to fund the interstate highway system, had championed using federal funds to improve the nation's infrastructure, and President Johnson recognized the importance of planning for further growth. In addition to overseeing the federal role in highway expansion, the new department was given responsibility for establishing and implementing regulations covering air, water, and rail transport.

## Other Initiatives

Other Great Society legislation addressed air and water quality; guaranteed Vietnam veterans assistance in pursuing higher education, housing, health, and job benefits; and recognized the arts and academic communities by creating the National Endowment for the Arts and the National Endowment for the Humanities. In addition, it established the Legal Services Corporation to expand legal representation for the poor, and it enacted child nutrition programs and laws mandating rent supplements, truth in packaging, a teacher corps, tire safety standards, and protective caps for prescription drugs. In the opinion of Senate majority leader Mike Mansfield, speaking at the time, "Johnson has outstripped Roosevelt, no doubt about that. He has done more than FDR ever did or ever thought of doing" (Leuchtenburg 1990). This, of course, was music to President Johnson's ears.

Johnson knew that his most controversial proposals, such as voting rights, the War on Poverty, and aid to secondary schools, had to be passed first, and they were. Despite his loss of influence in Congress with the passage of time and the rising costs and controversy engendered by the war in Vietnam, he continued to win congressional approval of components of his Great Society long into his presidency. Even as a lame duck president, after announcing his decision not to seek reelection, Congress passed the Housing Rights Act; a health manpower bill; an act for assistance to handicapped children in secondary schools; consumer protection bills; an extension of the food stamps program; conservation statutes; vocational education legislation; and the bill creating the Woodrow Wilson Center for Scholars at the Smithsonian Institution.

## FOREIGN POLICIES

Looking beyond domestic policy, Johnson maintained pressure on Congress during his presidency for a number of initiatives reaching beyond the nation's borders, and indeed, into outer space. Johnson had been associated with NASA and its moon-landing program since the agency's creation in 1958. As president, Johnson continued to support the race to the moon, a campaign launched with fanfare under President Kennedy. On December 21, 1968, just days before Johnson left office, Apollo 8 was launched into lunar orbit—the first manned mission to reach, if not land on, the moon.

In foreign affairs, more traditionally understood, Johnson's biggest policy decisions involved the Vietnam War (covered in Chapter 4). But the president had other foreign policy concerns as well and used military force in a variety of places throughout the world to advance U.S. objectives. One of the first was an explosive situation in Latin America.

### Latin America

From 1930 until his assassination in 1961, Rafael Trujillo Molina was the dictator of the Dominican Republic. Following his death, an intense power struggle absorbed the nation and complicated U.S.–Latin American relations. In 1963 a coup deposed Juan Bosch, the recently installed president. In 1965 pro-Bosch rebels besieged the government and civil war erupted among Dominicans. Johnson worried that Bosch was overly sympathetic to the communists who were numbered among his supporters and assumed that Fidel Castro, the communist dictator of Cuba, was providing support to the pro-Bosch factions. So Johnson sent some 22,000 troops to the country to evacuate U.S. citizens and defend the nation's military government against leftist-supported rebels.

The president's penchant for hyperbole got him into trouble in the Dominican crisis when he claimed that "some fifteen hundred innocent people were murdered and shot and their heads cut off." The president phoned the U.S. ambassador and pleaded, "For God's sake, see if you can find some headless bodies" (LBJL). The ambassador was able to confirm the discovery of two.

Twenty-five U.S. soldiers were killed in action in the Dominican intervention. The public was impatient with the president's policy, but Sen. William Fulbright, chairman of the Senate Foreign Relations Committee, was outright incredulous and publicly questioned the president's statements justifying the troop deployment (see Documents 3.8–3.11).

Also in 1964 President Johnson faced a more direct challenge from Castro. When Johnson assumed the presidency, he ordered a halt to U.S. efforts to assassinate the Cuban dictator. At times, Johnson speculated that it was this clandestine effort that had led to the death of John Kennedy. Despite Johnson's efforts to ease U.S.–Cuba tensions early in 1964, Castro's troops cut off the water supply to the U.S. military base at Guantanamo Bay. President Johnson handled the situation quietly. Learning that contingency plans had been made for just such a provocation, Johnson ordered them into action. When Castro offered to restore water, the United States told him not to bother.

Later in 1964 the Johnson administration faced another problem in the region when anti-U.S. rioting in Panama led to the deaths of four U.S. soldiers. Again, it was widely believed that even if Castro's agents were not responsible, they would take advantage of the situation if it were not brought quickly under control.

In his oral history for the Johnson presidential library, Thomas Mann, the Latin America expert in the Johnson administration, speculated that the Panamanian government exploited U.S. anxieties about Cuba by secretly supporting the riots themselves while publicly blaming Castro for the troubles. The goal of the Panamanians, according to Mann, was to pressure the United States to renegotiate the treaty for control of the Panama Canal. Whether justified by events or not, President Johnson waited until after the November 1964 election and then instructed the State Department to seek a new treaty with Panama. Under the next Democratic president, Jimmy Carter, Panama and the United States signed a treaty in Washington, D.C., in 1974, which transferred the canal to Panamanian control in 1999.

The overall policy that the Johnson administration followed in Latin America was in line with how the president handled these incidents. He downplayed the Alliance for Progress, created under President Kennedy for the purpose of spreading democracy and prosperity, and emphasized the cold war stakes in Latin America. In remarks to U.S. ambassadors in March 1964, Thomas Mann articulated what came to be known as the Mann Doctrine. It might also have been called the Johnson Doctrine, for it encapsulated President Johnson's perspective on foreign affairs in Latin America. Economic growth and anticommunism were to be the top U.S. priorities in Latin America. The United States would support governments able to withstand or contain communists and to maintain order and, in the process, promote an orderly path toward economic development. This policy, according to critics, gave a green light to military coup plotters. Indeed, two weeks after Mann's remarks, a coup replaced the elected government of Latin America's largest country, Brazil. In less than twelve hours, the United States recognized the new government. The United States had, moreover, provided assistance to the leaders of the coup and had created military contingency plans to come to their assistance if necessary.

Elsewhere in South America, circumstances permitted the United States to be less brazen in demonstrating its priorities. In Chile, the United States gave considerable help to the centrist presidential candidate, Eduardo Frei Montalva, who won election in 1965 and implemented one of the region's more successful land reform programs. After Frei's assumption of power, increase in U.S. aid to Chile made it one of the world's leading recipients of U.S. aid, on a per capita basis.

The Johnson administration's Latin American policy, like its foreign policy in general, was clearly anticommunist. But it was not mindlessly so. At the time, Latin American governments were under pressure from communist revolutionaries. The administration's effort to contain and defeat communist guerrillas militarily was highly successful, at least while Johnson was in power. An important, if controversial, symbolic victory regarding this objective was achieved on October 9, 1967, when Bolivian special forces, trained by American Green Berets, captured and killed the revolutionary icon, Che Guevara.

## Europe

President Johnson inherited a changing European policy. To promote European integration, the United States under President Kennedy had backed a plan to create a nuclear Multilateral Force (MLF). By December 1964, however, the MLF's prospects had dissipated under the intransigence of various European powers, especially Great Britain. The North Atlantic Treaty Organization (NATO), a diplomatic and military alliance of the United States and the countries of Western Europe that sought to protect the West against encroachment from the Soviet Union, was also shaken early in Johnson's tenure by France's abrupt departure from NATO's military partnership. Charles de Gaulle's decision, based on his desire that France play an independent and forceful role in world affairs, effectively evicted NATO headquarters from Paris.

Johnson responded coolly to these events and kept his administration speaking with a single voice on European matters. NATO remained strong, and U.S. lobbying paid off when NATO adopted "flexible response" (see Chapter 4) as its own military strategy in 1967. Johnson also fought off NATO critics in the Senate who wanted to decrease the U.S. share of the financial burden of NATO. President Johnson, as he recounted in *The Vantage Point,* thought that the United States had no choice but to continue to pay a heavy financial price for European security. Maintaining American leadership in NATO ensured not only the strength of the U.S.–European alliance, important in the overall cold war strategy of the United States, but also served as a bulwark against the return of American isolationism. Without presidential leadership, Johnson wrote in retirement, the American people might retreat into isolationism "out of boredom, or frustration . . . lack of money, or out of simple foolishness" (Johnson 1971, 492).

## The Middle East

In the Middle East, the biggest challenge to the Johnson presidency came in the Six-Day War of June 1967 between Arabs and Israelis. U.S. policy had been cautiously pro-Israel since the state's creation in 1948. With the rise of Egyptian president Gamal Abdel Nasser and his Soviet-backed version of pan-Arabism, the United States had begun to work even more closely with Israel and with anti-Nasser governments, including Iran. Nasser's authorization of a Viet Cong mission in Cairo and his aid to Congolese rebels gave the United States additional reasons to work against him. The threat of nuclear proliferation in the Middle East provided the administration with another reason to work more closely with Israel. Israel, alone among Middle Eastern states, was reportedly developing such weapons. Johnson became the first U.S. president to send to Israel offensive military weapons, in large part to reassure that state of its security. Such reassurance, it was reasoned, would take the pressure off of Israel to arm itself with even more deadly munitions.

President Johnson and his foreign affairs advisers, in particular Secretary of State Dean Rusk, tried to avoid the Six-Day War. The decision, however, was not in their hands, and during the conflict, the United States could only seek to restrain the triumphant Israeli military. With stunning success, Israel occupied the Sinai Peninsula and the Gaza Strip, previously held by Egypt, and the West Bank of the Jordan River and East Jerusalem, previously claimed by Jordan. Israeli forces proved equally effective against the army of Syria, a Soviet-backed state. With Israeli troops fifty miles from the Syrian capital of Damascus, the Hot Line providing direct teletype communication between the leaders of the United States and the Soviet Union carried threats that the Soviets would send troops to protect that state. The United States responded by ordering the Sixth Fleet to sail toward the eastern Mediterranean. Ultimately, Israel agreed to claim from Syria only the strategically significant Golan Heights, and U.S. and Soviet forces stood down.

After this short but consequential war ended, U.S. problems in the region grew more severe. Soviet arms shipments flowed to Palestinians in Jordanian refugee camps. (Palestinians had been resettled into such camps in Jordan and Lebanon following the warfare that occasioned the establishment of the state of Israel.) Oil-rich Arab states, including Saudi Arabia, Iraq and Kuwait, imposed an oil embargo against the United States.

Fortunately for Johnson, this first Middle Eastern oil embargo failed before summer's end, and the president was able to mollify Arab resentment against U.S. support for Israel by increasing assistance to moderate Arab states. This was part of a policy described by National Security Adviser McGeorge Bundy as dividing "good Arabs" (especially the Saudis) from "bad Arabs" (Douglas Little, "Choosing Sides," in Divine 1994, 180). Because anti-Israel radicalism threatened the stability of moderate Arab states such as Saudi Arabia and its neighboring countries on the Arabian peninsula, these states were open after the Six-Day War to closer ties with the United States. The Johnson administration offered military aid to such states in return for their assistance in relaxing tensions in the region. Over the course of Johnson's last two years in office, his administration similarly increased the U.S. commitment to Israel, in exchange for a vague Israeli pledge not to "be the first" to "introduce" nuclear weapons into the conflict in the Middle East (Divine 1994, 181).

The legacy of Johnson's decisions on Middle East policy was a "three pillars" strategy. The United States would work through Israel, Saudi Arabia, and Iran, while the Soviets continued to exert considerable influence in Egypt, Syria, and within the Palestinian Liberation Organization (PLO), the dominant institution speaking for the stateless Palestinians. The United States thus placed Saudi Arabia and Iran in a better position to succeed Great Britain as the guarantors of regional stability in the Persian Gulf. (Britain had been the dominant imperial power in the Arab states since the end of the Ottoman Empire. As an example of its sense of responsibility in the region, when Kuwait was threatened with invasion by Iraq shortly after Kuwait became independent from Britain in 1961, the British sent troops to force Iraq to back off from an apparent invasion.) Israel was not entirely dissuaded from pursuing a nuclear option, but no other state in the region would seek to develop nuclear weapons until Iraq did so in the 1980s. Under President Johnson, U.S. financial aid and military supplies flowed more freely than ever before to the "pillars." U.S. policy in the region would continue along the lines laid out in the aftermath of the Six-Day War until President Jimmy Carter's historic role in bringing Egypt and Israel to the bargaining table.

## Nuclear Strategy

The United States and the Soviet Union had rattled their sabers against one another in the Six-Day War. If the United States had not pressured Israel to cease its battle against Syria, a direct confrontation between the superpowers may have ensued. This near war underscored the importance of the Soviet–U.S. relationship and the threat that war between the two superpowers would pose to the entire world.

President Johnson was aware that he was the one who would have to, as he liked to say, "mash the button" in the event of a nuclear war. The Johnson administration consequently worked to consolidate and compromise its way to a workable policy on nuclear arms control. The Joint Chiefs of Staff wanted the United States to commit itself to an ambitious antiballistic missile (ABM) program to counter a Soviet ABM effort that was being built around Moscow. The envisioned program would protect, first and foremost, the U.S. first-strike capacity, that is, it would defend its offensive weapons. ABM technology was then, as it remains today, of debatable effectiveness. Nobody imagined that even the best ABM technology could destroy all incoming nuclear missiles. The very uncertainty of an ABM defense led Secretary of Defense Robert McNamara to strongly oppose ABM. McNamara reasoned that the Soviets, to counter an extensive U.S. ABM effort, would simply be encouraged to deploy more and more offensive missiles, against which the United States would deploy more and more defensive missiles, and so on. As an alternative, McNamara favored adding to the U.S. offensive threat by placing multiple, independently guided nuclear warheads on U.S. strategic missiles (MIRV). McNamara's preference for offensive weapons reflected the curious logic of "mutual assured destruction" (MAD), which held that, as long as each side in the cold war could obliterate the other, neither would risk war. From this perspective, the vulnerability of the U.S. population made the nation more, not less, secure.

In January 1967 Johnson began a diplomatic effort to engage the Soviets in arms talks that would encompass ABM. In June of that year Johnson and Soviet premier Aleksei Kosygin met at Glassboro, New Jersey. Johnson's effort to negotiate with Kosygin was complicated, however, by a power struggle within the Soviet Union, pitting Kosygin against the Soviet first secretary, Leonid Brezhnev. Until a clear winner in that internal Soviet struggle emerged, Johnson was powerless to come to an agreement with the Soviets. Exasperated, and under pressure from the U.S. military, the president ordered his secretary of defense to develop a limited ABM defense. McNamara, though he believed ABM technology too primitive to offer a realistic deterrent, was loyal to his commander in chief and reluctantly gave the Pentagon the go-ahead. The United States would build a "light" ABM system, ostensibly aimed at protecting the United States against China, but in reality designed to stiffen U.S. missile sites and national command centers against a first strike by the Soviet Union, the nation's only true nuclear rival. Continued work on ABM defense took the issue out of the 1968 presidential race. Politically, Johnson had succeeded. The Republicans would not be able to decry a "missile gap," as the Democrats had in running against President Eisenhower in 1960.

In 1967 and 1968 Johnson kept up the pressure within his administration to develop a position on strategic arms limitations (SALT) that the Soviets might accept as a starting point for negotiations. Strategic weapons pose different military and diplomatic risks than do the missiles that make up an ABM defense. ABM missiles are designed to thwart incoming weapons. Strategic nuclear weapons are designed to attack from a great distance and are targeted not at weapons in flight but at sites in enemy territory. In July 1968 President Johnson signed a limited nuclear nonproliferation treaty, to stop non-nuclear nations from developing their own nuclear weapons, and announced at the same time the start of SALT talks. In a setback, the August 1968 Soviet invasion of Czechoslovakia forced the administration to cancel an October SALT summit. Then, and even after Richard Nixon's victory in November 1968, President Johnson continued to press for a summit meeting. Only President-elect Nixon's communication to the Soviets warning against an eleventh-hour deal with the Johnson administration finally closed the door for good on Johnson's efforts to enter the history texts as a peace president, not a war president.

## Africa

The entire region of sub-Saharan Africa was a footnote to U.S. foreign policy during the cold war, particularly in the 1960s. The period from 1957 to the mid-1960s saw the departure of Britain and France from their colonial dominion over numerous African states. The United States generally supported the independence of new African states, including Ghana, Congo, Uganda, and Kenya, but it did not become heavily involved in African affairs until later events (including the collapse of Portuguese imperialism, which occurred only in 1974) opened the way for the superpowers to test one another by supporting proxies in the region, without worrisome interference from European colonial governments. Moreover, in President Johnson's time there was no consensus in this nation to support a major effort on the part of the United States in Africa.

Johnson did ask State Department officials to devise a plan for Africa, similar to the plan that he had put forward for Vietnam: a TVA–style program for comprehensive development of power and industry. (The Tennessee Valley Authority, or TVA, was a massive government program begun during the New Deal. The program provided electrical power to one of the nation's poorest regions and, in the process, gave employment and encouragement to thousands.) After delivering an exhortatory speech on the subject in May 1966, President Johnson assigned the U.S. ambassador to Ethiopia, Edward Korry, the lead in devising a program. Korry found little support within the government for an African initiative. Throughout the Johnson administration, therefore, policy toward Africa remained ad hoc and reactive.

## India and Pakistan

On the Indian subcontinent, the United States took a more active role. The 1962 Sino-Indian War (between China and India) had given the

United States a chance to bring India, considered a nonaligned nation because of its neutrality in the U.S.–Soviet cold war conflict, closer to the United States. U.S. ties to India's rival, Pakistan, however, caused considerable trouble for U.S. diplomats. Pakistan was a signatory to the Southeast Asian Treaty Organization (SEATO) (see Chapter 4), and was the site of important U.S. intelligence gathering facilities. Pakistan responded to the U.S. initiative with India by establishing closer ties with Communist China, antagonist of both India and the United States.

During his vice presidency, Johnson had developed a warm friendship with Pakistani president Mohammad Ayub Kahn, but he proved unable to charm the Pakistani leader into relaxing his fears of India. When Pakistan invaded the disputed territory of Kashmir in 1965, igniting another in a series of border wars with India, U.S. officials grew discouraged enough to accept a Soviet offer to mediate the dispute. The Soviets had their own reasons to want the conflict brought under control. If India overspent in its war to the north against Pakistan, it would be weakened in the east against China. The Soviets wanted a militarily strong India to balance China, which the Soviets feared was gaining in military strength. In the midst of this confusing state of affairs, President Johnson rethought the historic U.S. commitment to both India and Pakistan. After all, had Vietnam not turned into a nightmare because of the indelible commitments made to South Vietnam by a succession of U.S. presidents?

At the least, President Johnson wanted the United States to get more for itself out of its relationship with India and Pakistan. When a food shortage in India reached catastrophic proportions in 1965, President Johnson instituted stringent controls on American food aid. Under Johnson, U.S. commitment to aid India would run for only two to three months at a time and would then be reviewed for renewal. This "short tether" policy went against the advice of the State Department and the Agency for International Development, but Johnson responded to their opposition by assigning the food program to the Department of Agriculture.

The administration's policy toward India and Pakistan had several consequences. First, the Indian government was forced to prioritize agricultural production. Second, the U.S. symbolic commitment to India was cast in a more modest light. In fact, the new Indian prime minister, Indira Gandhi, turned toward the Soviet Union for military assistance in response to the "short tether." With Pakistan, a less severe food crisis was resolved in the same manner, with similar results. The U.S. commitment to Pakistan was diminished but by no means exhausted, and Pakistan compensated for the cooling of its relationship with the United States by turning to China for supplemental military aid. The short-tether approach failed to get the administration more out of its relationship with India and Pakistan. Rather, it backfired and worsened U.S. relations with both India and Pakistan.

## Korea

The major issues between the United States and South Korea during the Johnson years were Korea's relations with Japan, South Korean troop deployments to Vietnam, and the continued threat posed to South Korea by the communist state of North Korea, a conflict that had erupted into the Korean War in the early 1950s. When Johnson assumed the presidency, South Korea had recently turned to civilian rule and shifted its economic policy toward the promotion of exports. The resulting boom in the Korean economy was a relief to the executive branch in the U.S. government, always conscious of congressional opposition to large foreign aid budgets.

The Johnson administration eased its own budgetary pressure for Korean aid by pressuring South Korea to establish normal relations with Japan, which would open the way toward Japanese aid to Korea. On the other two issues of U.S.–Korean diplomacy, the nations struck a relatively straightforward bargain. South Korea gave into U.S. pressure to send troops to South Vietnam, and the United States kept at least an equal number of U.S. troops on Korean soil to aid in protection against North Korean aggression. Over the course of the war in Vietnam, the Republic of Korea sent more than 300,000 soldiers, with as many as 48,000 at any one time. The South Koreans also successfully pressured the United States for civilian contracts in South Vietnam, such as services for trash collection in Saigon. By 1969 fully one-fifth of South Korea's foreign currency earnings came from civilian enterprises in South Vietnam.

A crisis with North Korea developed in the last year of the Johnson presidency, when, two days after a North Korean commando raid against the executive mansion in Seoul, the North Korean military took the *Pueblo,* a U.S. intelligence ship, and its eighty-two crewmen captive. One goal of the assault on the *Pueblo* may have been to drive a wedge between the United States and its Korean ally, which the incident did, as South Koreans came to resent the enormous attention the United States gave to its eighty-two crewmen, relative to the millions of South Koreans who lived under daily threat of attack. For eleven difficult months, while the North Koreans held their U.S. captives, President Johnson kept the hawks at bay in Washington and allowed time for a diplomatic solution to be found.

In the end, a farcical resolution was agreed to. The United States would issue a formal apology to North Korea. The North Koreans would distribute this apology internally, thus claiming a propaganda victory against the leader of the anticommunist world. The United States would simultaneously be permitted to repudiate its apology, and the coerced confessions of its crewmen, thus saving face among its friends and allies. Of course, the people of North Korea, a highly repressive communist state, would see only the apology and would never learn of the U.S. repudiation. All in all, it was a humiliating episode for the Western superpower and its beleaguered president.

## China

When Lyndon Johnson looked at U.S.–Chinese relations, he was aware of several things. He knew that the People's Republic of China supported the North Vietnamese in their war against South Vietnam and the United States. He knew that China had become a nuclear power in 1964. And he knew that China publicly proclaimed support for "wars of national liberation," thereby promising aid to communist rebels seeking to overthrow Western-controlled, pro-Western, or even neutral governments. Under this policy, China in 1964 assisted the would-be liberators of not just South Vietnam but Thailand, Indonesia, Cambodia, and Laos as well. Chinese policy toward Asian rebel factions was an important factor leading President Johnson to fear that if one Asian state fell to communist forces, others would soon follow (the "domino theory").

Early in 1965 Johnson therefore had reason for alarm when President Sukarno of Indonesia led his country out of the United Nations and into alliance with Beijing. (Until 1971 Taiwan, the noncommunist island nation to which the Nationalist Party supporters had fled when Mao Zedong's army took control of mainland China, held the "Chinese seat" in the United Nations.) Would Indonesia be the first domino to fall in Southeast Asia? The Indonesian crisis evaporated, however, in October when General Suharto put down a communist coup and forced Sukarno from power. In a nationwide reaction against the Indonesian communist party, tens of thousands, possibly hundreds of thousands, Indonesians were killed.

The Johnson administration is sometimes criticized for believing in the supposedly monolithic nature of international communism. But the tension in Chinese–Soviet relations was plain to see in the Johnson years. It only reinforced U.S. fear of China, however, as Chinese bellicosity looked worse when contrasted with the newly cautious and sometimes even cooperative behavior of the Soviets. Indeed, in the Johnson years, it seemed that the United States might have better prospects of breaking the Soviets cleanly away from China than vice versa. This was particularly true when Mao plunged his nation in 1966 into a decade of chaos in the Cultural Revolution. The rift in Chinese–Soviet relations paved the way for a relaxation of cold war tensions under President Nixon but did little to assuage President Johnson's difficulties in the Vietnam War.

During China's experiment with the militant, street-level communism that embodied the Cultural Revolution, members of the Red Guard looted and burned the British embassy in Beijing, symbolizing the futility that Western nations felt in attempting to deal rationally with Mao's government. The Senate Foreign Relations Committee promoted "containment without isolation" as an appropriate U.S. response. Essentially, this meant waiting and seeing what would happen next in domestic Chinese politics. Ironically, the Johnson administration's failure in the Vietnam War helped create a better atmosphere for the United States and China, which President Nixon capitalized on in his historic renegotiation of U.S.–Chinese relations.

In its relations with Taiwan, the United States continued to stand by its Nationalist (Guomindang) government. The Taiwanese government proposed broadening the war against Vietnam by attacking Chinese territory. Instead, the United States agreed to use Taiwanese personnel in covert operations and to deploy Taiwanese troops, dressed in South Vietnamese uniforms, to South Vietnam (just as some of the Chinese troops in North Vietnam wore the uniforms of their host country).

## Southeast Asia

On August 7, 1967, the Association of South East Asian Nations (ASEAN) was formed, bringing together Thailand, the Philippines, Malaysia, Indonesia, and Singapore. After Johnson's decision of March 31, 1968, unilaterally halting bombing throughout almost all of North Vietnam, the ASEAN nations began to work more closely with one another to forge a regional response to the war in Vietnam.

Thailand and the Philippines, in particular, warned the United States that if it backed away from its promises in South Vietnam, ASEAN might have no choice but to explore détente with China. By the end of the Johnson presidency, events in the Vietnam War, specifically the U.S. pullback from its original objectives, had weakened U.S. influence in Asia. (For a thorough discussion of the war in Vietnam, see Chapter 4).

BIBLIOGRAPHY

Johnson's domestic and foreign policies are analyzed in three volumes edited by University of Texas historian Robert A. Divine, *Exploring the Johnson Years: Foreign Policy, the Great Society, and the White House Years* (Austin: University of Texas Press, 1981); *The Johnson Years,* Vol. 2, *Vietnam, the Environment, and Science* (Lawrence: University Press of Kansas, 1987); and *The Johnson Years,* Vol. 3, *LBJ at Home and Abroad* (Lawrence: University Press of Kansas, 1994).

Johnson's domestic policy is reviewed as well in Barbara C. Jordan and Elspeth D. Rostow, *The Great Society: A Twenty-Year Critique* (Austin: Lyndon B. Johnson School of Public Affairs, 1986). Contributors include Great Society veterans, academics, and conservative critics of the administration. This volume is based on a conference held at the school in 1985. See also Marvin E. Gettleman and David Mermelstein, eds., *The Great Society Reader: The Failure of American Liberalism* (New York: Random House, 1967). This volume is especially useful for its combination of contemporary criticism and reaction with excerpts from the president's speeches and other administration sources. Another source is James McGregor Burns, *To Heal and to Build: The Programs of President Lyndon B. Johnson* (New York: McGraw-Hill, 1968).

For contrasting perspectives on the effectiveness of the Great Society, see Charles A. Murray, *Losing Ground: American Social Policy, 1950–1980,* 10th anniversary edition (New York: Basic Books, 1995); and John E. Schwarz, *America's Hidden Success: A Reassessment of Twenty Years of Public Policy,* rev. ed. (New York: Norton, 1988). See also Elba K. Brown-Collier, "Johnson's Great Society: Its Legacy in the 1990s," *Review of Social Economy* 56 (fall 1998): 259–277.

A 1990 issue of *American Heritage* featured an interview with President Johnson conducted by historian William Leuchtenburg in September 1965, "A Visit with LBJ: An Hour and a Half of Growing Astonishment in the Presence of the President of the United States, as Recorded by a Witness Who Now Publishes a Record of It for the First Time," *American Heritage,* May–June 1990, 49–50.

Also of note are Allen J. Matusow, et al., *The Unraveling of America: A History of Liberalism in the 1960s* (New York: HarperCollins, 1985); and Hugh Davis Graham's comprehensive civil rights political history, *The Civil Rights Era: Origins and Development of National Politics, 1960–1970* (New York: Oxford University Press, 1990).

On Johnson's foreign policies, see the Divine volumes as well as Warren I. Cohen and Nancy Bernkopf Tucker, eds., *Lyndon Johnson Confronts the World: American Foreign Policy, 1963–1968* (New York: Cambridge University Press, 1994); H. W. Brands, ed., *The Foreign Policies of Lyndon Johnson: Beyond Vietnam* (College Station: Texas A&M University Press, 1999); and John Lewis Gaddis, *Strategies of Containment: A Critical Appraisal of Postwar American National Security Policy* (New York: Oxford University Press, 1982).

Other works cited in this chapter include Doris Kearns Goodwin, *Lyndon Johnson and the American Dream* (New York: St. Martin's Press, 1991); Lyndon Johnson, *The Vantage Point: Perspectives on the Presidency, 1963–1969* (New York: Holt, Rinehart, and Winston, 1971), and *Economic Report of the President, 1965* (Washington, D.C.: U.S. Government Printing Office, 1965); "Man of the Year," *Time*, January 1, 1965, 14; Robert Metz, "Affluence Spurs a Big Debate," *New York Times*, June 21, 1964, sec. 3, p. 1; Bill D. Moyers, "What a Real President Was Like," *Washington Post*, November 13, 1988, C5; and Herbert Stein, "Myth and Math: How Cutting Taxes Trims the Truth," *Washington Post*, August 30, 1992, C1.

## Document 3.1    The Kennedy-Johnson Tax Cut

*Federal income tax rates rose significantly during World War II. Under the pressure of the cold war, they remained high through the 1950s. President Kennedy proposed the first sizable tax reduction since the war. In the document excerpted below, syndicated columnist Bruce Bartlett reviews the effects of the Revenue Act of 1964, commonly known as the Kennedy-Johnson tax cut.*

*Bartlett asks whether the tax cut actually increased the amount of money the government received from taxes, due to the stimulation of the economy. It is difficult to say, he acknowledges, because we cannot truly know what tax receipts would have been under different conditions. Nevertheless, in Table II he cites figures that suggest the tax cut helped raise revenues. Budget receipts during the years immediately following the tax cut were consistently higher than the government's economists thought they would be.*

*In Table III Bartlett displays data from another analysis of the tax cut, this time showing the the cut's effect on people in different income brackets. Relatively wealthy taxpayers were seemingly most influenced. In Table IV, Bartlett compares estimated revenues from taxes with actual government receipts. Revenues exceeded expectations, especially for more well-to-do citizens.*

It was not until 1963, under the leadership of President John F. Kennedy, that a major effort was made to bring tax rates down to peacetime levels. In a message to Congress on January 24, he asked for a reduction in the top tax rate from 91 percent to 65 percent and a cut in the bottom rate from 20 percent to 14 percent, along with other tax measures. This proposal was signed into law, essentially as Kennedy proposed it, on February 26, 1964, shortly after his death.

The first analysis of the economic impact of the Kennedy tax cut was made by the Council of Economic Advisors. In its 1965 Annual Report, the CEA estimated that the tax cut had increased the rate of real economic growth by 50 percent. In the absence of the tax cut, the rate of real economic growth (adjusted for inflation) would have been 3 percent. With the tax cut, it was 4.5 percent. Subsequent revisions, however, put the rate of real economic growth in 1964 at 5.8 percent—almost twice the CEA forecast of economic growth without the tax cut.

A 1967 estimate by Arthur Okun found that the tax cut increased GNP by $25 billion through mid-1965, and ultimately increased the level of GNP by $36 billion. A 1969 study of the tax cut by Lawrence Klein found a somewhat smaller impact on GNP—about $13 billion in 1958 dollars—but a larger reduction in unemployment attributable to the tax cut. According to Klein, the tax cut reduced the unemployment rate by between 0.5 and 0.8 percentage points below what it otherwise would have been.

Table I   Economic Indicators, 1960–1968

| Year | Real GDP growth | Unemployment rate | Inflation rate |
|------|-----------------|-------------------|----------------|
| 1960 | 2.4% | 5.5% | 1.4% |
| 1961 | 2.3 | 6.7 | 0.7 |
| 1962 | 6.1 | 5.5 | 1.3 |
| 1963 | 4.3 | 5.7 | 1.6 |
| 1964 | 5.8 | 5.2 | 1.0 |
| 1965 | 6.4 | 4.5 | 1.9 |
| 1966 | 6.5 | 3.8 | 3.5 |
| 1967 | 2.5 | 3.8 | 3.0 |
| 1968 | 4.7 | 3.6 | 4.7 |

*Source:* Bureau of Economic Analysis and Bureau of Labor Statistics.

In 1978, the House Budget Committee and the Joint Economic Committee of Congress contracted with Data Resources, Inc. (DRI) and Wharton Econometric Forecasting Associates to estimate the impact of the Kennedy tax cut. The Wharton study found real GNP (in 1972 dollars) to be $8.2 billion higher in 1964, $18.5 billion higher in 1965, $20.2 billion higher in 1966, and $19.4 billion higher in 1967. The unemployment rate was found to be 0.4 percent lower the first year, 0.9 percent lower the second year, and 1.1 percent lower the third and fourth years. The DRI study estimated real GNP growth to be 0.8 percent higher in 1964, 1.3 percent higher in 1965, 1.3 percent higher in 1966, and 0.9 percent higher in 1967. The unemployment rate was found to have been 0.2 percent lower in 1964, 0.5 percent lower in 1965 and 1966, and 0.4 percent lower in 1967.

One limitation of these studies is that they all essentially employ a Keynesian framework for their analysis. That is to say, they analyzed the effect of the tax largely through its impact on aggregate demand, rather than supply. Professor Paul Evans of the University of Houston, however, has done a study that argues that the Kennedy tax cut did not stimulate consumption much, if at all. In short, there was no demand-side effect. The main impact, according to Evans, was on aggregate supply. To the extent that demand was stimulated, it was due to the effects of a looser monetary policy, rather than fiscal policy.

**Table II  Estimated and Actual Budget Receipts, 1964–1967 (billions of dollars)**

| Year | Estimate | Actual | Difference |
|------|----------|--------|------------|
| 1964 | $109.3 | $112.7 | +3.4 |
| 1965 | 115.9 | 116.8 | +0.9 |
| 1966 | 119.8 | 130.9 | +11.1 |
| 1967 | 141.4 | 149.6 | +8.2 |

*Source:* Congressional Budget Office, *A Review of the Accuracy of Treasury Revenue Forecasts, 1963–1978* (February 1981), 4.

**Table III    Revenues from High-Income Taxpayers, 1961–1966 (millions of dollars)**

| Income class | 1961 | 1962 | 1963 | 1964 | 1965 | 1966 |
|---|---|---|---|---|---|---|
| $100,000 to $500,000 | 1,970 | 1,740 | 1,890 | 2,220 | 2,752 | 3,176 |
| $500,000 to $1 million | 297 | 243 | 243 | 306 | 408 | 457 |
| Over $1 million | 342 | 311 | 427 | 603 | 590 | 326 |

*Source:* Michael K. Evans, "Taxes, Inflation and the Rich," *Wall Street Journal,* August 7, 1978.

**Table IV    Estimated vs. Actual Revenues by Income Class, 1965 (millions of dollars)**

| Income class[a] | Estimated | Actual | Difference | Percent |
|---|---|---|---|---|
| $0–5 | 4,374 | 4,337 | –37 | –0.8% |
| 5–10 | 13,213 | 15,434 | 2,221 | 16.8 |
| 10–15 | 6,845 | 10,711 | 3,886 | 56.5 |
| 15–20 | 2,474 | 4,188 | 1,714 | 69.3 |
| 20–50 | 5,104 | 7,440 | 2,336 | 45.8 |
| 50–100 | 2,311 | 3,654 | 1,343 | 58.1 |
| 100+ | 2,086 | 3,764 | 1,678 | 80.4 |

[a]Adjusted gross income in thousands of dollars.

*Source:* Estimated revenues calculated from Joseph A. Pechman, "Evaluation of Recent Tax Legislation: Individual Income Tax Provisions of the Revenue Act of 1964," *Journal of Finance* 20 (May 1965): 268. Actual revenues are from Internal Revenue Service, *Statistics of Income—1965,* Individual Income Tax Returns, 8.

*Source:* Bruce R. Bartlett, "The Impact of Federal Tax Cuts on Economic Growth," April 1999, The Lexington Institute, April 3, 2002, http://www.lexingtoninstitute.org/whatworks/whtwrks1.htm.

## Document 3.2    First Address to a Joint Session of Congress, November 27, 1963

*In President Kennedy's inaugural address, he asked the nation to "let us begin" building a stronger America and a peaceful world. In Johnson's first address to Congress, he urged "let us continue" the work Kennedy had begun. The following speech was the first step of Johnson's masterly political maneuvering that resulted in the passage of the Kennedy-Johnson tax cut and the formerly stalled Civil Rights Act.*

Mr. Speaker, Mr. President, Members of the House, Members of the Senate, my fellow Americans:

All I have I would have given gladly not to be standing here today.
The greatest leader of our time has been struck down by the foulest deed of our time. Today John Fitzgerald Kennedy lives on in the immortal words and works that he left behind. He lives on in the mind and memories of mankind. He lives on in the hearts of his countrymen.

No words are sad enough to express our sense of loss. No words are strong enough to express our determination to continue the forward thrust of America that he began.

The dream of conquering the vastness of space—the dream of partnership across the Atlantic—and across the Pacific as well—the dream of a Peace Corps in less developed nations—the dream of education for all of our children—the dream of jobs for all who seek them and need them—the dream of care for our elderly—the dream of an all-out attack on mental illness—and above all, the dream of equal rights for all Americans, whatever their race or color—these and other American dreams have been vitalized by his drive and by his dedication.

And now the ideas and the ideals which he so nobly represented must and will be translated into effective action.

Under John Kennedy's leadership, this Nation has demonstrated that it has the courage to seek peace, and it has the fortitude to risk war. We have proved that we are a good and reliable friend to those who seek peace and freedom. We have shown that we can also be a formidable foe to those who reject the path of peace and those who seek to impose upon us or our allies the yoke of tyranny.

This Nation will keep its commitments from South Viet-Nam to West Berlin. We will be unceasing in the search for peace; resourceful in our pursuit of areas of agreement even with those with whom we differ; and generous and loyal to those who join with us in common cause.

In this age when there can be no losers in peace and no victors in war, we must recognize the obligation to match national strength with national restraint. We must be prepared at one and the same time for both the confrontation of power and the limitation of power. We must be ready to defend the national interest and to negotiate the common interest. This is the path that we shall continue to pursue. Those who test our courage will find it strong, and those who seek our friendship will find it honorable. We will demonstrate anew that the strong can be just in the use of strength; and the just can be strong in the defense of justice.

And let all know we will extend no special privilege and impose no persecution. We will carry on the fight against poverty and misery, and disease and ignorance, in other lands and in our own.

We will serve all the Nation, not one section or one sector, or one group, but all Americans. These are the United States—a united people with a united purpose.

Our American unity does not depend upon unanimity. We have differences; but now, as in the past, we can derive from those differences strength, not weakness, wisdom, not despair. Both as a people and a government, we can unite upon a program, a program which is wise and just, enlightened and constructive.

For 32 years Capitol Hill has been my home. I have shared many moments of pride with you, pride in the ability of the Congress of the United States to act, to meet any crisis, to distill from our differences strong programs of national action.

An assassin's bullet has thrust upon me the awesome burden of the Presidency. I am here today to say I need your help; I cannot bear this burden alone. I need the help of all Americans, and all America. This Nation has experienced a profound shock, and in this critical moment, it is our duty, yours and mine, as the Government of the United States, to do away with uncertainty and doubt and delay, and to show that we are capable of decisive action; that from the brutal loss of our leader we will derive not weakness, but strength; that we can and will act and act now.

From this chamber of representative government, let all the world know and none misunderstand that I rededicate this Government to the unswerving support of the United Nations, to the honorable and determined execution of our commitments to our allies, to the maintenance of military strength second to none, to the defense of the strength and the stability of the dollar, to the expansion of our foreign trade, to the reinforcement of our programs of mutual assistance and cooperation in Asia and Africa, and to our Alliance for Progress in this hemisphere.

On the 20th day of January, in 1961, John F. Kennedy told his countrymen that our national work would not be finished "in the first thousand days, nor in the life of this administration, nor even perhaps in our lifetime on this planet. But," he said, "let us begin."

Today, in this moment of new resolve, I would say to all my fellow Americans, let us continue.

This is our challenge—not to hesitate, not to pause, not to turn about and linger over this evil moment, but to continue on our course so that we may fulfill the destiny that history has set for us. Our most immediate tasks are here on this Hill.

First, no memorial oration or eulogy could more eloquently honor President Kennedy's memory than the earliest possible passage of the civil rights bill for which he fought so long. We have talked long enough in this country about equal rights. We have talked for one hundred years or more. It is time now to write the next chapter, and to write it in the books of law.

I urge you again, as I did in 1957 and again in 1960, to enact a civil rights law so that we can move forward to eliminate from this Nation every trace of discrimination and oppression that is based upon race or color. There could be no greater source of strength to this Nation both at home and abroad.

And second, no act of ours could more fittingly continue the work of President Kennedy than the early passage of the tax bill for which he fought all this long year. This is a bill designed to increase our national income and Federal revenues, and to provide insurance against recession. That bill, if passed without delay, means more security for those now working, more jobs for those now without them, and more incentive for our economy.

In short, this is no time for delay. It is a time for action—strong, forward-looking action on the pending education bills to help bring the light of learning to every home and hamlet in America—strong, forward-looking action on youth employment opportunities; strong, forward-looking action on the pending foreign aid bill, making clear that we are not forfeiting our responsibilities to this hemisphere or to the world, nor erasing Executive flexibility in the conduct of our foreign affairs—and strong, prompt, and forward-looking action on the remaining appropriation bills.

In this new spirit of action, the Congress can expect the full cooperation and support of the executive branch. And in particular, I pledge that the expenditures of your Government will be administered with the utmost thrift and frugality. I will insist that the Government get a dollar's value for a dollar spent. The Government will set an example of prudence and economy. This does not mean that we will not meet our unfilled needs or that we will not honor our commitments. We will do both.

As one who has long served in both Houses of the Congress, I firmly believe in the independence and the integrity of the legislative branch. And I promise you that I shall always respect this. It is deep in the marrow of my bones. With equal firmness, I believe in the capacity and I believe in the ability of the Congress, despite the divisions of opinions which characterize our Nation, to act—to act wisely, to act vigorously, to act speedily when the need arises.

The need is here. The need is now. I ask your help.

We meet in grief, but let us also meet in renewed dedication and renewed vigor. Let us meet in action, in tolerance, and in mutual understanding. John Kennedy's death commands what his life conveyed—that America must move forward. The time has come for Americans of all races and creeds and political beliefs to understand and to respect one another. So let us put an end to the teaching and the preaching of hate and evil and violence. Let us turn away from the fanatics of the far left and the far right, from the apostles of bitterness and bigotry, from those defiant of law, and those who pour venom into our Nation's bloodstream.

I profoundly hope that the tragedy and the torment of these terrible days will bind us together in new fellowship, making us one people in our hour of sorrow. So let us here highly resolve that John Fitzgerald Kennedy did not live—or die—in vain. And on this Thanksgiving eve, as we gather together to ask the Lord's blessing, and give Him our thanks, let us unite in those familiar and cherished words:

> America, America,
>    God shed His grace on thee,
> And crown thy good with brotherhood
>    From sea to shining sea.

*Source: Public Papers of the Presidents of the United States: Lyndon B. Johnson, 1963–64, (Washington, D.C.: U.S. Government Printing Office, 1965), 1:8–10.*

## Document 3.3    Proposing the "Great Society," May 22, 1964

*Johnson declared "unconditional war on poverty" during his first State of the Union address in January 1964. Four months later, he went a step further while delivering a commencement address at the University of Michigan. Basking in America's economic success, the president professed a commitment not just to maintaining economic progress but to using America's prosperity to improve the quality of life for all citizens. The term "Great Society" became commonplace after articles in the* New Republic *and the* Washington Post *highlighted it after the University of Michigan speech.*

President Hatcher, Governor Romney, Senators McNamara and Hart, Congressmen Meader and Staebler, and other members of the fine Michigan delegation, members of the graduating class, my fellow Americans: . . .

I have come today from the turmoil of your Capital to the tranquility of your campus to speak about the future of your country.

The purpose of protecting the life of our Nation and preserving the liberty of our citizens is to pursue the happiness of our people. Our success in that pursuit is the test of our success as a Nation.

For a century we labored to settle and to subdue a continent. For half a century we called upon unbounded invention and untiring industry to create an order of plenty for all of our people.

The challenge of the next half century is whether we have the wisdom to use that wealth to enrich and elevate our national life, and to advance the quality of our American civilization.

Your imagination, your initiative, and your indignation will determine whether we build a society where progress is the servant of our needs, or a society where old values and new visions are buried under unbridled growth. For in your time we have the opportunity to move not only toward the rich society and the powerful society, but upward to the Great Society.

The Great Society rests on abundance and liberty for all. It demands an end to poverty and racial injustice, to which we are totally committed in our time. But that is just the beginning.

The Great Society is a place where every child can find knowledge to enrich his mind and to enlarge his talents. It is a place where leisure is a welcome chance to build and reflect, not a feared cause of boredom and restlessness. It is a place where the city of man serves not only the needs of the body and the demands of commerce but the desire for beauty and the hunger for community.

It is a place where man can renew contact with nature. It is a place which honors creation for its own sake and for what it adds to the understanding of the race. It is a place where men are more concerned with the quality of their goals than the quantity of their goods.

But most of all, the Great Society is not a safe harbor, a resting place, a final objective, a finished work. It is a challenge constantly renewed, beckoning us toward a destiny where the meaning of our lives matches the marvelous products of our labor.

So I want to talk to you today about three places where we begin to build the Great Society—in our cities, in our countryside, and in our classrooms.

Many of you will live to see the day, perhaps 50 years from now, when there will be 400 million Americans—four-fifths of them in urban areas. In the remainder of this century urban population will double, city land will double, and we will have to build homes, highways, and facilities equal to all those built since this country was first settled. So in the next 40 years we must rebuild the entire urban United States.

Aristotle said: "Men come together in cities in order to live, but they remain together in order to live the good life." It is harder and harder to live the good life in American cities today.

The catalog of ills is long: there is the decay of the centers and the despoiling of the suburbs. There is not enough housing for our people or transportation for our traffic. Open land is vanishing and old landmarks are violated.

Worst of all expansion is eroding the precious and time honored values of community with neighbors and communion with nature. The loss of these values breeds loneliness and boredom and indifference.

Our society will never be great until our cities are great. Today the frontier of imagination and innovation is inside those cities and not beyond their borders.

New experiments are already going on. It will be the task of your generation to make the American city a place where future generations will come, not only to live but to live the good life.

I understand that if I stayed here tonight I would see that Michigan students are really doing their best to live the good life.

This is the place where the Peace Corps was started. It is inspiring to see how all of you, while you are in this country, are trying so hard to live at the level of the people.

A second place where we begin to build the Great Society is in our countryside. We have always prided ourselves on being not only America the strong and America the free, but America the beautiful. Today that beauty is in danger. The water we drink, the food we eat, the very air that we breathe, are threatened with pollution. Our parks are overcrowded, our seashores overburdened. Green fields and dense forests are disappearing.

A few years ago we were greatly concerned about the "Ugly American." Today we must act to prevent an ugly America.

For once the battle is lost, once our natural splendor is destroyed, it can never be recaptured. And once man can no longer walk with beauty or wonder at nature his spirit will wither and his sustenance be wasted.

A third place to build the Great Society is in the classrooms of America. There your children's lives will be shaped. Our society will not be great until every young mind is set free to scan the farthest reaches of thought and imagination. We are still far from that goal. . . .

Each year more than 100,000 high school graduates, with proved ability, do not enter college because they cannot afford it. And if we cannot educate today's youth, what will we do in 1970 when elementary school enrollment will be 5 million greater than 1960? And high school enrollment will rise by 5 million. College enrollment will increase by more than 3 million.

In many places, classrooms are overcrowded and curricula are outdated. Most of our qualified teachers are underpaid, and many of our paid teachers are unqualified. So we must give every child a place to sit and a teacher to learn from. Poverty must not be a bar to learning, and learning must offer an escape from poverty.

But more classrooms and more teachers are not enough. We must seek an educational system which grows in excellence as it grows in size. This means better training for our teachers. It means preparing youth to enjoy their hours of leisure as well as their hours of labor. It means exploring new techniques of teaching, to find new ways to stimulate the love of learning and the capacity for creation.

These are three of the central issues of the Great Society. While our Government has many programs directed at those issues, I do not pretend that we have the full answer to those problems.

But I do promise this: We are going to assemble the best thought and the broadest knowledge from all over the world to find those answers for America. I intend to establish working groups to prepare a series of White House conferences and meetings—on the cities, on natural beauty, on the quality of education, and on other emerging challenges. And from these meetings and from this inspiration and from these studies we will begin to set our course toward the Great Society.

The solution to these problems does not rest on a massive program in Washington, nor can it rely solely on the strained resources of local authority. They require us to create new concepts of cooperation, a creative federalism, between the National Capital and the leaders of local communities.

Woodrow Wilson once wrote: "Every man sent out from his university should be a man of his Nation as well as a man of his time."

Within your lifetime powerful forces, already loosed, will take us toward a way of life beyond the realm of our experience, almost beyond the bounds of our imagination.

For better or for worse, your generation has been appointed by history to deal with those problems and to lead America toward a new age. You have the chance never before afforded to any people in any age. You can help build a society where the demands of morality, and the needs of the spirit, can be realized in the life of the Nation.

So, will you join in the battle to give every citizen the full equality which God enjoins and the law requires, whatever his belief, or race, or the color of his skin?

Will you join in the battle to give every citizen an escape from the crushing weight of poverty?

Will you join in the battle to make it possible for all nations to live in enduring peace—as neighbors and not as mortal enemies?

Will you join in the battle to build the Great Society, to prove that our material progress is only the foundation on which we will build a richer life of mind and spirit?

There are those timid souls who say this battle cannot be won; that we are condemned to a soulless wealth. I do not agree. We have the power to shape the civilization that we want. But we need your will, your labor, your hearts, if we are to build that kind of society.

Those who came to this land sought to build more than just a new country. They sought a new world. So I have come here today to your campus to say that you can make their vision our reality. So let us from this moment begin our work so that in the future men will look back and say: It was then, after a long and weary way, that man turned the exploits of his genius to the full enrichment of his life.

Thank you. Goodbye.

*Source: Public Papers of the Presidents of the United States: Lyndon B. Johnson, 1963–64, vol. 1* (Washington, D.C.: U.S. Government Printing Office, 1965).

## Document 3.4    The Elementary and Secondary Education Bill, April 11, 1965

*Johnson chose meaningful locations to sign Great Society legislation into law. He traveled to the Statue of Liberty to sign the Immigration Act; Independence, Missouri, the hometown of Harry Truman, to sign the Medicare bill; and to the Capitol Rotunda, where Abraham Lincoln signed the Emancipation Proclamation, to sign the Voting Rights Act. On April 11, 1965, Johnson returned to the one-room schoolhouse where he first attended class to sign the Elementary and Secondary Education Act.*

Ladies and gentlemen:

I want to welcome to this little school of my childhood many of my former schoolmates and many who went to school with me at Cotulla and Houston and San Marcos, as well as some of my dear friends from the educational institutions of this area. . . .

. . . I do not wish to delay by a single day the program to strengthen this Nation's elementary and secondary schools. I devoutly hope that my sense of urgency will be communicated to Secretary Celebrezze, Commissioner Keppel, and the other educational officers throughout the country who will be responsible for carrying out this program.

. . . I felt a very strong desire to go back to the beginnings of my own education—to be reminded and to remind others of that magic time when the world of learning began to open before our eyes.

In this one-room schoolhouse Miss Katie Deadrich taught eight grades at one and the same time. Come over here, Miss Katie, and sit by me, will you? Let them see you. I started school when I was 4 years old, and they tell me, Miss Kate, that I recited my first lessons while sitting on your lap.

From our very beginnings as a nation, we have felt a fierce commitment to the ideal of education for everyone. It fixed itself into our democratic creed.

Over a century and a quarter ago, the President of the Republic of Texas, Mirabeau B. Lamar, proclaimed education as "the guardian genius of democracy . . . the only dictator that free men acknowledge and the only security that free men desire."

But President Lamar made the mistaken prophecy that education would be an issue "in which no jarring interests are involved and no acrimonious political feelings excited." For too long, political acrimony held up our progress. For too long, children suffered while jarring interests caused stalemate in the efforts to improve our schools. Since 1946 Congress tried repeatedly, and failed repeatedly, to enact measures for elementary and secondary education.

Now, within the past 3 weeks, the House of Representatives, by a vote of 263 to 153, and the Senate, by a vote of 73 to 18, have passed the most sweeping educational bill ever to come before Congress. It represents a major new commitment of the Federal Government to quality and equality in the schooling that we offer our young people. I predict that all of those of both parties of Congress who supported the enactment of this legislation will be remembered in history as men and women who began a new day of greatness in American society.

We are delighted that Senator McCarthy could be speaking at the University of Texas yesterday, and he came up and had lunch with me today, and is returning to Washington with me at 7:30 in the morning. Senator McCarthy is an old friend of mine from Minnesota. Stand up, Senator, and let them see you. He has been working for this educational bill ever since the first day he came to the House of Representatives, and ever since he has been in the Senate.

I am delighted to have another good friend of mine who spent the weekend in his home district—McAlester, Oklahoma—and who came down here to spend the evening with me, and is returning in the morning, the distinguished majority leader of the House, without whose efforts we would never have passed this bill—Carl Albert of Oklahoma.

By passing this bill, we bridge the gap between helplessness and hope for more than 5 million educationally deprived children.

We put into the hands of our youth more than 30 million new books, and into many of our schools their first libraries.

We reduce the terrible time lag in bringing new teaching techniques into the Nation's classrooms.

We strengthen State and local agencies which bear the burden and the challenge of better education.

And we rekindle the revolution—the revolution of the spirit against the tyranny of ignorance.

As a son of a tenant farmer, I know that education is the only valid passport from poverty.

As a former teacher—and, I hope, a future one—I have great expectations of what this law will mean for all of our young people.

As President of the United States, I believe deeply no law I have signed or will ever sign means more to the future of America.

To each and everyone who contributed to this day, the Nation is indebted. . . .

So it is not the culmination but only the commencement of this journey. Let me urge, as Thomas Jefferson urged his fellow countrymen one time to, and I quote, "Preach, my dear sir, a crusade against ignorance; establish and improve the law for educating the common people. . . ."

We have established the law. Let us not delay in putting it to work.

*Source: Public Papers of the Presidents of the United States: Lyndon B. Johnson, 1965,* vol. 1 (Washington, D.C.: U.S. Government Printing Office, 1966).

## Document 3.5    Legislative Accomplishments in the Eighty-ninth Congress

*Johnson's skill at pushing bills through Congress is evidenced by the productivity of the Eighty-ninth Congress. Republicans griped that Johnson "bullied, badgered, and brainwashed" them, reducing their role to a mere rubber stamp (Eric F. Goldman,* The Tragedy of Lyndon Johnson, *New York: Knopf, 1969). The following report details the legislative accomplishments of the Eighty-ninth Congress.*

In a word, this was a fabulous and remarkable Congress. We say this not because of its unprecedented productivity—but because what was passed has deep meaning and significance for every man, woman and child in this country—and for future generations. A particularly striking feature about the 89th was that its second session was equally as productive as the first . . .

| | |
|---|---|
| *First session:* | 87 measures |
| | 84 passed |
| *Second session:* | 113 measures |
| | 97 passed |
| *Grand total:* | 200 measures |
| | 181 passed |
| | 19 did not |
| *Batting average:* | .905 |

Of the list of 181 measures passed, we regard the following 60 as of landmark and historic significance:

## THE FIRST SESSION

Medicare

Elementary and Secondary Education

Higher Education

Farm Bill

Department of Housing and Urban Development

Omnibus Housing Act (including rent supplements and low and moderate income housing)

Social Security Increases

Voting Rights

Immigration Bill

Older Americans Act

Heart Disease, Cancer and Stroke Research and Facilities

Law Enforcement Assistance Act

National Crime Commission

Drug Controls

Mental Health Research Facilities

Health Professions Education

Medical Library Facilities

Vocational Rehabilitation

Inter-American Bank Fund increases

Stepping Up the War Against Poverty

Arts and Humanities Foundation

Appalachia, Highway Beautification

Air Pollution (auto exhausts and research)

Water Pollution Control (water quality standards)

High speed ground transportation

Extension and strengthening of MDTA

Presidential Disability and Succession

Child Health Medical Assistance

Regional Development

## THE SECOND SESSION

The Department of Transportation

Truth in Packaging

Demonstration Cities

Funds for Rent Supplements

Funds for Teacher Corps

Asian Development Bank

Water Pollution (Clean Rivers)

Food for Peace

March Anti-inflation package

Narcotics Rehabilitation

Child Safety

Viet-Nam Supplemental

Foreign Aid Extension

Traffic Safety

Highway Safety

Public Health Service Reorganization

Community Relations Service Reorganization

Water Pollution Control Administration Reorganization

Mine Safety

Allied Health Professions Training

International Education

Child Nutrition

*(continued)*

The Second Session *continued*

Bail Reform

Civil Procedure Reforms

Tire Safety

Protection for Savers (increase in
Federal Insurance for savings
accounts)

The GI Bill

Minimum Wage Increase

Urban Mass Transit

Elementary and Higher Education
Funds

The Unfinished Agenda

Civil Rights

Repeal of 14b

Unemployment Insurance
Amendments

D.C. Home Rule

Truth in Lending

Election Reform

Four Year Term for Members of
the House

East-West Trade

Gun Bill

International Health

Special Amortization Formula for
Hospital Modernization

Rural Community Development
Districts

Electoral College Reform

Consolidated Federal Correc-
tional System

National Wild Rivers System

Transportation User Charges

Three Stockpile Bills

*Source:* Lawrence F. O'Brien and Joseph A. Califano Jr., "Final Report to President
Lyndon B. Johnson on the 89th Congress," in "Remarks on the Accomplishments
of the 89th Congress" (15 October 1966), *Public Papers of the Presidents of the
United States: Lyndon B. Johnson, 1966* (Washington, D.C.: U.S. Government
Printing Office, 1967), 2:1193–1194.

## Document 3.6    The American Promise, March 15, 1965

*The following speech, delivered just one week after the assault on peaceful dem-
onstrators in Selma, Alabama, marked the beginning of Johnson's push for the
Voting Rights Act of 1965, which ended with the act's passage on August 6.*

Mr. Speaker, Mr. President, Members of the Congress, I speak tonight for
the dignity of man and the destiny of democracy.

I urge every member of both parties, Americans of all religions and of
all colors, from every section of this country, to join me in that cause.

At times history and fate meet at a single time in a single place to shape a turning point in man's unending search for freedom. So it was at Lexington and Concord. So it was a century ago at Appomattox. So it was last week in Selma, Alabama. . . .

There is no cause for pride in what has happened in Selma. There is no cause for self-satisfaction in the long denial of equal rights of millions of Americans. But there is cause for hope and for faith in our democracy in what is happening here tonight.

For the cries of pain and the hymns and protests of oppressed people have summoned into convocation all the majesty of this great Government—the Government of the greatest Nation on earth.

Our mission is at once the oldest and the most basic of this country: to right wrong, to do justice, to serve man. . . .

The issue of equal rights for American Negroes is such an issue. And should we defeat every enemy, should we double our wealth and conquer the stars, and still be unequal to this issue, then we will have failed as a people and as a nation. . . .

There is no Negro problem. There is no Southern problem. There is no Northern problem. There is only an American problem. And we are met here tonight as Americans—not as Democrats or Republicans—we are met here as Americans to solve that problem.

This was the first nation in the history of the world to be founded with a purpose. The great phrases of that purpose still sound in every American heart, North and South: "All men are created equal"— "government by consent of the governed"— "give me liberty or give me death." Well, those are not just clever words, or those are not just empty theories. In their name Americans have fought and died for two centuries, and tonight around the world they stand there as guardians of our liberty, risking their lives.

Those words are a promise to every citizen that he shall share in the dignity of man. This dignity cannot be found in a man's possessions; it cannot be found in his power, or in his position. It really rests on his right to be treated as a man equal in opportunity to all others. It says that he shall share in freedom, he shall choose his leaders, educate his children, and provide for his family according to his ability and his merits as a human being.

To apply any other test—to deny a man his hopes because of his color or race, his religion or the place of his birth—is not only to do injustice, it is to deny America and to dishonor the dead who gave their lives for American freedom.

## The Right to Vote

Our fathers believed that if this noble view of the rights of man was to flourish, it must be rooted in democracy. The most basic right of all was the right to choose your own leaders. The history of this country, in large measure, is the history of the expansion of that right to all of our people.

Many of the issues of civil rights are very complex and most difficult. But about this there can and should be no argument. Every American citizen must have an equal right to vote. There is no reason which can excuse the denial of that right. There is no duty which weighs more heavily on us than the duty we have to ensure that right.

Yet the harsh fact is that in many places in this country men and women are kept from voting simply because they are Negroes. . . .

Experience has clearly shown that the existing process of law cannot overcome systematic and ingenious discrimination. No law that we now have on the books—and I have helped to put three of them there—can ensure the right to vote when local officials are determined to deny it.

In such a case our duty must be clear to all of us. The Constitution says that no person shall be kept from voting because of his race or his color. We have all sworn an oath before God to support and to defend that Constitution. We must now act in obedience to that oath.

## Guaranteeing the Right to Vote

Wednesday I will send to Congress a law designed to eliminate illegal barriers to the right to vote. . . .

This bill will strike down restrictions to voting in all elections—Federal, State, and local—which have been used to deny Negroes the right to vote.

This bill will establish a simple, uniform standard which cannot be used, however ingenious the effort, to flout our Constitution.

It will provide for citizens to be registered by officials of the United States Government if the State officials refuse to register them.

It will eliminate tedious, unnecessary lawsuits which delay the right to vote.

Finally, this legislation will ensure that properly registered individuals are not prohibited from voting. . . .

To those who seek to avoid action by their National Government in their own communities; who want to and who seek to maintain purely local control over elections, the answer is simple:

Open your polling places to all your people.

Allow men and women to register and vote whatever the color of their skin.

Extend the rights of citizenship to every citizen of this land.

## THE NEED FOR ACTION

There is no constitutional issue here. The command of the Constitution is plain.

There is no moral issue. It is wrong—deadly wrong—to deny any of your fellow Americans the right to vote in this country.

There is no issue of States rights or national rights. There is only the struggle for human rights.

I have not the slightest doubt what will be your answer.

The last time a President sent a civil rights bill to the Congress it contained a provision to protect voting rights in Federal elections. That civil rights bill was passed after 8 long months of debate. And when that bill came to my desk from the Congress for my signature, the heart of the voting provision had been eliminated.

This time, on this issue, there must be no delay, no hesitation and no compromise with our purpose.

We cannot, we must not, refuse to protect the right of every American to vote in every election that he may desire to participate in. And we ought not and we cannot and we must not wait another 8 months before we get a bill. We have already waited a hundred years and more, and the time for waiting is gone.

So I ask you to join me in working long hours—nights and weekends, if necessary—to pass this bill. And I don't make that request lightly. For from the window where I sit with the problems of our country I recognize that outside this chamber is the outraged conscience of a nation, the grave concern of many nations, and the harsh judgment of history on our acts.

## WE SHALL OVERCOME

But even if we pass this bill, the battle will not be over. What happened in Selma is part of a far larger movement which reaches into every section and State of America. It is the effort of American Negroes to secure for themselves the full blessings of American life.

Their cause must be our cause too. Because it is not just Negroes, but really it is all of us, who must overcome the crippling legacy of bigotry and injustice.

And we shall overcome.

As a man whose roots go deeply into Southern soil I know how agonizing racial feelings are. I know how difficult it is to reshape the attitudes and the structure of our society.

But a century has passed, more than a hundred years, since the Negro was freed. And he is not fully free tonight.

It was more than a hundred years ago that Abraham Lincoln, a great President of another party, signed the Emancipation Proclamation, but emancipation is a proclamation and not a fact.

A century has passed, more than a hundred years, since equality was promised. And yet the Negro is not equal.

A century has passed since the day of promise. And the promise is unkept.

The time of justice has now come. I tell you that I believe sincerely that no force can hold it back. It is right in the eyes of man and God that it should come. And when it does, I think that day will brighten the lives of every American.

For Negroes are not the only victims. How many white children have gone uneducated, how many white families have lived in stark poverty, how many white lives have been scarred by fear, because we have wasted our energy and our substance to maintain the barriers of hatred and terror? . . .

AN AMERICAN PROBLEM

Now let none of us in any sections look with prideful righteousness on the troubles in another section, or on the problems of our neighbors. There is really no part of America where the promise of equality has been fully kept. In Buffalo as well as in Birmingham, in Philadelphia as well as in Selma, Americans are struggling for the fruits of freedom.

This is one Nation. What happens in Selma or in Cincinnati is a matter of legitimate concern to every American. But let each of us look within our own hearts and our own communities, and let each of us put our shoulder to the wheel to root out injustice wherever it exists. . . .

And I have not the slightest doubt that good men from everywhere in this country, from the Great Lakes to the Gulf of Mexico, from the Golden Gate to the harbors along the Atlantic, will rally together now in this cause to vindicate the freedom of all Americans. For all of us owe this duty; and I believe that all of us will respond to it. . . .

## PROGRESS THROUGH THE DEMOCRATIC PROCESS

The real hero of this struggle is the American Negro. His actions and protests, his courage to risk safety and even to risk his life, have awakened the conscience of this Nation. His demonstrations have been designed to call attention to injustice, designed to provoke change, designed to stir reform.

He has called upon us to make good the promise of America. And who among us can say that we would have made the same progress were it not for his persistent bravery, and his faith in American democracy.

For at the real heart of battle for equality is a deep-seated belief in the democratic process. Equality depends not on the force of arms or tear gas but upon the force of moral right; not on recourse to violence but on respect for law and order. . . .

We do have a right to protest, and a right to march under conditions that do not infringe the constitutional rights of our neighbors. And I intend to protect all those rights as long as I am permitted to serve in this office. . . .

In Selma as elsewhere we seek and pray for peace. We seek order. We seek unity. But we will not accept the peace of stifled rights, or the order imposed by fear, or the unity that stifles protest. For peace cannot be purchased at the cost of liberty. . . .

## RIGHTS MUST BE OPPORTUNITIES

The bill that I am presenting to you will be known as a civil rights bill. But, in a larger sense, most of the program I am recommending is a civil rights program. Its object is to open the city of hope to all people of all races.

Because all Americans just must have the right to vote. And we are going to give them that right.

All Americans must have the privileges of citizenship regardless of race. And they are going to have those privileges of citizenship regardless of race.

But I would like to caution you and remind you that to exercise these privileges takes much more than just legal right. It requires a trained mind and a healthy body. It requires a decent home, and the chance to find a job, and the opportunity to escape from the clutches of poverty. . . .

So we want to open the gates to opportunity. But we are also going to give all our people, black and white, the help that they need to walk through those gates.

## The Purpose of This Government

... This is the richest and most powerful country which ever occupied the globe. The might of past empires is little compared to ours. But I do not want to be the President who built empires, or sought grandeur, or extended dominion.

I want to be the President who educated young children to the wonders of their world. I want to be the President who helped to feed the hungry and to prepare them to be taxpayers instead of taxeaters.

I want to be the President who helped the poor to find their own way and who protected the right of every citizen to vote in every election.

I want to be the President who helped to end hatred among his fellow men and who promoted love among the people of all races and all regions and all parties.

I want to be the President who helped to end war among the brothers of this earth. ...

Above the pyramid on the great seal of the United States it says—in Latin—"God has favored our undertaking."

God will not favor everything that we do. It is rather our duty to divine His will. But I cannot help believing that He truly understands and that He really favors the undertaking that we begin here tonight.

*Source: Public Papers of the Presidents of the United States: Lyndon B. Johnson, 1965* (Washington, D.C.: U.S. Government Printing Office, 1966), 1:281–287.

## Document 3.7   Estimated Percentage of Blacks Registered to Vote in Eleven Southern States, 1956–1976

*The Voting Rights Act of 1965 led to a dramatic increase in voter registration among formerly disenfranchised citizens in the South. The following table displays the estimated percentage of eligible black voters who were registered in various years in eleven southern states. Within three years of the Voting Rights Act, there was nearly a 50 percent increase in the number of eligible blacks registered to vote in the South.*

| State | 1956 | 1964 | 1968 | 1976 |
|---|---|---|---|---|
| Alabama | 11.0% | 23.0% | 56.7% | 58.4% |
| Arkansas | 36.0 | 49.3 | 67.5 | 94.0 |
| Florida | 32.0 | 63.8 | 62.1 | 61.1 |
| Georgia | 27.0 | 44.0 | 56.1 | 74.8 |
| Louisiana | 31.0 | 32.0 | 59.3 | 63.0 |
| Mississippi | 5.0 | 6.7 | 59.4 | 60.7 |
| North Carolina | 24.0 | 46.8 | 55.3 | 54.8 |
| South Carolina | 27.0 | 38.7 | 50.8 | 56.5 |
| Tennessee | 29.0 | 69.4 | 72.8 | 66.4 |
| Texas | 37.0 | 57.7 | 83.1 | 65.0 |
| Virginia | 19.0 | 45.7 | 58.4 | 54.7 |
| **Total** | **24.9** | **43.1** | **62.0** | **63.1** |

*Source:* Chandler Davidson and Bernard Grofman, eds., *Quiet Revolution in the South: The Impact of the Voting Rights Act, 1965–1990* (Princeton: Princeton University Press, 1994), 374.

## Document 3.8    The Dominican Republic

*On June 17, 1965, peace was restored to the Dominican Republic. Johnson gave a televised speech that evening, stating that he had sent troops to the country to protect the lives of Americans, aid a government that had requested assistance, and to prevent a communist victory in the region. In his first public remarks on the invasion, J. William Fulbright, head of the Senate Foreign Relations Committee, noted differences between what presidential aides told his committee and what the president had said on television, and he suggested that the president might be lying to the people.*

. . . U.S. policy in the Dominican crisis was characterized initially by over-timidity and subsequently by overreaction. Throughout the whole affair, it has also been characterized by a lack of candor.

These are general conclusions I have reached from a painstaking review of the salient features of the extremely complex situation. These judgments are made, of course, with the benefit of hindsight and, in fairness, it must be conceded there were no easy choices available to the United States in the Dominican Republic. Nonetheless, it is the task of diplomacy to make wise decisions when they need to be made and U.S. diplomacy failed to do so in the Dominican crisis. . . .

This decision [to send troops] seems to me to have been based on exaggerated estimates of Communist influence in the rebel movement in the initial stages and on distaste for the return to power of Juan Bosch or of a government controlled by Bosch's party, the PRD—Dominican Revolutionary Party.

The question of the degree of Communist influence is of critical importance and I shall comment on it later. The essential point, however, is that the United States, on the basis of ambiguous evidence, assumed almost from the beginning that the revolution was Communist dominated, or would certainly become so. It apparently never occurred to anyone that the United States could also attempt to influence the course which the revolution took. We misread prevailing tendencies in Latin America by overlooking or ignoring the fact that any reform movement is likely to attract Communist support. We thus failed to perceive that if we are automatically to oppose any reform movement that Communists adhere to, we are likely to end up opposing every reform movement, making ourselves the prisoners of reactionaries who wish to preserve the status quo—and the status quo in many countries is not good enough.

*Source:* Sen. William Fulbright, D-Ark., "The Situation in the Dominican Republic," in U.S. Congress, Senate, *Congressional Record,* daily ed., 89th Cong., 2d sess. September 15, 1965, S23855–23861.

## Document 3.9    Foreign Aid

*Like all cold war presidents, Johnson used the carrot of foreign aid as well as the stick of military intervention to shape events in developing countries. America's military campaign in Vietnam was paralleled by a humanitarian aid program that, at its peak, consumed more than 20 percent of the foreign aid budget. That still left considerable sums to distribute in other countries, particularly elsewhere in Asia and in Latin America. Listed below are the official Agency for International Development expenditures (in millions of dollars) to the top ten recipient countries from 1964 to 1969. (Total country aid includes aid to countries not listed in the top ten. Total aid includes aid not directed toward particular countries.)*

### 1964

| | |
|---|---|
| India | $344 |
| Pakistan | 236 |
| Brazil | 179 |
| Viet Nam | 166 |
| Turkey | 132 |
| Korea | 109 |
| Colombia | 79 |
| Chile | 79 |
| Bolivia | 58 |
| Nigeria | 46 |
| Total country aid | 1,988 |
| Total aid | 2,271 |

### 1966

| | |
|---|---|
| Viet Nam | $591 |
| India | 310 |
| Brazil | 243 |
| Korea | 147 |
| Turkey | 133 |
| Pakistan | 127 |
| Dominican Republic | 94 |
| Chile | 93 |
| Colombia | 87 |
| Laos | 51 |
| Total country aid | 2,334 |
| Total aid | 2,665 |

### 1965

| | |
|---|---|
| India | $265 |
| Brazil | 235 |
| Viet Nam | 225 |
| Pakistan | 188 |
| Turkey | 151 |
| Korea | 123 |
| Chile | 99 |
| Dominican Republic | 53 |
| Laos | 51 |
| ROCAP | 43 |
| Total country aid | 1,864 |
| Total aid | 2,178 |

### 1967

| | |
|---|---|
| Viet Nam | $494 |
| Brazil | 214 |
| India | 212 |
| Turkey | 139 |
| Pakistan | 137 |
| Korea | 115 |
| Colombia | 105 |
| Laos | 57 |
| Dominican Republic | 54 |
| Thailand | 53 |
| Total country aid | 2,063 |
| Total aid | 2,415 |

| 1968 | | 1969 | |
| --- | --- | --- | --- |
| Viet Nam | $400 | Viet Nam | $314 |
| India | 301 | India | 203 |
| Brazil | 194 | Pakistan | 104 |
| Pakistan | 132 | Colombia | 101 |
| Colombia | 77 | Indonesia | 56 |
| Korea | 75 | Laos | 52 |
| Turkey | 72 | Korea | 45 |
| Laos | 63 | Nigeria | 44 |
| Chile | 58 | Turkey | 44 |
| Thailand | 47 | Thailand | 36 |
| Total country aid | 1,794 | Total country aid | 1,259 |
| Total aid | 2,178 | Total aid | 1,690 |

*Source:* Statistics and Reports Division, Agency for International Development, "Operations Report," FY 1964, 1965, 1966, 1967, 1968, and 1969.

## Document 3.10    Major Foreign Policy Accomplishments

*Shortly after Johnson announced he would not seek reelection, he asked his staff to prepare reports summarizing the accomplishments of his administration. This report highlights foreign policy. Naturally, it represents the most positive of all plausible assessments of the administration's actions.*

Increased the power and prestige of the U.S. abroad by ending the uncertainty resulting from the assassination of President Kennedy
— Reaffirmation of international commitments, military policies and alliances
— Restoration of foreign confidence in U.S. leadership by establishing personal relations with world leaders and addressing the U.N. General Assembly

Speeding up development in the Western Hemisphere
— Punta Del Este Conference agreed to create a common Latin American market
— Alliance for Progress extended, tightened, and accelerated

Focusing on Asia
— Defense of national interest, U.S. commitments in Vietnam and Korea
— March 31 initiative leads to beginning of peace discussions in Paris
— Tightening of relations with Pacific allies by means of conferences and visits
— Leadership and support for the new Asia—the Mekong Project—Asian Development Bank—ASPAC
— International food assistance to meet Indian needs

Managing and resolving crises
— Restoration of normal relations with Panama; negotiation of new Canal Treaty
— War over Cyprus staved off—outbreak of fighting between two U.S. allies avoided
— Congo aided in defeating rebels by use of U.S. transport planes

Meeting Communist threat in Dominican Republic on multi-lateral basis
— Democratic government restored through OAS action
— U.S. forces withdrawn

Achieving improved and correct relations with the Soviet Union
— Outer Space Treaty negotiated and signed
— Consular Convention ratified
— Non-Proliferation Treaty formulated, agreed in Geneva, and introduced jointly to the U.N. General Assembly
— Conference with Premier Kosygin at Glassboro

Modernizing NATO
— Successful realignment of Alliance following French withdrawal
— Agreement on troop contributions and financing with Germany and Great Britain
— Nuclear planning group organized

Limiting spread of war in Mid East and leading drive to achieve peace
— U.S.–Soviet confrontation avoided
— Renewal of fighting staved off
— Leadership in finding a peace settlement on basis of Five Points of June 19 speech

Management of balance of payments problem, through international
   cooperation
— Liberal trade gains and Kennedy Round progress maintained
— Breakdown in international monetary system avoided

Creating a new basis for neighborly relations with Mexico
— Signing of Chamizal Boundary Treaty first year in office
— President-to-President tie created by discussion of mutual problems in
   Mexico City and in the United States

*Source:* "The Ten Major Foreign Policy Accomplishments of Lyndon Johnson,"
May 17, 1968, Foreign Affairs Highlights reference file, LBJL.

### Document 3.11     Foreign Affairs Highlights

*Johnson declared "continuity" the theme of his first year in office. Once he
received a mandate in the 1964 election, however, he began to develop his own
policies. The following report lists the major foreign affairs highlights of his
presidency from 1963 to 1967, as viewed from within the administration.*

MAJOR FOREIGN ACCOMPLISHMENTS IN 1963
Maintained continuity and foreign confidence in U.S. leadership
Established personal relations with major western leaders
Established a single authoritative U.S. voice on Latin American affairs
Moved forward on a number of outstanding issues involving Germany
   (MLF, troop offset, etc.)

MAJOR FOREIGN ACCOMPLISHMENTS IN 1964
U.S. Soviet-British agreement on mutual cuts in production of nuclear
   weapons materials
Successful handling of the Panama crisis
Leading role (with George Ball and Dean Acheson as Presidential
   envoys) in the settlement of the Cyprus crisis
Repulsion of the Tonkin attacks and passage of the Tonkin Resolution
Calm resolution of problems caused by Cuban denial of water to Guan-
   tanamo Naval Base
Smallest Congressional cut in the President's foreign aid request in the
   history of the program

Conclusion of a Consular Treaty with the Soviet Union, the first bilateral treaty in the history of U.S.–Soviet relations

Calm weathering of fall of Khruschev and first Chicom nuclear explosion

Stanleyville (Congo) paradrop

Establishment of relations with Harold Wilson, and deft finesse of the MLF issue which threatened to split the Atlantic Alliance

MAJOR FOREIGN ACCOMPLISHMENTS IN 1965

Decision to begin bombing North Vietnam (after communist mortaring of U.S. base at Pleiku)

Baltimore speech, laying out a full and humane plan for the peaceful development of free Asia

Successful intervention in the Dominican Republic

Founding of the Asian Development Bank

Leading role in stopping the brief war between India and Pakistan (Cessation of U.S. arms to aid both sides)

Beginning of 37-day bombing pause

Peace offensive which sent Presidential emissaries around the world

Maintenance of solid relations with Erhard and Germany, despite slow fade of MLF proposal

MAJOR FOREIGN ACCOMPLISHMENTS IN 1966

Thirty-seven day bombing pause in Vietnam, accompanied by all-out efforts to start negotiations

Recasting of the foreign aid program to emphasize the roots of international poverty—backward farming, ignorance, and disease

New proposals to promote international health and education

Calm, strong handling of the NATO crisis caused by de Gaulle's decision to pull France out of NATO organizations and to order NATO troops and installations out of France

The Honolulu Conference with Thieu and Ky; the beginnings of the solution to Vietnam's economic crisis, and of long-term Vietnamese efforts to bring economic and social progress to the countryside

Recasting and renewal of the Food for Peace Program, moving from surplus disposal to a world-wide integrated War on Hunger

Reformulation of U.S. policy toward Red China, offering a route to reconciliation as well as an uncompromising stand against aggression in Asia

Proposal of legislation to authorize expansion of trade with the Soviet
Union and Eastern Europe

Repeated cooperative and successful efforts to hold the line against pressure on the pound sterling

President's trip to Asia, reaffirming the solidarity of the Allied stand in
Vietnam and the U.S. interest in Asian progress

MAJOR FOREIGN ACCOMPLISHMENTS IN 1967

Glassboro Summit with Kosygin

Signing of treaty banning nuclear weapons from outer space

Great military and economic progress in Vietnam, and installation of
Ellsworth Bunker, Eugene Locke and other top-flight people to maintain the strength of the U.S. effort

Successful completion of tri-lateral conversations (U.S.–U.K.–FRG) which
met the problems of financial burden-sharing and troop maintenance
without the predicted split in the alliance

Re-definition and reaffirmation of the Alliance for Progress

Successful completion of the Kennedy Round with agreement upon the
largest tariff cuts in history

Agreement on international monetary reform

Leading role in staving off war in the Middle East as long as possible, and
then in bringing hostilities to a rapid close

The San Antonio speech and a clear and reasonable formula for peace in
Vietnam

Successful weathering of the devaluation of the pound sterling

*Source:* "The Presidency of Lyndon Baines Johnson: Foreign Affairs Highlights,"
May 13, 1968, Foreign Affairs Highlights reference file, LBJL.

*Judge Sarah Hughes swears in Johnson* on Air Force One *after the death of John F. Kennedy, November 22, 1963. At Johnson's side are his wife, Lady Bird (left), and Jacqueline Kennedy (right).*

# CHAPTER FOUR

# Crises and Flashpoints

L yndon Johnson was a good man in a crisis. In fact, when he did not have a crisis to focus his manic energies, Johnson could be difficult to the point of self-destructiveness. In his 1948 race for the Senate, Johnson at one point thought he could coast to victory. His demeanor on the campaign trail turned from irascible but charming to imperious and demeaning. He would explode in public at his aides and with crude behavior and high-handedness offend delegations of leading citizens who made the pilgrimage to his hotel suite in isolated Texas towns. When polls showed the race tightening, Johnson composed himself. He was once again gracious and imploring to those whose support he needed, and he confined the routine abuse of his aides to private situations. When serving in the purgatory of the vice presidency, Johnson underwent another, more lasting, period of self-pity and reckless personal behavior, including excessive drinking. But at the moment when the assassin's bullets struck in Dallas, Johnson was back in a crisis atmosphere and back in charge of himself and his situation.

## ASSUMING THE PRESIDENCY

In November 1963 Vice President and Lady Bird Johnson accompanied President Kennedy and the first lady on a campaign trip to Texas. Kennedy had been pressing Johnson to arrange the trip for months. Texas would be a critical battleground in Kennedy's reelection campaign, and he wanted to hit the state early to raise money for the lengthy campaign ahead. The significance of the trip was apparent in Mrs. Kennedy's presence. It would be her first political trip of the campaign and her first time ever in the Lone Star State.

On Friday, November 22, Lee Harvey Oswald shot and killed President Kennedy and wounded Texas governor John Connally as the presidential motorcade made its way through the streets of Dallas. When the reality of the situation had sunk in—after seconds of hesitation—the Secret Service agents driving the president's and the vice president's cars raced to Parkland Hospital. At the hospital the vice president and the head of his Secret Service detail, Rufus Youngblood, were eager to leave for Washington, D.C. No one knew at the time who had shot the president or whether it was part of a wider assault on the U.S. government. After learning that the president was dead, the vice president, his wife, and his few aides who were present left the hospital for *Air Force One.*

On the tarmac at the airport the crew and passengers waited on the plane for the body of the late president and his widow. Mrs. Kennedy and President Kennedy's aides and Secret Service detail were back at the hospital, fighting their way out. The Dallas medical examiner refused to authorize the removal of the body until an autopsy was performed. Kennedy had been murdered in Dallas, and the law stated that in a murder an autopsy must be performed. Feeling under siege, and eager to leave the city where the president had been shot, Kennedy's men forced their way past the officious doctor and headed toward the airport with Mrs. Kennedy and the body of the late president.

On the plane, Lyndon Johnson had been waiting for a federal district court judge, Sarah Hughes, an old friend and recent federal appointee, to come to administer the oath of office. When Judge Hughes arrived, the oath was administered in the crowded cabin of the plane, with Jacqueline Kennedy by the new president's side, her dress still bearing the stains of her husband's killing (see Document 4.1).

When Mrs. Kennedy joined in Johnson's swearing in, some of the Kennedy aides thought Johnson was using her opportunistically to seize power and the limelight from the grieving family and administration. But Jackie Kennedy seems to have understood even then that she and Johnson were on a common mission. Together, they would shape through their actions and words in the coming days the nation's lasting impression of John F. Kennedy.

Airborne at last, Johnson began to take charge of his accidental presidency. He recalled later, "I think the first thought I had was that this is a terrifying thing that may have international consequences, that this might be an international conspiracy of some kind. And I knew, of course, that I was on my own and that it was my responsibility and it was a thing that had to be dealt with very quickly and as calmly as could be. And I had tried to think it out, recognize the problems that faced me and the necessity of giving the nation and the world confidence as soon as I could" (Miller 1980, 315). Liz Carpenter, a reporter working on the vice presidential campaign staff, drafted a brief note of consolation, which the president read at Andrews Air Force Base, the Maryland airfield that serves as the home base for *Air Force One*. As Johnson recalled in his memoirs, "the people would want to know there was leadership and purpose and continuity in their government" (Johnson 1971, 16).

From the moment Johnson set foot on the ground as president, he worked to win the loyalty of Kennedy's top advisers in order to demonstrate the continuity he felt the country yearned for. "I want you all to stay on. I need you," Johnson told one Kennedy appointee after another (Dallek 1998, 56). "I need you far more than John Kennedy ever needed you," he flatteringly implored (Manchester 1967, 639). The night of November 22, after working the phones in the vice president's offices in the Old Executive Office Building, Johnson returned to The Elms, his Washington home. (Vice presidents would not have an official residence at the Naval Observatory in Washington, D.C., until 1974.) From there, Johnson placed calls to the living former presidents and touched base late into the night with many other political leaders and friends. "That whole night," Bill Moyers recalled, "he seemed to have several chambers of his mind operating simultaneously. It was formidable, very formidable" (Miller 1980, 325)

After a few hours' sleep, Johnson received his first daily intelligence briefing as president. Learning that no pressing international issues demanded his attention, Johnson was free to turn his mind to domestic matters. The first, still pressing, issue was to demonstrate continuity and establish his legitimacy as president. That afternoon, he met with his inherited cabinet, where he again urged all members of the Kennedy government to remain in their posts. "I knew each of these men," the president recalled, "and I respected them. In the top echelon I had no desire to replace any of them. I wanted all of them to stay" (Miller 1980, 330).

On Sunday, November 24, two days after the assassination, and immediately following President Kennedy's burial at Arlington National Ceme-
tery, Johnson met with foreign heads of state and ministers at a State
Department reception and spoke privately with former president Dwight
D. Eisenhower. Eisenhower suggested that Johnson arrange soon for a
speech to the nation and deliver the address before both chambers of Congress. Abe Fortas, who had been a friend of the Johnsons' from the New
Deal years (see Chapter 1), recounted the conversations Johnson held with
his staff and associates about whether to use the occasion of the speech to
press for passage of the stalled Kennedy agenda, in particular a civil rights
bill that would attack local and state laws that excluded blacks from public facilities in the South. "At one point there were a lot of us sitting around
at the table at The Elms discussing that with him for hours. And the incident that I remember, which renewed my pride in him, was this. One of
the wise, fine, practical people around the table said, 'Mr. President, you
ought not to urge Congress to pass this. You oughtn't to make this one of
the imperatives of your program because the president has only a certain
amount of coinage to expend, and you oughtn't expend it on this.' . . .
There was a moment of silence as I recall, and Johnson looked at this fellow—'Well, what the hell's the presidency for?'" (Miller 1980, 337; for
Johnson's sanitized version, see Johnson 1971, 38).

President Johnson addressed Congress and the nation on November
27, 1963 (see Document 3.2). In that speech the president urged Congress to pass the civil rights bill and other measures of the late president's
agenda, as the most suitable "eulogy" for Kennedy. As Johnson recalled in
his memoirs, "Teddy Roosevelt used to call the Presidency a 'bully pulpit.'
During my first thirty days in office I preached many sermons from that
pulpit" (Johnson 1971, 29). Following the address to Congress, the president held high-profile talks in the White House with leaders from the civil
rights movement, business, and labor. The president had the advantage,
he realized, of "a genuine desire for national unity on the part of most
people" (Johnson 1971, 33).

On the eve of President Kennedy's trip to Dallas, there had been omi-
nous forebodings of trouble. Reactionary Texas conservatives had
denounced the Kennedy administration for alleged radicalism and appease-
ment of communism. Dealing with the popular view that the poisoned
atmosphere of Dallas had somehow been responsible for the actions of Lee
Harvey Oswald, Johnson used that perception to appeal for support of his

agenda. The American people, he reflected, had learned "in the cruelest way possible, where hatred and divisiveness could lead the nation, and I think they were ready to try another route. My task was to show the way" (Johnson 1971, 33).

The final matter that Johnson had to deal with during this period was the possibility that popular suspicion of an international plot behind the killing of the president might push the nation into a dangerous confrontation with a foreign power. Johnson had seen before, in World War II and during the Korean War, how quickly a war fever could grip the nation, and he knew that ultraconservatives in Congress and the military longed to turn up the heat in the cold war. If speculation about Cuban or Soviet involvement in the assassination were to get out of hand, Johnson might have difficulty restraining an aroused nation. Though Johnson harbored suspicions until his death that Kennedy's assassination was indeed part of a wider conspiracy, as president he did not want to encourage such thinking. Without proof that Oswald had not acted alone, Johnson was eager to lay the matter to rest, and he urged the members of the so-called Warren Commission, named for its chair, Chief Justice Earl Warren, to work calmly but quickly to review the evidence concerning the assassination. President Johnson praised their work when, after ten months, they concluded that Oswald had operated by and for himself.

The assumption of power that began in Dallas was a crisis that Johnson proved highly capable of mastering. Indeed, Johnson thought his marshaling of unity following the assassination "one of the great satisfactions" of his presidency (Johnson 1971, 41). There would be other dilemmas during his presidency, including riots at home and revolutions abroad. In most of these as well, Johnson typically displayed a calm resolve. But the president met his match in Vietnam, a crisis that went on for so long and created so many divisions within his own government and within the nation that it ultimately forced him to abandon the presidency.

## THE VIETNAM WAR

The war in Vietnam continues to cast a large shadow over the accomplishments of the Johnson presidency. Thirty-two years after Johnson left office, 69 percent of Americans told Gallup pollsters (November 17, 2000) that it had been a mistake to send troops to fight in Vietnam. The war is remembered by many, moreover, as "one of the most important events of the century." (In a Gallup poll released December 6, 1999, 37 percent of Americans thought so; another 31 percent said it was "important, but not the *most* important event of the century.") An incredible one in four Americans, Gallup reported in November 17, 2000, has visited the Vietnam War Memorial in Washington, D.C.

Commentary on Johnson's part in the war typically condemns the president for a range of alleged failings. H. R. McMaster, a military historian and army officer, portrays the president as conniving with his civilian secretary of defense, Robert McNamara, to shut the military out of decision making for the war (McMaster 1997). McMaster's account complements the widespread belief of conservatives that in Vietnam those in the military were forced to fight with "one-arm-behind-the-back restraint" (Baldwin 1978, xiii). The political scientist Irving Bernstein, meanwhile, joins a number of scholars in seeing the war as a reflection of Johnson's troubled personality. Johnson, the story goes, was an oversized Texan fond of making up ancestors who had died at the Alamo. With such a man in the White House, the unreasoned pursuit of even the most suicidal "victory" was a foregone conclusion. Because Lyndon "Davy Crockett" Johnson could brook no dissent, he froze out of White House discussions his few dovish advisers (Bernstein 1996).

Much of the prevailing commentary on President Johnson and the Vietnam War, then, expresses what might be termed counterfactual angst. "If only Kennedy had lived." "If only Johnson had listened to his hawkish advisers." "If only Johnson had listened to his dovish advisers." But what actually happened in "Lyndon Johnson's" Vietnam War? What decisions did the president make, why, and to what effect? (See Document 4.15 for definitions of "dove" and "hawk.")

## Let Us Continue

Lyndon Johnson knew he was inheriting a mess in Vietnam. The new president thought that U.S. complicity in the removal (and assassination) of South Vietnam's president, Ngo Dinh Diem, three weeks before Kennedy's death had been a tragic mistake. Johnson had foreseen that removing Diem for general incompetence and lack of popularity would produce political chaos in South Vietnam and that without a stable government the rebels there, the Viet Cong (VC), and their supporters, the North Vietnamese enemy, would gain strength. Johnson also knew why the United States was in this mess in the first place. He had watched as successive presidents starting with Harry Truman had supported the fight against the communists in what was then French Indochina, and he, like everyone else, had heard both Eisenhower and Kennedy boldly vow that America would not let South Vietnam fall to communism. He was vice president when the Kennedy administration drew a line in the sand in Vietnam after suffering cold war humiliations in Cuba, Berlin, and Laos. This, Kennedy decided, would be the place to demonstrate U.S. resolve to stand up against communism and to prove that there was a vigorous, flexible, alternative in military policy to President Eisenhower's reliance on nuclear gamesmanship. Johnson also knew that the United States was obligated by its own creation, the Southeast Asia Treaty Organization (see Document 4.2), to come to the aid of South Vietnam. "We are party to a treaty," Johnson reminded his old friend, Sen. Richard Russell, D-Ga., "And if we don't pay attention to this treaty, why, I don't guess they [world opinion] think we pay attention to any of them" (Beschloss 1997, 364).

On November 26, 1963, the new administration expressed its policy in National Security Action Memorandum 273 (see Document 4.3). The memorandum affirmed the U.S. commitment to South Vietnam, as well as the late president's initiative to withdraw 1,000 of the 16,000 U.S. advisers in South Vietnam by the end of the year.

The partial withdrawal has convinced some observers, such as John M. Newman, that President Kennedy had a secret plan to pull out of Vietnam after the election (Newman 1992). Others, including Gen. Maxwell Taylor, a key member of Kennedy's inner circle, thought the partial withdrawal a ploy to pressure the South Vietnamese government to devote more of its own resources to the war. A third possibility is that the action was taken for the reasons stated in Kennedy's National Security Action Memorandum 263—namely, that the South Vietnamese were thought to be doing well in the conflict and that U.S. forces could begin to pull back. However Kennedy had intended it, the withdrawal of 1,000 troops lost all significance as Viet Cong and North Vietnamese successes on the battlefield forced a response from the United States.

During the remainder of 1963, and until the election of the following year, Johnson pursued a consistent approach in the war. His aim was to prevent the collapse of South Vietnam. Although he authorized Operation Plan 34A, a series of covert actions, and sent thousands of additional advisers, as long as the election was in progress Johnson deferred a decision on just how far the U.S. might go to prevent defeat.

Johnson put off making tough choices on Vietnam in part to avoid a potentially damaging political fight. If he openly escalated the war in the midst of the campaign, both hawks and doves would assail him. "I just spent a lot of time with the Joint Chiefs," Johnson recounted in a phone conversation with his national security adviser, McGeorge Bundy, during the 1964 campaign. "The net of it—they say, get in or get out. And I told them. . . . We haven't got any Congress that will go with us, and we haven't got any mothers that will go with us in a war. And nine months I'm just an inherited—I'm a trustee. I've got to win an election, or Nixon or somebody else has. And then you can make a decision. But in the meantime, let's see if we can't find enough things to do to keep them off base" (Beschloss 1997, 266).

To keep the issue of Vietnam out of the election, Johnson engineered a nearly unanimous congressional resolution of support. During a covert mission in August 1964 in the Gulf of Tonkin, U.S. vessels reported that they were under torpedo attack. Within hours, limited U.S. reprisal bombing was under way. Within days, Congress rushed to the president's side in the Tonkin Gulf Resolution, granting support for "all necessary measures to repel any armed attack against the forces of the U.S. and to prevent further aggression" (H.J. RES 1145, 1964; see Document 4.4). Despite the fact that the assault on the ship was evidenced only by ambiguous radar signals (see Document 4.5) and that the resolution did not explicitly authorize the war to come, Johnson read a great deal into this expression of support. "I made it clear from the day I took office," he recounted in his memoirs, "I was not a 'peace at any price man.' The American people knew what they were voting for in 1964" (Johnson 1971, 68).

## Americanizing the War

After the election, Johnson called for a consideration of options in the war. Now John McNaughton, assistant secretary of defense for international security affairs, drafted a paper, endorsed by Johnson's national security team, that presented the president with the choices he had been deferring. Option A called for more tit-for-tat reprisal bombings, such as the one ordered immediately after the incident in the Tonkin Gulf. Option B, described as a "fast full squeeze" of bombing and perhaps even the use of U.S. combat troops, was the Joint Chiefs' preference. Option C, labeled "progressive squeeze-and-talk," was the one the president chose, a gradually escalating air war designed to pressure the North Vietnamese leadership.

All that was needed for the implementation of the president's decision was the necessary provocation from North Vietnam. It came in February 1965, with a joint North Vietnamese–Viet Cong attack at Pleiku. The air war was under way. Under the name "Rolling Thunder," it quickly broadened into full-scale bombing by B-52s of large areas surrounding defined targets, or so-called carpet bombing.

The next step in the U.S. escalation, the introduction of U.S. troops into ground combat, followed close on the heels of the decision to launch the air war. Air bases required a level of security that the South Vietnamese were not competent to provide. Two months after Pleiku, the president, in National Security Action Memorandum 328, approved a request for marine land and helicopter battalions to engage in the active defense of the air base at Da Nang (see Document 4.6). Once on the ground, the line between defense and offense soon blurred, as the marines sought out the enemy before he could attack the air base.

Despite these steps, by the summer of 1965 the situation in South Vietnam was deteriorating, and the U.S. commander there, Gen. William Westmoreland, sent the president an urgent request for reinforcements. On the hawkish side, the Joint Chiefs and General Westmoreland made a plea for a massive force increase and a free hand to maneuver U.S. troops far afield from U.S. bases. On the dovish side, the president received the advice of George Ball, undersecretary of state, who urged a "base defense and reserve strategy" to set the stage for U.S. withdrawal altogether. The president, on July 27, 1965, approved the deployment of about 100,000 more U.S. troops, but he decided to downplay the decision. He would not call the nation's military reservists to active duty (see Document 4.7). The following day, in the words of Irving Bernstein, President Johnson "sort of informed the American people that their nation was at war." (Bernstein 1996, 348; see Document 4.8.)

## Waging Limited War

President Johnson had made a momentous decision. He had greatly deepened U.S. involvement in the war in Vietnam, but he denied any change in policy. The Joint Chiefs wanted the president to mobilize the reserve forces, the nation's part-time soldiers, sailors, airmen, and marines who train on weekends and during summers in case they are needed to respond to war or a national emergency. Defense Secretary McNamara recommended that Johnson return to Congress for a tax increase to offset inflationary pressures that were certain to flow from the military buildup. Johnson refused to do either of these things. Why?

One reason was the Great Society (see Chapter 3). As McNamara recounted in a January 8, 1975, interview for the Johnson presidential library, the president thought Congress would vote down a war tax. As Johnson told McNamara, "if you know so damn much, you go up there [to Congress] and make your own check." McNamara did and came back to tell the president he had been right. Johnson then elaborated on his difficulties. Not only would a proposal to raise taxes fail, the president said, "but in the process of failure it would impose severe penalties on the Great Society programs," because many members of Congress were eager for an excuse to jump off Johnson's domestic bandwagon. As the president liked to remind his advisers, he had seen for himself how, after Roosevelt and Truman had become war presidents, they "could not get Congress to pass the time of day" (LBJL).

At the same time, Johnson persuaded himself that further debate would be superfluous. Congress had passed the Tonkin Gulf Resolution and, moreover, the old choice of "guns or butter" was obsolete. A nation as wealthy as the United States in the 1960s had the resources to do anything it put its mind to. "I believe," the president told Congress on January 12, 1966, "that we can continue the Great Society while we fight in Vietnam" (Johnson 1971, 326). Even in retirement, Johnson insisted that "We have enough to do it all" (Goodwin 1991, 213).

Still, why did President Johnson take for granted not only the nation's wealth and Congress's support but also the willpower of the American people? Did not the president have a responsibility to lead the public to "put their mind to" the problem of Vietnam? Perhaps, but here Johnson ran up against a fundamental difficulty of limited war. To wage such a war requires perseverance more than passion. An excess of passion, in fact, might lead the nation into World War III.

## Many Wars at Once

The war in Vietnam embodied many wars at once. It was a war of national liberation, a civil war, and a proxy war pitting the United States against the People's Republic of China and the Soviet Union. It was this last war that most concerned U.S. policymakers. Johnson worried endlessly that if he pushed too far, if he bombed the wrong target, if his forces stumbled across some hidden trip wire identified in secret agreements between the North

Vietnamese and their patrons, the United States would find itself in direct confrontation with China or the Soviet Union, or both.

Recent research into the archives of the former Soviet Union, in which are filed away documents reporting on communication between China and its allies, suggests that Johnson had reason to worry. In 1962 Chairman Mao Zedong promised that China would come to the aid of North Vietnam if the United States attacked, and he pledged that during the war the North Vietnamese could count on China as "the strategic rear." In 1964 and 1965, as the United States Americanized the war, Chinese promises became more explicit. If the United States attacked North Vietnam with ground troops, the Chinese would enter on the ground as well, as they had in Korea. As it was, during the course of Johnson's war, the Chinese provided the North Vietnamese with antiaircraft artillery battalions and thousands of engineering troops. The Chinese were sufficiently influential as a result of their aid that in 1966, as the U.S. buildup began to batter the North Vietnamese and the Viet Cong, China extracted from North Vietnam a promise not to end the war. During the Johnson phase of the American war, only 3,000 Soviet advisers were present in Vietnam, but the North Vietnamese were adept at playing one of their patrons against the other, and in launching the Tet offensive in the winter of 1967–1968, the Soviets gave North Vietnam additional critical support.

Mao himself was incredulous at President Johnson's public restraint on the subject of the proxy war. "Why have the Americans not made a fuss about the fact," Mao remarked on September 23, 1968, in a conversation with the North Vietnamese premier Pham Van Dong in Beijing, "that more than 100,000 Chinese troops help you in building railways, roads, and airports although they knew about it?" As his guest suggested, it was simple: "Of course, they are afraid," said the Vietnamese premier (Westad and others 1998, 177). Mao's point was that the president feared revelation of such facts might excite an uncontrollable war fever in the United States, which could lead the United States to war against China, as had happened in the Korean War, a conflict that no American statesman wanted to repeat.

## Patience Wears Thin

The military chafed at the restraints that Johnson placed on its conduct of the war. But Johnson had his own complaints about the military. "Bomb, bomb, bomb," Johnson exploded in a meeting of military strategists. "You generals have been educated at the taxpayers' expense, and you're not giving me any ideas and solutions for this damn little piss-ant country. Now, I don't need ten generals to come in here ten times and tell me to bomb" (Lind 1999, 93).

The air war was not without effect, but it could never be so thorough as to succeed completely, to block infiltration of South Vietnam from the north, especially given the porous sanctuaries of Laos and Cambodia. The North Vietnamese, throughout the war, ferried equipment and personnel into battle along the Ho Chi Minh and the Sihanouk "trails," off-limits in Johnson's presidency to American military planners (see Document 4.9). Nor could bombing destroy the industrial base of the North Vietnamese war effort because that base was in China and the Soviet Union. On the ground was where the war would be won or lost—and where President Johnson made his most critical decisions.

The U.S. ground war strategy was consistent throughout the Johnson presidency. The United States would provide security against regular forces. In the fight against the "guerrilla, the assassin, the terrorist and the informer," wrote General Westmoreland to the president in the summer of 1965, the South Vietnamese would bear primary responsibility (LBJL). Westmoreland's strategy called for U.S. ground forces gradually to extend their range of operations. First, they would protect the cities and the planes and build up an infrastructure for military expansion. Then the United States would take the fight to the enemy in "search and destroy" operations, while the South Vietnamese patrolled the villages in "pacification" missions designed to root out the VC from villages and towns and to encourage local support for the war among the peasantry. Finally, U.S. forces would destroy the enemy in large-scale warfare.

The army's plan was for what the military calls a "war of attrition." American soldiers would simply kill the enemy forces until they came to their senses and surrendered. This meant a war of no fixed front, where the job of a typical soldier was, in effect, to be ambushed. The strategy was based on the superiority of U.S. firepower. And indeed, throughout the war, U.S. forces killed far more enemy troops than they lost. The search for combat was so intense that even fortified positions would be attacked, as at Ap Bia Mountain, the infamous "Hamburger Hill," because such an assault promised an opportunity to "attrit" the enemy. To Westmoreland, the only alternative to attrition was an unthinkable war of annihilation. As Carl Bernard, a former U.S. province adviser in South Vietnam, explained in 1969, while U.S. forces concentrated on looking for and killing enemy soldiers, the VC concentrated on controlling the people. "Each succeeds" Bernard observed (Lind 1999, 97).

By pursuing a war of attrition, in which it aimed to win by not losing, the United States left the initiative in the war to the enemy. What would the United States have to do to win? That depended largely on what the VC and the North Vietnamese decided to do. How many enemy troops could the U.S. soldiers kill? That too depended on the enemy's willingness to stand and fight. President Johnson's choice of strategy left him little choice but to respond to the enemy and to continue to pour bombs on the north and troops into the south.

From autumn 1965 to the end of 1967, the situation in Vietnam continually challenged the United States to increase its efforts. North Vietnamese and VC troops gained ground in the countryside and seemed able to replace as many men as they lost to the U.S. and South Vietnamese forces. The Joint Chiefs urged greater bombing and were rewarded in 1967 when the president ordered a "hard knock" strike against formerly off-limit targets in North Vietnam. The army urgently requested more ground troops, and the United States sent hundreds of thousands of draftees to Vietnam, until U.S. troop deployment peaked at 671,616 in March 1967.

Ironically, the Chinese and the North Vietnamese on one side and the Americans and the South Vietnamese on the other were growing anxious about the war at the same time. By the end of 1967, Chairman Ho Chi Minh, the leader of North Vietnam, had grown weary of stalemate. Ho and his military advisers decided that during the Tet holiday, the North Vietnamese and VC would launch what their war planners termed a "General Offensive/General Uprising" throughout South Vietnam. In Washington, President Johnson too was worn out by the war and by the rise of the antiwar movement, which climaxed during his administration with a massive protest at the Pentagon in the fall of 1967. Throwing aside some of his caution about exciting popular emotions, the president unleashed a peace offensive aimed at domestic opinion. Though he might have meant to stimulate the will of the people to sustain long-term combat—Johnson lectured the public that they could not expect this war to end quickly and conclusively like a football game—his message was widely read as one of reassurance and optimism. We are winning the war. We just need to stay the course.

## Tet

The Tet offensive failed in every respect but one. The anticipated uprising of the South Vietnamese population did not occur, and the Viet Cong were in fact routed so extensively that in the remainder of the war the opposition would rely on regular North Vietnamese army units to carry the burden of the fight. In Tet, moreover, North Vietnamese soldiers subjected themselves to horrendous casualties, as the American superiority in firepower continued to prove decisive in combat. Even the much-maligned army of the Republic of Vietnam (the South Vietnamese) put in a solid performance. Earle Wheeler, chairman of the Joint Chiefs, in fact, told the president in numerous White House meetings that the situation in Vietnam following Tet was fraught with opportunities, not just dangers. In strictly military terms, Tet was a catastrophe for the communists.

But this was not a strictly military war. In their effort to "erode the resolve of the American people," the president noted in his memoirs, the enemy got "exactly the reaction they sought" (Johnson 1971, 384). The nightly scenes of combat on television left Americans little doubt that they were involved in a bigger war than their president's optimistic rhetoric had prepared them to accept. Within the administration, Johnson was buffeted by the discordant voices of an administration being torn apart (see Document 4.10). One of the strongest supporters of the president through the years had been Drew Pearson, a highly respected newspaper columnist. In a letter of March 11, Pearson put the president on notice that he was "preparing a series of columns in disagreement with your Far Eastern policy" (Barrett 1997, 664; see Document 4.11). The revered newscaster Walter Cronkite gave the president no such warning before he ended a special broadcast on the war by recommending that the United States negotiate a withdrawal "not as victors" but as a nation that had done its best, and come up short (Dallek 1998, 506; see Document 4.12). Even among young adults, a group that, despite stereotypes to the contrary, had been the most hawkish on the war, Tet proved a turning point in public opinion (see Document 4.13).

Stunned by the erosion of public support and the emergence of peace candidates such as Edmund Muskie and Robert Kennedy in the race for the Democratic Party nomination for president in 1968, Johnson desperately sought a way out of the agony that Vietnam had become. With chants of "Hey, hey, LBJ, how many kids did you kill today?" wafting into the White House, and the military calling for 206,000 more troops, the president made a dramatic announcement from the Oval Office on the last day of March 1968. He would unilaterally halt the bombing of almost all of North Vietnam, and he would not stand for reelection in 1968 (see Documents 4.14 and 6.1). From that point on the war stagnated on the ground, until the North Vietnamese Politburo voted in August 1972 to authorize a negotiated settlement (Isaacson 1992, 440).

## LYNDON JOHNSON'S WAR?

The war in Vietnam would end for the United States as it had begun, with ambiguity and doubt. In 1973 the Americans at last achieved a negotiated withdrawal at Paris. The South Vietnamese endured until North Vietnamese troops in Soviet tanks rolled virtually unopposed into Saigon in 1975. Vietnamese war deaths, North and South, during the American phase of the war, 1965–1975, numbered almost 900,000. American deaths numbered over 58,000.

Was this Lyndon Johnson's war? In a sense, no. South Vietnam was one of three Asian states (the others being Korea and China) divided in two during the cold war between communist and noncommunist territories. The Democrats had been in power when the United States, as Republicans said, "lost China." Many Democrats joined with Republican critics of U.S. policy in urging greater efforts the next time a divided Asian state was threatened. When North Korea invaded South Korea, the United States fought both North Korea and the People's Republic of China to a desultory stalemate. After the Korean conflict, almost no one in Washington wanted to fight another ground war in Asia, certainly not one that might pit the United States against the massive Chinese infantry. But U.S. policy, history, and treaty obligations made it impossible for a president not to come to the aid of South Vietnam when it, too, was attacked by communist forces.

But Vietnam was Johnson's war in other ways. It was the decisive event in undermining the president's quest to achieve a reputation for greatness in the White House that would rival that of his idol and former mentor, Franklin Roosevelt (see Chapter 1). It was also the event that consumed Johnson's attention and drove him from the White House after a single elective term. Could it have been otherwise?

President Johnson was not irrational in believing that he had no choice but to fight in Vietnam. But he did not have to fight the war the way he did. The president constantly searched for consensus among his advisers and often assumed consensus among the public. The demand for consensus in the government led the president to castigate dovish advisers as near traitors and to compromise even when what was called for were tough choices, not middle-of-the-road caution. Johnson compromised the conflict between his civilian secretary of defense, who disputed bombing's effectiveness, and the Joint Chiefs, who put great faith in the air war. Johnson also sought to compromise his way to a winning strategy in the ground war, giving critics of attrition within the military a limited chance to experiment with an alternative pacification strategy but never enough support to make the experiment a real test.

Under Johnson, the United States would neither go all out nor consider withdrawing. It would simply persevere. Such a strategy required a great deal of patience, perhaps even stoicism, among the public. But Americans, as Johnson knew, were not stoic by nature, which is why he was so fearful of creating a "war psychosis" if he were to speak openly to the public about the war. Johnson waited too long to take his case for public support aggressively before the public. When at last he spoke up, his message of caution was drowned by his message of optimism. In the face of the Tet offensive, it was too little, too late.

It is time, then, to return to the great "what if" questions about this war. What if President Johnson had unleashed a wider war? Evidence from the archives of the communist states from the cold war suggests that he might have inadvertently launched World War III. What if he had spoken more candidly to the public about the war and the depth of the U.S. commitment? He might well have lost Congress, as he feared, but he would possibly have gained public support for the war. Even so, public support would likely have been limited.

The political scientist John Mueller has observed that U.S. support for the Vietnam War declined principally in response to one thing, U.S. casualties (see Documents 4.15 and 4.16). The trend in support for the war in Vietnam in this respect almost exactly mirrored support for the Korean War. If the president had spoken with greater credibility about the war, he may have earned greater public backing, even sufficient to withstand Tet, but there is no reason to believe that the United States could have been persuaded to "bear any burden" in the war. Again, we are faced with the problem of a war of attrition. How much is enough? What if the United States could have won the perpetual sovereignty of South Vietnam with the loss of, say, 100,000 U.S. soldiers? It is doubtful that any president could have sustained public support for a proxy war in the face of such losses. And how could Johnson have known if 100,000 U.S. deaths would have been sufficient?

Would President Kennedy have done things differently? On the one hand, Kennedy would certainly have had a freer hand than Johnson in making decisions for the war. Johnson said he was continuing Kennedy's policies. If he had decided to do less in Vietnam, he knew he would be pilloried (by none other than the then-hawkish Robert Kennedy) for departing from John Kennedy's legacy. President Kennedy, on the other hand, could at least have changed his mind. Still, would Kennedy have taken the risks involved in withdrawal, or even the risks of responding less aggressively than Johnson did to the pressures of the North Vietnamese and Viet Cong? If he had dared to do so, he would likely have lost all influence with Congress, as well as with his own party, and he would have added to an already long list of cold war embarrassments for the United States.

There is, however, one thing that Kennedy might have done differently. Kennedy was the biggest supporter within the government of the Special Forces, the vaunted Green Berets. The Special Forces, according to the military analyst Eliot Cohen, might have joined with the marines in pursuing an alternative to a war of attrition (Cohen 1985). If the United States had used not more force, in other words, but less—over an admittedly long time—it might have had a superior outcome in Vietnam. Could Kennedy have forced a reluctant military establishment to pursue such a strategy, surrendering its advantage in firepower and large-scale operations? We cannot truly know. But because of Kennedy's special interest in counterinsurgency warfare, and because he was more skeptical generally of military expertise than was Johnson, it remains at least a tantalizing possibility.

Fittingly, the war, and President Johnson's role in it, will in many ways remain an enigma. John Roche, a White House aide in the later years of the Johnson presidency, recounted in an interview that the president would repeatedly ask him, "What does Ho want?" In a highly publicized speech at Johns Hopkins University, April 7, 1965, Johnson had offered Ho a better life for his people—billions in aid, even a Mekong River equivalent to the great New Deal project, the Tennessee Valley Authority (see Document 4.17). "He wants to win," Roche would reply. "He couldn't understand," Roche continued. "You know, maybe he wanted three post offices, a dam, a Mekong River TVA . . ." (Roche 1987, n.p.).

BIBLIOGRAPHY

Important documentation about the Vietnam War and Lyndon Johnson's role in it is contained in *The Pentagon Papers, as Published by the New York Times* (New York: Quadrangle, 1971); and David M. Barrett, ed., *Lyndon B. Johnson's Vietnam Papers: A Documentary Collection* (College Station: Texas A&M University Press, 1997).

On the cold war setting of the Vietnam War, see the works produced by the Cold War International History Project, including Odd Arne Westad, Chen Jian, Stein Tonnesson, Nguyen Vu Tung, and James G. Hershberg, "77 Conversations between Chinese and Foreign Leaders on the Wars in Indochina, 1964–1977," Cold War International History Project Working Paper no. 22 (Washington, D.C.: Woodrow Wilson International Center for Scholars, May 1998).

A superb brief account of Lyndon Johnson's decision making for Vietnam is George C. Herring, "The Reluctant Warrior: Lyndon Johnson as Commander in Chief," in *Shadow on the White House: Presidents and the Vietnam War, 1945–1975*, ed. David L. Anderson, (Lawrence: University Press of Kansas, 1993), 87–112.

The best of the recent books on Vietnam are Michael Lind, *Vietnam: The Necessary War* (New York: Free Press, 1999); and H. R. McMaster, *Dereliction of Duty: Lyndon Johnson, Robert McNamara, the Joint Chiefs of Staff, and the Lies That Led to Vietnam* (New York: Harper Perennial, 1997). See also Andrew F. Krepenevich Jr., *The Army in Vietnam* (Baltimore: Johns Hopkins University Press, 1986).

Other important books include Larry Berman, *Lyndon Johnson's War: The Road to Stalemate in Vietnam* (New York: Norton, 1989); David Halberstam's journalistic classic, *The Best and the Brightest* (New York: Random House, 1972); Robert S. McNamara, *Mea Culpa, in Retrospect: The Tragedy and Lessons of Vietnam* (New York: Times Books, 1995); Irving Bernstein, *Guns or Butter: The Presidency of Lyndon Johnson* (New York: Oxford University Press, 1996); John E. Mueller, *War, Presidents, and Public Opinion* (New York: Wiley, 1973); and Eliot A. Cohen, *Citizens and Soldiers: The Dilemmas of Military Service* (Ithaca: Cornell University Press, 1985).

Additional works cited in this chapter are Hanson W. Baldwin, foreword to Ulysses Grant Sharp, *Strategy for Defeat* (San Rafael, Calif.: Presidio Press, 1978); Michael Beschloss, ed., *Taking Charge: The Johnson White House Tapes, 1963–1964* (New York: Simon and Schuster, 1997); Robert

Dallek, *Flawed Giant: Lyndon Johnson and His Times, 1960–1973* (New York: Oxford University Press, 1998); Walter Isaacson, *Kissinger* (New York: Simon and Schuster, 1992); Lyndon Johnson, *The Vantage Point: Perspectives on the Presidency, 1963–1969* (New York: Holt, Rinehart, and Winston, 1971); Doris Kearns Goodwin, *Lyndon Johnson and the American Dream* (New York: St. Martin's, 1991); William Manchester, *Death of a President, November 20–November 25, 1963* (New York: Harper and Row, 1967); Merle Miller, *Lyndon: An Oral Biography* (New York: Ballantine, 1980); John M. Newman, *JFK and Vietnam* (New York: Warner Books, 1992); and John Roche, interview with author, Medford, Mass., 1987.

**Document 4.1    The Kennedy Assassination**
*The Democratic National Committee raised little money from Texas in the 1960 election. Recognizing the importance of the state in the 1964 contest, President Kennedy decided a visit was necessary. In November 1964 he set out to attend fund-raising events and make public appearances with leading Democrats, including Sen. Ralph Yarborough and John Connally, his vice president's longtime friend and ally and the governor of Texas. The following excerpt is from Lady Bird Johnson's first entry in her White House diary. She recorded these thoughts on a tape recorder at her home, The Elms, just a few days after Kennedy's assassination.*

Friday, November 22, 1963

Dallas: It all began so beautifully. After a drizzle in the morning, the sun came out bright and clear. We were driving into Dallas. In the lead car were President and Mrs. Kennedy, John and Nellie Connally, a Secret Service car full of men, and then our car with Lyndon and me and Senator Ralph Yarborough.

The streets were lined with people—lots and lots of people—the children all smiling, placards, confetti, people waving from windows. One last happy moment I had was looking up and seeing Mary Griffith leaning out of a window waving at me. (Mary for many years had been in charge of altering the clothes which I purchased at Neiman-Marcus.)

Then, almost at the edge of town, on our way to the Trade Mart for the Presidential luncheon, we were rounding a curve, going down a hill, and suddenly there was a sharp, loud report. It sounded like a shot. The sound seemed to me to come from a building on the right above my shoulder. A moment passed, and then two more shots rang out in rapid succession. There had been such a gala air about the day that I thought the noise must come from firecrackers—part of the celebration. Then the Secret Service men were suddenly down in the lead car. Over the car radio system, I heard "Let's get out of here!" and our Secret Service man, Rufus Youngblood, vaulted over the front seat on top of Lyndon, threw him to the floor, and said, "Get down."

Senator Yarborough and I ducked our heads. The car accelerated terrifically—faster and faster. Then, suddenly, the brakes were put on so hard that I wondered if we were going to make it as we wheeled left and went around the corner. We pulled up to a building. I looked up and saw a sign, "HOSPITAL." Only then did I believe that this might be what it was, Senator Yarborough kept saying in an excited voice, "Have they shot the President? Have they shot the President?" I said something like, "No, it can't be."

As we ground to a halt—we were still the third car—Secret Service men began to pull, lead, guide, and hustle us out. I cast one last look over my shoulder and saw in the President's car a bundle of pink, just like a drift of blossoms, lying on the back seat. It was Mrs. Kennedy lying over the President's body.

The Secret Service men rushed us to the right, then to the left, and then onward into a quiet room in the hospital—a very small room. It was lined with white sheets, I believe.

People came and went—Kenny O'Donnell, the President's top aide, Congressman Homer Thornberry, Congressman Jack Brooks. Always there was Rufe right there and other Secret Service agents—Emory Roberts, Jerry Kivett, Lem Johns, and Woody Taylor. People spoke of how widespread this might be. There was talk about where we should go—to the plane, to our house, back to Washington.

Through it all Lyndon was remarkably calm and quiet. He suggested that the Presidential plane ought to be moved to another part of the field. He spoke of going back out to the plane in unmarked black cars. Every face that came in, you searched for the answer. I think the face I kept seeing the answer on was the face of Kenny O'Donnell, who loved President Kennedy so much.

It was Lyndon who spoke of it first, although I knew I would not leave without doing it. He said, "You had better try to see Jackie and Nellie." We didn't know what had happened to John.

I asked the Secret Service if I could be taken to them. They began to lead me up one corridor and down another. Suddenly I found myself face to face with Jackie in a small hallway. I believe it was right outside the operating room. You always think of someone like her as being insulated, protected. She was quite alone. I don't think I ever saw anyone so much alone in my life. I went up to her, put my arms around her, and said something to her. I'm sure it was something like "God, help us all," because my feelings for her were too tumultuous to put into words.

And then I went to see Nellie. There it was different, because Nellie and I have gone through so many things together since 1938. I hugged her tight and we both cried and I said, "Nellie, John's going to be all right." And Nellie said, "Yes, John's going to be all right." Among her many other fine qualities, she is also strong.

I turned and went back to the small white room where Lyndon was. Mac Kilduff, the President's pressman on this trip, and Kenny O'Donnell were coming and going. I think it was from Kenny's face that I first knew the truth and from Kenny's voice that I first heard the words "The President is dead." Mr. Kilduff entered and said to Lyndon, "Mr. President."

It was decided that we would go immediately to the airport. Hurried plans were made about how we should get to the cars and who was to ride in which car. Our departure from the hospital and approach to the cars was one of the swiftest walks I have ever made.

We got in. Lyndon told the agents to stop the sirens. We drove along as fast as we could. I looked at a building and there, already, was a flag at half-mast. I think that was when the enormity of what had happened first struck me.

When we got to the field, we entered *Air Force One* for the first time. There was a TV set on and the commentator was saying, "Lyndon B. Johnson, now President of the United States." The news commentator was saying the President had been shot with a 30-30 rifle. The police had a suspect. They were not sure he was the assassin.

On the plane, all the shades were lowered. We heard that we were going to wait for Mrs. Kennedy and the coffin. There was a telephone call to Washington—I believe to the Attorney General. It was decided that Lyndon should be sworn in here as quickly as possible, because of national and world implications, and because we did not know how widespread this was

as to intended victims. Judge Sarah Hughes, a Federal Judge in Dallas—
and I am glad it was she—was called and asked to come in a hurry to
administer the oath.

Mrs. Kennedy had arrived by this time, as had the coffin. There, in the
very narrow confines of the plane—with Jackie standing by Lyndon, her
hair falling in her face but very composed, with me beside him, Judge
Hughes in front of him, and a cluster of Secret Service people, staff, and
Congressmen we had known for a long time around him—Lyndon took
the oath of office.

*Source: Lady Bird Johnson: A White House Diary* (New York: Holt, Rinehart, and
Winston, 1970), 3–6.

## Document 4.2    Southeast Asia Collective Defense Treaty, September 8, 1954

*Johnson referred often to the Southeast Asia Collective Defense Treaty as oblig-
ing the United States to come to the defense of South Vietnam.*

The Parties to this Treaty,

Recognizing the sovereign equality of all the Parties,

Reiterating their faith in the purposes and principles set forth in the Charter of the United Nations and their desire to live in peace with all peoples
and all governments,

Reaffirming that, in accordance with the Charter of the United Nations,
they uphold the principle of equal rights and self-determination of peoples, and declaring that they will earnestly strive by every peaceful means
to promote self-government and to secure the independence of all countries whose peoples desire it and are able to undertake its responsibilities,

Desiring to strengthen the fabric of peace and freedom and to uphold the
principles of democracy, individual liberty and the rule of law, and to promote
the economic well-being and development of all peoples in the treaty area,

Intending to declare publicly and formally their sense of unity, so that any potential aggressor will appreciate that the Parties stand together in the area, and DESIRING further to coordinate their efforts for collective defense for the preservation of peace and security,

Therefore agree as follows:

Article I
The Parties undertake, as set forth in the Charter of the United Nations, to settle any international disputes in which they may be involved by peaceful means in such a manner that international peace and security and justice are not endangered, and to refrain in their international relations from the threat or use of force in any manner inconsistent with the purposes of the United Nations.

Article II
In order more effectively to achieve the objectives of this Treaty, the Parties, separately and jointly, by means of continuous and affective self-help and mutual aid will maintain and develop their individual and collective capacity to resist armed attack and to prevent and counter subversive activities directed from without against their territorial integrity and political stability.

Article III
The Parties undertake to strengthen their free institutions and to cooperate with one another in the further development of economic measures, including technical assistance, designed both to promote economic progress and social well-being and to further the individual and collective efforts of governments toward these ends.

Article IV
1. Each Party recognizes that aggression by means of armed attack in the treaty area against any of the Parties or against any State or territory which the Parties by unanimous agreement may hereafter designate, would endanger its own peace and safety, and agrees that it will in that event act to meet the common danger in accordance with its constitutional processes. Measures taken under this paragraph shall be immediately reported to the Security Council of the United Nations.

2. If, in the opinion of any of the Parties, the inviolability or the integrity of the territory or the sovereignty or political independence of any Party in the treaty area or of any other State or territory to which the provisions of paragraph 1 of this Article from time to time apply is threatened in any way other than by armed attack or is affected or threatened by any fact or situation which might endanger the peace of the area, the Parties shall consult immediately in order to agree on the measures which should be taken for the common defense.

3. It is understood that no action on the territory of any State designated by unanimous agreement under paragraph 1 of this Article or on any territory so designated shall be taken except at the invitation or with the consent of the government concerned. . . .

UNDERSTANDING OF THE UNITED STATES OF AMERICA

The United States of America in executing the present Treaty does so with the understanding that its recognition of the effect of aggression and armed attack and its agreement with reference thereto in Article IV, paragraph 1, apply only to communist aggression but affirms that in the event of other aggression or armed attack it will consult under the provisions of Article IV, paragraph 2. . . .

Done at Manila, this eighth day of September, 1954.

Source: "Southeast Asia Collective Defense Treaty," *Collective Security: Shield of Freedom* (Bangkok, Thailand: Southeast Asia Treaty Organization, 1963), 157–162.

## Document 4.3    Supporting Vietnam: National Security Action Memorandum 273, November 26, 1963

*Upon assuming office, Johnson communicated to members of his National Security Council his commitment to Kennedy's plans for South Vietnam. The following memorandum affirmed the central objective of the war—to assist the South Vietnamese in resisting North Vietnamese and domestic threats— and affirmed the decision made by Kennedy in NSAM 263, October 11, 1963, to withdraw one thousand U.S. military personnel by the end of the year. The document illustrates Johnson's concerns about continuity in government, unity of support, and the mixing of military actions with economic and political development efforts in the war.*

To:  The Secretary of State
     The Secretary of Defense
     The Director of Central Intelligence
     The Administrator, AID
     The Director, USIA

The President has reviewed the discussions of South Vietnam which occurred in Honolulu, and has discussed the matter further with Ambassador Lodge. He directs that the following guidance be issued to all concerned:

1. It remains the central object of the United States in South Vietnam to assist the people and Government of that country to win their contest against the externally directed and supported Communist conspiracy. The test of all U.S. decisions and actions in this area should be the effectiveness of their contribution to this purpose.

2. The objectives of the United States with respect to the withdrawal of U.S. military personnel remain as stated in the White House statement of October 2, 1963.

3. It is a major interest of the United States Government that the present provisional government of South Vietnam should be assisted in consolidating itself and in holding and developing increased public support. All U.S. officers should conduct themselves with this objective in view.

4. The President expects that all senior officers of the Government will move energetically to insure the full unity of support for established U.S. policy in South Vietnam. Both in Washington and in the field, it is essential that the Government be unified. It is of particular importance that express or implied criticism of officers of other branches be scrupulously avoided in all contacts with the Vietnamese Government and with the press. More specifically, the President approves the following lines of action developed in the discussions of the Honolulu meeting of November 20. The offices of the Government to which central responsibility is assigned are indicated in each case.

5. We should concentrate our own efforts, and insofar as possible we should persuade the Government of South Vietnam to concentrate its efforts, on the critical situation in the Mekong Delta. This concentration should include not only military but political, economic, social, educational and informational effort. We should seek to turn the tide not only of battle but of belief, and we should seek to increase not only the control of hamlets but the productivity of this area, especially where the proceeds can be held for the advantage of anti-Communist forces. . . .

6. Programs of military and economic assistance should be maintained at such levels that their magnitude and effectiveness in the eyes of the Vietnamese Government do not fall below the levels sustained by the United States in the time of the Diem Government. . . .

[signed] McGeorge Bundy

*Source:* National Security File, LBJ Library. Top Secret (declassified).

## Document 4.4    Tonkin Gulf Resolution, August 7, 1964

*When military leaders assured Johnson that the U.S.S.* Maddox, *a destroyer on intelligence patrol in the Gulf of Tonkin, was attacked by North Vietnamese PT boats, the president moved quickly to exploit the opportunity. The administration wanted Congress to sign off on the war, and it seemed to do so in this document, authorizing "all necessary steps" to assist South Vietnam.*

Resolved by the Senate and House of Representatives of the United States of America in Congress assembled,

That the Congress approves and supports the determination of the President, as Commander in Chief, to take all necessary measures to repel any armed attack against the forces of the United States and to prevent further aggression. . . .

Section 2. The United States regards as vital to its national interest and to world peace the maintenance of international peace and security in Southeast Asia. Consonant with the Constitution of the United States and the Charter of the United Nations and in accordance with its obligations under the Southeast Asia Collective Defense Treaty, the United States is, therefore, prepared, as the President determines, to take all necessary steps, including the use of armed force, to assist any member or protocol state of the Southeast Asia Collective Defense Treaty requesting assistance in defense of its freedom.

Section 3. This resolution shall expire when the President shall determine that the peace and security of the area is reasonably assured by international conditions created by action of the United Nations or otherwise, except that it may be terminated earlier by concurrent resolution of the Congress.

*Source:* Joint Resolution of Congress, H.J. RES 1145, August 7, 1964.

### Document 4.5    What Happened in Tonkin Gulf?

*Johnson's secretary of defense, Robert McNamara, took the opportunity in 1995 to inquire of the retired North Vietnamese strategist, General Vo Nguyen Giap, whether the Tonkin Gulf Resolution was based on an actual attack.*

HANOI, Vietnam (AP)—When former Defense Secretary Robert McNamara met the enemy's leading strategist Thursday, he raised a question he'd saved for 30 years: What really happened in the Tonkin Gulf on Aug. 4, 1964?

"Absolutely nothing," replied retired Gen. Vo Nguyen Giap.
Both sides agree that North Vietnam attacked a U.S. Navy ship in the gulf on Aug. 2 as it cruised close to shore. But it was an alleged second attack two days later that led to the first U.S. bombing raid on the North and propelled America deep into war.

Many U.S. historians have long believed either that the Johnson administration fabricated the second attack to win congressional support for widening the war, or that the White House had only flimsy evidence of a real attack.

McNamara was Johnson's secretary of defense at the time, but even he admitted Thursday that the administration may have made "serious misjudgments."

For McNamara, Giap's word was the clincher.

"It's a pretty damned good source," he said after the meeting.

*Source:* "McNamara Asks Giap: What Happened in Tonkin Gulf?" *Houston Chronicle,* November 19, 1995.

**Document 4.6    National Security Action Memorandum 328, April 6, 1965**

*In early 1965 Johnson authorized Operation Rolling Thunder, the sustained aerial bombardment of North Vietnam. To protect the U.S.–controlled air bases conducting the bombings, the president authorized the use of U.S. forces in ground combat. In NSAM 328 the president's national security adviser, McGeorge Bundy, reports his confidence in these decisions and urges the president's other top defense policymakers to toe the line in their public statements.*

Memorandum for
  The Secretary of State
  The Secretary of Defense
  The Director of Central Intelligence

On Thursday, April 1, the President made the following decisions with respect to Vietnam:

1. Subject to modifications in the light of experience, and to coordination and direction both in Saigon and in Washington, the President approved the 41-point program of non-military actions submitted by Ambassador Taylor in a memorandum dated March 31, 1965.
2. The President gave general approval to the recommendations submitted by Mr. Rowan in his report dated March 16, with the exception that the President withheld approval of any request for supplemental funds at this time—it is his decision that this program is to be energetically supported by all agencies and departments and by the reprogramming of available funds as necessary within USIA.
3. The President approved the urgent exploration of the 12 suggestions for covert and other actions submitted by the Director of Central Intelligence under date of March 31.
4. The President repeated his earlier approval of the 21-point program of military actions submitted by General Harold K. Johnson under date of March 14 and re-emphasized his desire that aircraft and helicopter reinforcements under this program be accelerated.
5. The President approved an 18–20,000 man increase in U.S. military support forces to fill out existing units and supply needed logistic personnel.

6. The President approved the deployment of two additional Marine Battalions and one Marine Air Squadron and associated headquarters and support elements.

7. The President approved a change of mission for all Marine Battalions deployed to Vietnam to permit their more active use under conditions to be established and approved by the Secretary of Defense in consultation with the Secretary of State. . . .

11. The President desires that with respect to the actions in paragraphs 5 through 7, premature publicity be avoided by all possible precautions. The actions themselves should be taken as rapidly as practicable, but in ways that should minimize any appearance of sudden changes in policy, and official statements on these troop movements will be made only with the direct approval of the Secretary of Defense, in consultation with the Secretary of State. The President's desire is that these movements and changes should be understood as being gradual and wholly consistent with existing policy.

[signed] McGeorge Bundy

*Source:* National Security File, LBJ Library, Top Secret (declassified).

## Document 4.7    Americanizing the War in Vietnam

*In the summer of 1965 Johnson made a momentous decision to "Americanize" the war in Vietnam—to make it more clearly an American responsibility. In doing so he rejected the advice of some of his advisers to mobilize the nation for war by calling up the reserves and requesting new funding from Congress. The president did not want to trade support for his domestic agenda for war support. The president also feared antagonizing the Soviets and the Chinese.*

Summary Notes of 553rd NSC Meeting
July 26, 1965—5:40 P.M.–6:20 P.M.
Subject: Deployment of Additional U.S. Troops to Vietnam

*The President:* Before formalizing decisions on the deployment of additional U.S. forces to Vietnam, he wished to review the present situation with Council members present. Secretary Rusk will deal with the political situation and Secretary McNamara will describe the military situation.

*Secretary Rusk:*
   a. Chinese Communists are most adamant against any negotiations be-
      tween the North Vietnamese and the U.S./South Vietnamese. The clash
      between the Chinese Communists and the Russians continues.
   b. We have asked many times what the North Vietnamese would do if we
      stopped the bombing. We have heard nothing to date in reply.
   c. There appear to be elements of caution on the other side—in Hanoi
      as well as Moscow. Our purpose is to keep our contacts open with the
      other side in the event that they have a new position to give us.
   d. The U.S. actions we are taking should be presented publicly in a low
      key but in such a way as to convey accurately that we are determined
      to prevent South Vietnam from being taken over by Hanoi. At the
      same time, we seek to avoid a confrontation with either the Chinese
      Communists or the Soviet Union.

*Secretary McNamara:* Summarized the military situation in Vietnam:
   a. The number of Viet Cong forces has increased and the percentage of
      these forces committed to battle has increased.
   b. The geographic area of South Vietnam controlled by the Viet Cong
      has increased.
   c. The Viet Cong have isolated the cities and disrupted the economy of
      South Vietnam. The cities are separated by the countryside.
   d. Increased desertions from the South Vietnamese Army have prevented
      an increase in the total number of South Vietnamese troops available
      for combat.
   e. About half of all U.S. Army helicopters are now in South Vietnam in
      addition to over 500 U.S. planes.

   The military requirements are:
   a. More combat battalions from the U.S. are necessary. A total of 13
      additional battalions need to be sent now. On June 15, we announced
      a total of 75,000 men, or 15 battalions. . . .

*The President:* The situation in Vietnam is deteriorating. Even though we
   now have 80 to 90,000 men there, the situation is not very safe. We
   have these choices:
   a. Use our massive power, including SAC, to bring the enemy to his
      knees. Less than 10% of our people urge this course of action.
   b. We could get out on the grounds that we don't belong there. Not very
      many people feel this way about Vietnam. Most feel our national
      honor is at stake and that we must keep our commitments there.

c. We could keep our forces at the present level, approximately 80,000 men, but suffer the consequences of losing additional territory and of accepting increased casualties. We could "hunker down." No one is recommending this course.

d. We could ask for everything we might desire from Congress—money, authority to call up the reserves, acceptance of the deployment of more combat battalions. This dramatic course of action would involve declaring a state of emergency and a request for several billion dollars. Many favor this course. However, if we do go all out in this fashion, Hanoi would be able to ask the Chinese Communists and the Soviets to increase aid and add to their existing commitments.

e. We have chosen to do what is necessary to meet the present situation, but not to be unnecessarily provocative to either the Russians or the Communist Chinese. We will give the commanders the men they say they need and, out of existing material in the U.S., we will give them the material they say they need. We will get the necessary money in the new budget and will use our transfer authority until January. We will neither brag about what we are doing or thunder at the Chinese Communists and the Russians.

This course of action will keep us there during the critical monsoon season and possibly result in some gains. Meanwhile, we will push on the diplomatic side. This means that we will use up our manpower reserves. We will not deplete them, but there will be a substantial reduction. Quietly, we will push up the level of our reserve force. We will let Congress push us but, if necessary, we will call the legislators back.

We will hold until January. The alternatives are to put in our big stack now or hold back until Ambassadors Lodge and Goldberg and the diplomats can work.

*Secretary Fowler:* Do we ask for standby authority now to call the reserves but not actually call them?

*The President:* Under the approved plan, we would not ask for such authority now.

*Source:* "Summary Notes of 553rd National Security Conference Meeting, July 27, 1965," *Public Papers of the Presidents of the United States: Lyndon B. Johnson, 1965* (Washington, D.C.: U.S. Government Printing Office, 1966), 2:388–389.

## Document 4.8    Press Conference Denying Increases in Troop Deployment, July 28, 1965

*The Vietnam War was as difficult to explain as it was to fight, with no fixed fronts and no serious option of simply annihilating the enemy. The president damaged his credibility in this press conference when he denied any change in policy after announcing that U.S. troop deployments would dramatically and rapidly increase, and that even more troops would be sent "as requested."*

My fellow Americans:

Not long ago I received a letter from a woman in the Midwest. She wrote:

"Dear Mr. President: In my humble way I am writing to you about the crisis in Viet-Nam. I have a son who is now in Viet-Nam. My husband served in World War II. Our country was at war, but now, this time, it is just something that I don't understand. Why?"

Well, I have tried to answer that question dozens of times and more in practically every State in this Union. I have discussed it fully in Baltimore in April, in Washington in May, in San Francisco in June. Let me again, now, discuss it here in the East Room of the White House.

Why must young Americans, born into a land exultant with hope and with golden promise, toil and suffer and sometimes die in such a remote and distant place?

The answer, like the war itself, is not an easy one, but it echoes clearly from the painful lessons of half a century. Three times in my lifetime, in two World Wars and in Korea, Americans have gone to far lands to fight for freedom. We have learned at a terrible and a brutal cost that retreat does not bring safety and weakness does not bring peace.

It is this lesson that has brought us to Viet-Nam. This is a different kind of war. There are no marching armies or solemn declarations. Some citizens of South Viet-Nam at times, with understandable grievances, have joined in the attack on their own government.

But we must not let this mask the central fact that this is really war. It is guided by North Viet-Nam and it is spurred by Communist China. Its goal is to conquer the South, to defeat American power, and to extend the Asiatic dominion of communism.

There are great stakes in the balance.

Most of the non-Communist nations of Asia cannot, by themselves and alone, resist the growing might and the grasping ambition of Asian communism.

Our power, therefore, is a very vital shield. If we are driven from the field in Vietnam, then no nation can ever again have the same confidence in American promise, or in American protection.

Nor would surrender in Viet-Nam bring peace, because we learned from Hitler at Munich that success only feeds the appetite of aggression. The battle would be renewed in one country and then another country, bringing with it perhaps even larger and crueler conflict, as we have learned from the lessons of history.

Moreover, we are in Vietnam to fulfill one of the most solemn pledges of the American Nation. Three Presidents—President Eisenhower, President Kennedy, and your present President—over 11 years have committed themselves and have promised to help defend this small and valiant nation.

Strengthened by that promise, the people of South Viet-Nam have fought for many long years. Thousands of them have died. Thousands more have been crippled and scarred by war. We just cannot now dishonor our word, or abandon our commitment, or leave those who believed in us and who trusted us to the terror and repression and murder that would follow.

This, then, my fellow Americans, is why we are in Vietnam. . . .
I have asked the Commanding General, General Westmoreland, what more he needs to meet this mounting aggression. He has told me. We will meet his needs.

I have today ordered to Viet-Nam the Air Mobile Division and certain other forces which will raise our fighting strength from 75,000 to 125,000 men almost immediately. Additional forces will be needed later, and they will be sent as requested. . . .

Q: Mr. President, does the fact that you are sending additional forces to Vietnam imply any change in the existing policy of relying mainly on the South Vietnamese to carry out offensive operations and using American forces to guard American installations and to act as an emergency backup?

THE PRESIDENT. It does not imply any change in policy whatever. It does not imply any change of objective.

*Source:* "The President's News Conference," July 28, 1965. *Public Papers of the Presidents of the United States: Lyndon B. Johnson, 1965* (Washington, D.C.: U.S. Government Printing Office, 1966), 2:794–803.

Document 4.9    Map of Vietnam during the
Johnson Administration

*Source:* Timothy J. Lomperis, *The War Everyone Lost—and Won,* rev. ed. (Washington, D.C.: CQ Press, 1993), ii.

## Document 4.10    Gen. William Westmoreland Requests Additional Troops

*General Westmoreland had requested an additional 205,000 troops for Vietnam, in response to what he argued were opportunities posed by the Tet offensive. Westmoreland's suggestions revealed dissension among Johnson's top advisers, who came together in the Cabinet Room on March 4, 1968, to discuss Westmoreland's request. These excerpted notes constitute an official record of the meeting. The only thing that all parties could agree on in their conversation with the president was that the president faced a momentous decision in the war. On March 26, 1968, the president met with Secretary Rusk, Gen. Earle Wheeler, and Gen. Creighton Abrams, preparatory to the generals' briefing to a group of informal senior advisers, "the Wise Men." In the notes from that meeting we hear the president pour out his concerns to some of his more hawkish advisers.*

Notes of the President's Meeting with Senior Foreign Policy Advisers (Cabinet Room). Attending were: The President, the Vice President, Secretary Rusk, Secretary Clifford, General Wheeler, Undersecretary Nitze, CIA Director Helms, General Maxwell Taylor, Secretary Henry Fowler, Mr. Walt Rostow, Mr. George Christian, Mr. Marvin Watson (joined for conclusion), Mr. Tom Johnson. The meeting began at 5:33 p.m. It ended at 7:20 p.m.
By: Tom Johnson.

*The President:* As I told you last week, I wanted you to return today with your recommendations in response to General Westmoreland's request. . . .
As I understand it, Clark Clifford, Secretary Rusk, and Rostow and others have been meeting on these questions in conjunction with the Joint Chiefs of Staff.
*Walt Rostow:* That is correct.
*Clark Clifford:* Paul Nitze and I started to work on this Friday night. As you could understand, with the time pressure we placed upon ourselves there still may need to be refinements and adjustments to the program I will discuss.
We have tried to make this document clear and understandable. (Undersecretary Nitze passed out prior to the meeting copies of a "Draft Memorandum for the President"). . . .

The subject is a very profound one, and I consider it advisable to out-line the difficulty we face and the central problem which your advisers see you facing.

As you know, from time to time, the military leaders in the field ask for additional forces. We have, in the past, met these requests until we are now at the point where we have agreed to supply up to 525,000 men to General Westmoreland. He has now asked for 205,000 addi-tional troops. . . .

Your senior advisers have conferred on this matter at very great length. There is a deep-seated concern by your advisers. There is a con-cern that if we say, yes, and step up with the addition of 205,000 more men that we might continue down the road as we have been without accomplishing our purpose—which is for a viable South Vietnam which can live in peace.

We are not convinced that our present policy will bring us to that objective.

As I said before, we spent hours discussing this matter. For a while, we thought and had the feeling that we understood the strength of the Viet Cong and the North Vietnamese. You will remember the rather optimistic reports of General Westmoreland and Ambassador Bunker last year.

Frankly, it came as a shock that the Vietcong-North Vietnamese had the strength of force and skill to mount the Tet offensive—as they did. They struck 34 cities, made strong inroads in Saigon and in Hue. There have been very definite effects felt in the countryside.

At this stage, it is clear that this new request by General Westmore-land brings the President to a clearly defined watershed:

1. Do you continue to go down the same road of "more troops, more guns, more planes, more ships?"
2. Do you go on killing more Viet Cong and more North Vietnamese and killing more Vietcong and more North Vietnamese?

There are grave doubts that we have made the type of progress we had hoped to have made by this time. As we build up our forces, they build up theirs. We continue to fight at a higher level of intensity.

Even were we to meet this full request of 205,000 men, and the pat-tern continues as it has, it is likely that by March he [General West-moreland] may want another 200,000 to 300,000 men with no end in sight. . . .

We recommend an immediate decision to deploy to Vietnam an estimated total of 22,000 additional personnel. We would agree to get them to General Westmoreland right away. It would be valuable for the general to know they are coming so he can make his plans accordingly. This is as far as we are willing to go. . . .

*The President:* Westmoreland is asking for 200,000 men, and you are recommending 20,000 or so?

*Clark Clifford:* The strategic reserves in the United States are deeply depleted. They must be built up. Senator Russell has said this. We do not know what might happen anywhere around the world, but to face an emergency we will need to strengthen the reserve. . . .

We are not sure the present strategy is the right strategy—that of being spread out all over the country with a seek and destroy policy.

We are not convinced that this is the right way, that it is the right long-term course to take. We are not sure under the circumstances which exist that a conventional military victory, as commonly defined, can be had. . . .

We can no longer rely just on the field commander. He can want troops and want troops and want troops. We must look at the overall impact on us, including the situation here in the United States. We must look at our economic stability, our other problems in the world, our other problems at home; we must consider whether or not this thing is tying us down so that we cannot do some of the other things we should be doing; and finally, we must consider the effects of our actions on the rest of the world—are we setting an example in Vietnam through which other nations would rather not go if they are faced with a similar threat? . . .

*Secretary Rusk:* Mr. President, without a doubt, this will be one of the most serious decisions you will have made since becoming President. This has implications for all of our society.

First, on the review of strategic guidance: we want the Vietnamese to do their full share and be able to survive when we leave. This was one of the things that saved us in Korea. The question is whether substantial additional troops would eventually increase or decrease South Vietnamese strength.

. . . Many of us would like to see the ARVN [Army of the Republic of Vietnam] equipped better and supplied with the M-16 rifles.

We must also consider what would happen to our NATO troop policies. To reduce NATO troops is a serious matter indeed.

We have also got to think of what this troop increase would mean in terms of increased taxes, the balance of payments picture, inflation, gold, and the general economic picture. . . .

*Fowler:* . . . The adoption of this program would require a new fiscal program. . . .

*Dick Helms:* I feel that the study of the last 3–4 days has shown that we must replenish our Strategic Reserve. If you look at the conditions throughout the world, you can easily see that we need it.

*Rusk:* I would go to Congress for specific actions, not for a statement of policy such as the Tonkin Gulf Resolution. We do not want a general declaration.

*President:* In the Senate we face a real problem. Anything that requires any authority may result in a filibuster.

*Wheeler:* If we *could* provide Westy with the troops he wants I would recommend they be sent. They cannot be provided. This [the 22,000] is what we can do by 15 June. . . .

*General Taylor:* We are all for this recommendation tonight—but all for different reasons. I frankly was startled to learn that we can't send more than 22,000 men.

I also want to know if this is a year of despair or a year of opportunity. I think it is the latter. Westy may get into trouble between now and June. He could lose a lot of politically valuable terrain.

We should bear this in mind. . . . Let's not delude ourselves about the ARVN. They will try—they will give us the right answers—but don't count on them to do too much in a short period of time.

*President:* Have you told Westmoreland you would only send this number and we could give no more by June 1?

*Wheeler:* No, I will tell him after this meeting.

*President:* Tell him to forget the 100,000 [sic]. Tell him 22,000 is all we can give at the moment. If the ARVN are not equipped as well as the Vietcong, isn't that a sad commentary on us?

Notes of the President's Meeting with General Earle Wheeler, JCS, and General Creighton Abrams, [and Sec. Rusk] March 26, 1968, Family Dining Room, Meeting began: 10:30 a.m., Meeting Ended: 12:15 p.m.

By: Tom Johnson

*The President:* I want you to meet with that group today. Stress that you have worked with the South Vietnamese closely. Tell them, in candor, we want to talk to you about the South Vietnamese. Give them the factual, cold honest picture as you see it. We don't want an inspirational talk or a gloom talk. Nitze won't even testify. It is the civilians that are cutting our guts out.

We weren't caught asleep during Tet. They lost 50,000. They are trying their damndest to recover.

Give them your plan, hope and belief.

[Sentence sanitized.] I want both of you at lunch. I want General Abrams to give us the whole pictures—pros and cons.

The bitterness has built up here. We hope we aren't attacked while this is going on.

General Ridgway said the strategic reserves are down to nothing. He said he thinks we have more commitments than we can handle.

*Secretary Rusk:* If we can't see some reasonable date, this country can't support a bottomless pit.

*General Wheeler:* The ARVN is doing well. The morale is good.

*The President:* Stress that.

*General Wheeler:* Westy said he understands the situation in the U.S. . . .

*The President:* Our fiscal situation is abominable. We have a deficit running over 20 [billion dollars]. We are not getting the tax bill. The deficit could be over 30. If it does, the interest rate will rise. The British pound may fall. The Canadian pound may fall. The dollar will be in danger. Unless we get a tax bill it will be unthinkable.

They say to get $10 in taxes we must get $10 in reductions of appropriations. We have to take one half from non-Vietnam defense expenditures. That will cause hell with Russell, if we don't do that we have hell. What happens when you cut poverty, housing and education?

This is complicated by the fact that it is an election year. I don't give a damn about the election. I will be happy just to keep doing what is right and lose the election.

There has been a panic in the last three weeks. It is caused by Ted Kennedy's report on corruption and the ARVN and the GVN [Government of (South) Vietnam] being no good. And now a release that Westmoreland wants 206,000 more men, and a call-up of 400,000. That would cost $15 billion. That would hurt the dollar and gold.

The leaks to the *New York Times* hurt us. The country is demoralized. You must know about it. It's tough you can't have communications. A worker writes a paper for Clifford group and it's all over Georgetown. The people are trying to save us from ourselves. You must bear this in mind. Bobby advocated: (1) Rusk resigning. (2) Placing the war in the hands of a Commission. I said no.

I will have overwhelming disapproval in the polls and elections. I will go down the drain. I don't want the whole alliance and military pulled in with it. . . .

How can we get this job done? We need more money in an election year, more taxes in an election year, more troops in an election year and more cuts in an election year.

As yet I cannot tell them what they expect to get in return. We have no support for the war. This is caused by the 206,000 troop request, leaks, Ted Kennedy and Bobby Kennedy.

I would give Westmoreland 206,000 men if he said he needed them and we could get them. . . .

I want you to tell them [the Wise Men] all the things that are true. Be sure it is factual. If you soldiers were as gloomy and doomy as the civilians you would have surrendered.

*Source:* David M. Barrett, ed., *Lyndon B. Johnson's Vietnam Papers: A Documentary Collection* (College Station: Texas A&M University Press, 1997), 643–651, 706–710.

## Document 4.11    Letter from Drew Pearson to the President, March 11, 1968

*Drew Pearson had been one of the few elite newspaper columnists who could count Johnson as a friend, and whom the president could rely upon for support. After Tet, Pearson came to believe that the war was too divisive at home to continue to support. As a courtesy, he let the president know beforehand that he was going to change his public stance on the war.*

March 11, 1968

To: The President
From: Drew Pearson, newspaper columnist

I have written this letter over half a dozen times, trying to decide whether to send it. I know it will hurt you. But as an old friend, I feel I owe it to you.

Regretfully, I have arrived at the conclusion that your policies in the Far East are taking us down a perilous road which can end only in disaster for you personally and for the nation; and that I must leave you. . . .

I cannot go along with you in your reasoning that this war is to stop the march of communism as World War II was to stop the march of Nazism. In Europe we are fighting for the ethnic groups which had settled the United States and given us our basic freedoms. All our cultural and historic ties have been with Europe, not with the Orient. Our immigration laws for nearly two centuries banned those ties.

Furthermore, the march of communism in Asia is actually a march of nationalism which we inspired originally in the Philippines and which Burma, India, Indonesia, Malaysia, et al. have followed. Vietnam, both North and South, want to be independent of China just as much as they do from the French or even from us, and I am convinced our intervention has driven the North partially into the hands of China.

I fear you have been led astray by such shortsighted advisers as Rostow and the military, while some of your other advisers have not spoken up.

In traveling around the country I have found increasing resentment, even bitterness, over the war, with much of it becoming personally directed against you. In my opinion we cannot continue tearing the country asunder over an issue so distant and so unrelated to the mainstream of our lives.

I shall continue to be your enthusiastic supporter in regard to domestic policy and your Latin American and European policy. But I am preparing a series of columns in disagreement with your Far Eastern policy.

*Source:* David M. Barrett, ed., *Lyndon B. Johnson's Vietnam Papers: A Documentary Collection* (College Station: Texas A&M University Press, 1997), 663–664.

## Document 4.12   Vietnam Special with Walter Cronkite, February 27, 1968

*Walter Cronkite returned from a trip to Vietnam following the Tet offensive and expressed to the nation his profound cynicism about U.S. political and military leadership and his skepticism about what good would come from continuing the war. When Johnson heard the broadcast, he said, "If I've lost Cronkite, I've lost Middle America" (Dallek 1998, 506).*

Tonight, back in more familiar surroundings in New York, we'd like to sum up our findings in Vietnam, an analysis that must be speculative, personal, subjective. Who won and who lost in the great Tet offensive against the cities? I'm not sure. The Vietcong did not win by a knockout, but neither did we. The referees of history may make it a draw. Another standoff may be coming in the big battles expected south of the Demilitarized Zone. Khesanh could well fall, with a terrible loss in American lives, prestige and morale, and this is a tragedy of our stubbornness there; but the bastion no longer is a key to the rest of the northern regions, and it is doubtful that the American forces can be defeated across the breadth of the DMZ with any substantial loss of ground. Another standoff. On the political front, past performance gives no confidence that the Vietnamese government can cope with its problems, now compounded by the attack on the cities. It may not fall, it may hold on, but it probably won't show the dynamic qualities demanded of this young nation. Another standoff.

We have been too often disappointed by the optimism of the American leaders, both in Vietnam and Washington, to have faith any longer in the silver linings they find in the darkest clouds. They may be right, that Hanoi's winter-spring offensive has been forced by the Communist realization that they could not win the longer war of attrition, and that the Communists hope that any success in the offensive will improve their position for eventual negotiations. It would improve their position, and it would also require our realization, that we should have had all along, that any negotiations must be that—negotiations, not the dictation of peace terms. For it seems now more certain than ever that the bloody experience of Vietnam is to end in a stalemate. This summer's almost certain standoff will either end in real give-and-take negotiations or terrible escalation; and for every means we have to escalate, the enemy can match us, and that applies to invasion of the North, the use of nuclear weapons, or the mere commitment of one hundred, or two hundred, or three hundred thousand more American troops to the battle. And with each escalation, the world comes closer to the brink of cosmic disaster.

To say that we are closer to victory today is to believe, in the face of the evidence, the optimists who have been wrong in the past. To suggest we are on the edge of defeat is to yield to unreasonable pessimism. To say that we are mired in stalemate seems the only realistic, yet unsatisfactory, conclusion. On the off chance that military and political analysts are right, in the next few months we must test the enemy's intentions, in case this is indeed his last big gasp before negotiations. But it is increasingly clear to this reporter that the only rational way out then will be to negotiate, not as victors, but as an honorable people who lived up to their pledge to defend democracy, and did the best they could.

*Source:* Robert Dallek, *Flawed Giant: Lyndon Johnson and His Times, 1960–1973* (New York: Oxford University Press, 1998); Ward Just, comp., *Reporting Vietnam, American Journalism 1959–1975* (New York: Library of America, 2000), 581–582.

# Document 4.13  Public Opinion Supporting the Vietnam War, May 1965–May 1971

*Young adults were typically more supportive of the war than were their elders, but support among all cohorts gradually declined over time.*

| | Age group | | | | | | | | |
|---|---|---|---|---|---|---|---|---|---|
| | Under 30 | | | 30–49 | | | Over 49 | | |
| | Support | Oppose | No opinion | Support | Oppose | No opinion | Support | Oppose | No opinion |
| May 1965 | 61% | 21% | 18% | 59% | 23% | 18% | 43% | 30% | 27% |
| August 1965 | 76 | 14 | 10 | 64 | 22 | 14 | 51 | 29 | 20 |
| November 1965 | 75 | 17 | 8 | 68 | 17 | 15 | 57 | 25 | 18 |
| March 1966 | 71 | 21 | 8 | 63 | 23 | 14 | 48 | 30 | 22 |
| May 1966 | 62 | 29 | 9 | 54 | 32 | 14 | 39 | 42 | 19 |
| September 1966 | 53 | 37 | 10 | 56 | 28 | 16 | 39 | 40 | 21 |
| November 1966 | 66 | 21 | 13 | 55 | 30 | 15 | 41 | 36 | 23 |
| May 1967 | 60 | 31 | 9 | 53 | 34 | 13 | 4 | 42 | 16 |
| July 1967 | 62 | 32 | 6 | 52 | 37 | 11 | 37 | 50 | 13 |
| October 1967 | 50 | 43 | 7 | 50 | 43 | 7 | 35 | 53 | 12 |
| Early February 1968 | 51 | 40 | 9 | 44 | 46 | 10 | 36 | 48 | 16 |
| March 1968 | 50 | 46 | 4 | 46 | 47 | 7 | 35 | 52 | 13 |

*continued*

**Document 4.13** (*continued*)

| | Age group | | | | | | | | |
| | Under 30 | | | 30–49 | | | Over 49 | | |
| | Support | Oppose | No opinion | Support | Oppose | No opinion | Support | Oppose | No opinion |
|---|---|---|---|---|---|---|---|---|---|
| April 1968 | 54 | 38 | 8 | 44 | 46 | 10 | 31 | 54 | 15 |
| August 1968 | 45 | 48 | 7 | 39 | 48 | 13 | 27 | 61 | 12 |
| Early October 1968 | 52 | 44 | 4 | 41 | 49 | 10 | 26 | 64 | 10 |
| February 1969 | 47 | 49 | 4 | 43 | 49 | 8 | 31 | 57 | 12 |
| September 1969 | 36 | 58 | 6 | 37 | 54 | 9 | 5 | 63 | 12 |
| January 1970 | 41 | 54 | 5 | 37 | 54 | 9 | 25 | 2 | 13 |
| April 1970 | 43 | 50 | 7 | 40 | 45 | 15 | 25 | 57 | 18 |
| March 1970 | 48 | 49 | 3 | 41 | 53 | 6 | 26 | 61 | 13 |
| January 1971 | 41 | 52 | 7 | 8 | 55 | 7 | 20 | 67 | 13 |
| May 1971 | 34 | 59 | 7 | 30 | 61 | 9 | 23 | 63 | 14 |

*Source:* John E. Mueller, *War, Presidents, and Public Opinion* (New York: Wiley, 1973), 139.

## Document 4.14     The Decision to Halt the Bombing, Recollections from February 6, 1970

*In retirement, Johnson gave a series of interviews to CBS news reporter Walter Cronkite. In the following interview Johnson built up a head of steam talking about his critics and the Tonkin Gulf Resolution, which he characterized as a "sky is the limit" authorization.*

I think I did a very poor job of pointing up to the American that one time, two times, a dozen times we made substantial overtures to Ho Chi Minh—willing to go anywhere, anytime, talk about anything; just please let's talk instead of fight. And in not one single instance, not one did we get anything but an arrogant, tough, unyielding rebuff. And yet the next day I would be attacked that I hadn't handled it the right way, that I didn't present it the right way—and not one word about Ho Chi Minh.

And I read the papers now, and I see the people that are critical, and I just wonder how they must feel, how their children are going to feel, when they see that their fathers are up there and here we are engaged in a war where 38,000 of our men have given their lives. And they're up there on the sidelines kicking and crying and mouthing; and if they are experts in that field, why is it they never find anything that the Communists have done that's wrong? . . . And we have said from the very beginning that all of us believed that Hitler's aggression almost destroyed the world. And we believe that Communist aggression will destroy it if somebody doesn't stand up to it.

So we all go in, in the Southeast Asia Resolution, which they misnamed—they called it the Tonkin Gulf Resolution. It was a shame somebody didn't think of calling it the Fulbright Resolution, like the Fulbright Scholars thing, with his approval, his consent. He passed it. He voted for it, eighty-two to one. Don't tell me a Rhodes Scholar didn't understand everything in that Resolution, because we said to him at the White House and every other member of that Committee that the President of the United States is not about to commit forces and undertake actions to deter aggression in South Vietnam to prevent this Communist conspiracy, unless and until the American people through their Congress sign on to go in. If the President's going in, as he may be required to do, he wants the Congress to go in right by the side of him. Why? Because that's the course of action I'd recommended for President Eisenhower when I was a senator, when I was the leader and he wanted the commitment for Formosa. That was the action I recommended in the Middle East Resolution. . . .

Anyone served in Congress twenty-five years, as I had served in Congress, wasn't about to undertake the responsibilities and the dangers I had in South Vietnam without the Congress being with me. And the Congress was with me; before that Resolution went up, every single man in that room recommended it and advocated it. And when the roll was called there were 504 that voted for it. And that's something we insisted on—committee hearings before the Armed Services and Foreign Affairs, where Secretary Rusk answered every question. He didn't hurry that committee hearing. But then they called the roll, and Senator Morse—and I respect him—he stood right up and said, "I think this is equivalent of a declaration of war. This authorizes the president to do whatever is necessary to prevent aggression." Well, he was a teacher too. He was from Oregon, he could read that language and understand it.

But when the going got hard, when the road got longer and dustier, when the casualties started coming in, why there were certain folk started looking for the cellar. . . . I don't question their right to do so. I don't even criticize them for taking that position, if that's what their conscience dictates. But I just wish their conscience had been operating when they were making all these other decisions, because the Congress gave us this authority in August, 1964 to do "whatever may be necessary"—that's pretty far-reaching; that's "the sky's the limit"—to protect your troops and prevent aggression.

Now I never used that authority—our troops didn't go in—until July 1965, almost a year later. I agonized, I explored every possible way. I tried to get these people to talk reason. I tried to keep them from coming in attacking our camps, and killing their people. I tried to get them not to infiltrate. But they were determined to do one thing, and that's take over this little country. And if they take that one over, they were determined to take over others, in my judgment, just as Hitler was.

*Source:* CBS News Special, "LBJ: The Decision to Halt the Bombing," CBS broadcast, February 6, 1970, LBJ Library.

## Document 4.15  Hawks, Doves, and Vietnam

*The Tet offensive initially led to increased support for the war in Vietnam. But by March 1968, "doves" outnumbered "hawks" for the first time. From that moment on, support for the war declined.*

People are called "hawks" if they want to step up our military effort in Vietnam. They are called "doves" if they want to reduce our military effort in Vietnam. How would you describe yourself—as a "hawk" or a "dove?"

|  | December 1967 | Late January 1968 | Early February 1968 | Late February 1968 | March 1968 | April 1968 | Early October 1968 | November 1969 |
|---|---|---|---|---|---|---|---|---|
| Hawk | 52% | 56% | 61% | 58% | 41% | 41% | 44% | 31% |
| Dove | 35 | 28 | 23 | 26 | 42 | 41 | 42 | 55 |
| No opinion | 13 | 16 | 16 | 16 | 17 | 18 | 14 | 14 |

*Source:* John E. Mueller, *War, Presidents, and Public Opinion* (New York: Wiley, 1973), 107.

**Document 4.16     Support and Opposition in the Vietnam War**

*Until 1965 the situation in Vietnam was not a salient topic in America. A Gallup Poll from May 27, 1964, indicated that 63 percent of Americans were uninterested in news about Vietnam. By the latter half of 1965, Americans were paying attention and showed strong support for the military intervention. John Mueller attributes public approval to "rally-around-the-flag syndrome." But, as the table indicates, support for the war peaked early and declined steadily throughout Johnson's presidency.*

Question A: "In view of the developments since we entered the fighting in Vietnam, do you think the U.S. made a mistake sending troops to fight in Vietnam?"

Question B: "Some people think we should not have become involved with our military forces in Southeast Asia, while others think we should have. What is your opinion?"

Question C: "Do you think we did the right thing in getting into the fighting in Vietnam or should we have stayed out?"[1]

[1]In 1964 and 1966 [the survey] asked only of those who said they had been paying attention to what was going on in Vietnam: 80 percent of the sample in 1964, 93 percent in 1966.

For each question the numbers represent, in order, the percentages in support of the war (Pro), in opposition (Con), and with no opinion (DK; don't know).

| | A | | | B | | | C | | |
|---|---|---|---|---|---|---|---|---|---|
| | Pro | Con | DK | Pro | Con | DK | Pro | Con | DK |
| November 1964 | | | | | | | 47% | 30% | 23% |
| January 1965 | | | | 50% | 28% | 22% | | | |
| May 1965 | | | | 52 | 26 | 22 | | | |
| August 1965 | 61% | 24% | 15% | | | | | | |
| November 1965 | | | | 64 | 21 | 15 | | | |
| March 1966 | 59 | 25 | 16 | | | | | | |
| May 1966 bombing oil dumps | 49 | 36 | 15 | | | | | | |

*continued*

**Document 4.16** *(continued)*

| | A | | | B | | | C | | |
|---|---|---|---|---|---|---|---|---|---|
| | Pro | Con | DK | Pro | Con | DK | Pro | Con | DK |
| September 1966 | 48 | 35 | 17 | | | | | | |
| November 1966 | 51 | 31 | 18 | | | | 47 | 31 | 22 |
| Early February 1967 | 52 | 32 | 16 | | | | | | |
| May 1967 | 50 | 37 | 13 | | | | | | |
| July 1967 | 48 | 41 | 11 | | | | | | |
| October 1967 bunker, Westmoreland visit | 44 | 46 | 10 | | | | | | |
| December 1967 Tet offensive | 46 | 45 | 9 | | | | | | |
| Early February 1968 | 42 | 46 | 12 | | | | | | |
| March 1968 | 42 | 49 | 10 | | | | | | |
| April 1968 GOP convention | 40 | 48 | 12 | | | | | | |
| August 1968 Democratic convention | 35 | 53 | 12 | | | | | | |
| Early October 1968 Nixon elected | 37 | 54 | 9 | | | | 30 | 52 | 18 |
| February 1969 | 39 | 52 | 9 | | | | | | |
| September 1969 | 32 | 58 | 10 | | | | | | |
| January 1970 | 33 | 57 | 10 | | | | | | |
| March 1970 | 32 | 58 | 10 | | | | | | |
| April 1970 | 34 | 51 | 15 | | | | | | |
| May 1970 | 36 | 56 | 18 | | | | | | |

*Source:* John E. Mueller, "Popular Support for the Wars in Korea and Vietnam." *American Political Science Review* 65 (June 1971): 363.

## Document 4.17    Peace without Conquest, April 7, 1965

*In early 1965 critics of Johnson's Vietnam policy charged he was a "warmonger" operating without a coherent plan. He responded in a televised speech at Johns Hopkins University. Johnson laid out his plan for Vietnam with the hope that Ho Chi Minh would accept Johnson's peace offer. If Ho did not, Johnson's speech would serve, he hoped, to bolster support for an escalation of the war.*

. . . Viet-Nam is far away from this quiet campus. We have no territory there, nor do we seek any. The war is dirty and brutal and difficult. And some 400 young men, born into an America that is bursting with opportunity and promise, have ended their lives on Viet-Nam's steaming soil.

Why must we take this painful road?

Why must this Nation hazard its ease, and its interest, and its power for the sake of a people so far away?

We fight because we must fight if we are to live in a world where every country can shape its own destiny. And only in such a world will our own freedom be finally secure.

This kind of world will never be built by bombs or bullets. Yet the infirmities of man are such that force must often precede reason, and the waste of war, the works of peace.

We wish that this were not so. But we must deal with the world as it is, if it is ever to be as we wish.

THE NATURE OF THE CONFLICT

. . . The first reality is that North Viet-Nam has attacked the independent nation of South Viet-Nam. Its object is total conquest.

Of course, some of the people of South Viet-Nam are participating in attack on their own government. But trained men and supplies, orders and arms, flow in a constant stream from north to south. . . .

And it is a war of unparalleled brutality. Simple farmers are the targets of assassination and kidnapping. Women and children are strangled in the night because their men are loyal to their government. And helpless villages are ravaged by sneak attacks. Large-scale raids are conducted on towns, and terror strikes in the heart of cities. . . .

Over this war—and all Asia—is another reality: the deepening shadow of Communist China. The rulers in Hanoi are urged on by Peking. This is a regime which has destroyed freedom in Tibet, which has attacked India, and has been condemned by the United Nations for aggression in Korea. It is a nation which is helping the forces of violence in almost every continent. The contest in Viet-Nam is part of a wider pattern of aggressive purposes.

### WHY ARE WE IN VIET-NAM?
Why are these realities our concern? Why are we in South Viet-Nam?

We are there because we have a promise to keep. Since 1954 every American President has offered support to the people of South Viet-Nam. We have helped to build, and we have helped to defend. Thus, over many years, we have made a national pledge to help South Viet-Nam defend its independence.

And I intend to keep that promise.

To dishonor that pledge, to abandon this small and brave nation to its enemies, and to the terror that must follow, would be an unforgivable wrong.

We are also there to strengthen world order. Around the globe, from Berlin to Thailand, are people whose well-being rests, in part, on the belief that they can count on us if they are attacked. To leave Viet-Nam to its fate would shake the confidence of all these people in the value of an American commitment and in the value of America's word. The result would be increased unrest and instability, and even wider war.

We are also there because there are great stakes in the balance. Let no one think for a moment that retreat from Viet-Nam would bring an end to conflict. The battle would be renewed in one country and then another. The central lesson of our time is that the appetite of aggression is never satisfied. To withdraw from one battlefield means only to prepare for the next. We must say in southeast Asia—as we did in Europe—in the words of the Bible: "Hitherto shalt thou come, but no further." . . .

### OUR OBJECTIVE IN VIET-NAM
Our objective is the independence of South Viet-Nam, and its freedom from attack. We want nothing for ourselves—only that the people of South Viet-Nam be allowed to guide their own country in their own way.

We will do everything necessary to reach that objective. And we will do only what is absolutely necessary. . . .

We will not be defeated. We will not grow tired.

We will not withdraw, either openly or under the cloak of a meaningless agreement. . . .

We hope that peace will come swiftly. But that is in the hands of others besides ourselves. And we must be prepared for a long continued conflict. It will require patience as well as bravery, the will to endure as well as the will to resist.

I wish it were possible to convince others with words of what we now find it necessary to say with guns and planes: Armed hostility is futile. Our resources are equal to any challenge. Because we fight for values and we fight for principles, rather than territory or colonies, our patience and our determination are unending.

Once this is clear, then it should also be clear that the only path for reasonable men is the path of peaceful settlement.

Such peace demands an independent South Viet-Nam—securely guaranteed and able to shape its own relationships to all others—free from outside interference—tied to no alliance—a military base for no other country. . . .

## A COOPERATIVE EFFORT FOR DEVELOPMENT

These countries of southeast Asia are homes for millions of impoverished people. Each day these people rise at dawn and struggle through until the night to wrestle existence from the soil. They are often wracked by disease, plagued by hunger, and death comes at the early age of 40.

Stability and peace do not come easily in such a land. Neither independence nor human dignity will ever be won, though, by arms alone. It also requires the work of peace. The American people have helped generously in times past in these works. Now there must be a much more massive effort to improve the life of man in that conflict-torn corner of our world.

The first step is for the countries of Southeast Asia to associate themselves in a greatly expanded cooperative effort for development. We would hope that North Viet-Nam would take its place in the common effort just as soon as peaceful cooperation is possible.

The United Nations is already actively engaged in development in this area. As far back as 1961 I conferred with our authorities in Viet-Nam in connection with their work there. And I would hope tonight that the Secretary General of the United Nations could use the prestige of his great office, and his deep knowledge of Asia, to initiate, as soon as possible, with the countries of that area, a plan for cooperation in increased development.

For our part I will ask the Congress to join in a billion dollar American investment in this effort as soon as it is underway.

And I would hope that all other industrialized countries, including the Soviet Union, will join in this effort to replace despair with hope, and terror with progress.

The task is nothing less than to enrich the hopes and the existence of more than a hundred million people. And there is much to be done. . . .

CONCLUSION

We often say how impressive power is. But I do not find it impressive at all. The guns and the bombs, the rockets and the warships, are all symbols of human failure. They are necessary symbols. They protect what we cherish. But they are witness to human folly.

A dam built across a great river is impressive. . . .

A rich harvest in a hungry land is impressive.

The sight of healthy children in a classroom is impressive.

These—not mighty arms—are the achievements which the American Nation believes to be impressive. . . .

Every night before I turn out the lights to sleep I ask myself this question: Have I done everything that I can do to unite this country? Have I done everything I can to help unite the world, to try to bring peace and hope to all the peoples of the world? Have I done enough?

Ask yourselves that question in your homes—and in this hall tonight. Have we, each of us, all done all we could? Have we done enough? . . .

This generation of the world must choose: destroy or build, kill or aid, hate or understand.

We can do all these things on a scale never dreamed of before.

Well, we will choose life. In so doing we will prevail over the enemies within man, and over the natural enemies of all mankind.

*Source:* "Address at Johns Hopkins University: Peace Without Conquest," April 7, 1965. In *Public Papers of the Presidents of the United States: Lyndon B. Johnson, 1965* (Washington, D.C.: U.S. Government Printing Office, 1966), 2:394–399.

*Johnson and Gen. William Westmoreland tour the U.S. military base at Camh Ran Bay, South Vietnam, October 26, 1966.*

# CHAPTER FIVE

# Institutional Relations

President Johnson's relationships with the major political institutions of his time were shaped by his opportunities, by his personality, and by events beyond his control. The Democratic majorities Johnson enjoyed on Capitol Hill ensured that he would have the chance to work closely with Congress. The optimism of intellectuals and policy experts in the 1960s guaranteed that his administration would receive a helping hand from liberal interest groups and academics. A supportive federal judiciary eased the way, moreover, for the administration's efforts in civil rights. In foreign affairs, a similar optimism prevailed at the start of the Johnson presidency, and Johnson was receptive, as President Kennedy had been, to the idea that the United States had to act with vigor to regain the initiative in the cold war.

Johnson's personality earned him both allies and enemies. His energetic attempts to make the government a magnet for reform brought into the lawmaking process a host of talented people, including the leaders of the major civil rights organizations, who had formerly been kept away from the White House. But the president's insecurities regarding criticism ironically magnified the influence of those who refused to join in his search for consensus.

Although many of his detractors made quite personal criticisms of the president, Johnson should not have taken their comments personally. The emerging protest movement of the 1960s was after all not simply a protest against Lyndon Johnson or his policies. Even if he had pursued different

217

policies for civil rights and poverty, Johnson would likely have faced violent demonstrations in the cities. Dissatisfaction with the status quo in civil rights and anger at the economic decay of inner cities had grown deep roots in the 1960s, and radical groups, such as the Black Panthers and Students for a Democratic Society, that exploited this dissatisfaction had their own histories and purposes that were independent of events in Washington.

The radical protest against the president's foreign policies was more clearly related to decisions made in the White House. But even the antiwar movement ranged far beyond the Johnson administration's policies in its condemnation of U.S. government misdeeds. The antiwar movement targeted not just the war in Vietnam but the cold war worldview that had been the foundation of each of Johnson's predecessors from Harry Truman through John Kennedy. So, even if Johnson had found a way out of Vietnam, he would likely have had difficulty with those individuals and organizations opposed to America's role in the cold war.

Taken together, then, President Johnson's political environment, his personality, and the flowering of protest in the 1960s made his relationship with the major political institutions of his time a story of achievement for liberalism but disappointment and puzzlement for the president. In this chapter, the president's interaction with select political institutions is chronicled, beginning with Congress, the organization that nurtured Johnson in his long path to the White House.

## CONGRESS

Lyndon Johnson was a master at handling Congress. As Barbara Kellerman noted in *The Political Presidency,* Johnson typically used earthy language to explain the tactics of persuasion he employed when "working" the Congress. "Give a man a good reason for voting with you, and he'll try," Johnson once said. "Try to force it down his throat and he'll gag. A man can take a little bourbon without getting drunk, but if you hold his mouth open and pour in a quart, he'll get sick on you" (Kellerman 1984, 121). Especially after the election of 1964, with a 68 percent overall majority in Congress, the president was in an enviable position to give legislators a reason for voting with him. He was popular, and the new liberal majority in Congress was as eager as he was to get things done. Under these conditions, Johnson had a historic opportunity to put his expertise at congressional relations to effective use (see Document 5.1). The Johnson administration's approach to lawmaking included much more than lobbying. It started with extensive White House involvement in policy development.

## The Johnson Task Forces

Even in policy areas where Congress had been deliberating for years, the Johnson White House convened task forces to draft new legislation. The task force operation, headed first by Bill Moyers and then by Joseph Califano and his aides, brought together academics, senior civil servants, Budget Bureau staff members, and, on high-profile issues, members of Congress as well. The task forces worked in secrecy, with small staffs, and were charged by the president to think big and leave the politics to the White House.

Once the president gave the go-ahead to a proposal or set of ideas that emerged from one of these outside task forces, an interagency task force of administration officials would coordinate plans for the division of responsibility within the government for the proposed initiatives and work out a budgetary guideline.

This extensive task force operation was part of a wider process of innovation that involved the widest possible solicitation of policy proposals. The White House even kept files on "BYM," bright young men within the government. All were asked to contribute ideas in each year's search for new legislative proposals. Califano and his assistants, when they took over the operation, would additionally tour select college campuses to meet with "idea men." The proposals that came from such methods were all summarized—one page per idea—and reviewed by Califano, his staff, and other members of the administration brought in on an ad hoc basis. The president personally studied the proposals that survived this gauntlet.

The Johnson task forces were important in generating and defining the president's legislative agenda. They also served the obvious political purpose of flattering the intellectual community, whose devotion Johnson was eager to win.

## The Arts of Persuasion

The president's involvement in the legislative process intensified once the White House began working with members of Congress to draft bills. At this stage, Johnson's leadership was in using the arts of persuasion. This included changing the fine print in a bill to make it attractive to as many members of Congress as possible. In preparing the legislative package to wage war on poverty, for example, the president was responsible for reducing the program's startup costs and for broadening the categories of beneficiaries so that virtually every congressional district might reap rewards.

Johnson worked to refine the political attractiveness of his legislation in order to get Congress committed to the goal of a piece of legislation. If the compromises that the president put forward in making his bills attractive to a diverse audience within Congress diminished a law's effectiveness, improvements to the law might be made later.

Johnson's persuasive skills were often instrumental in winning passage of his most controversial proposals. Unlike more rhetorically gifted presidents, Johnson did not often attempt to pressure Congress as a whole through appeals to the public. The most notable exceptions to this tendency were the president's nationally televised address days after Kennedy was assassinated, when he urged passage of the late president's domestic agenda, which had stalled in Congress, and his speech on behalf of the Voting Rights Act of 1965 (see Documents 3.2 and 3.6).

More typically, Johnson refrained from such tactics. He was not at his best before large audiences, and he preferred backroom politics to the open-air variety. Speechmaking, to Lyndon Johnson, was suspect, associated as it was with the open discussion of beliefs. As Johnson told his biographer, Doris Kearns Goodwin, "What the man in the street wants is *not* a big debate on fundamental issues; he wants a little medical care, a rug on the floor, a picture on the wall, a little music in the house, and a place to take Molly and the grandchildren when he retires" (Goodwin 1991, 152). As Goodwin explains, this attitude led Johnson both to seek consensus and to distrust dissent. After all, who could object to a little music in the house?

Still, Johnson knew that members of Congress would not follow him blindly. So he would bargain, cajole, and if need be cry, plead, and threaten to get the votes he needed. To collect votes in Congress, sometimes the entire White House staff, not just the president and the legislative liaison team, would devote themselves to round-the-clock lobbying. As Johnson said to Goodwin, "There is only one way for a president to deal with Congress, and that is continuously, incessantly, and without interruption. . . . He's got to know them even better than they know themselves" (Goodwin 1991, 226). Routine weekly breakfasts with the congressional leadership were transformed in the Johnson White House into intense lobbying sessions, with the president and his top liaison officer, Lawrence O'Brien, using charts and an easel to review the status of the president's pending legislation.

The president also took every opportunity to draw attention to cooperating members of Congress. No member of Congress was beneath the president's personal notice when a vote was coming up. A freshman member of the House, for instance, whose vote was counted as uncertain, might be hurried off the floor to take a phone call from the president, wishing him a happy birthday or giving him advance notice that his local newspaper was running a favorable story on how productive he was becoming in Washington—a story originating, naturally, in the White House.

Johnson was at his most effective in one-on-one sessions in the White House. "He would," recounts O'Brien in his oral history for the Johnson library, "devote an inordinate amount of time to the sales pitch, and he would put it on a truly personal basis: 'I'm pleading with you. You've got to help me. You can't walk away from this. Come on, you've just—' And that would get to the arm around the shoulder, the close proximity and the pitch that could be lengthy at times. A member would be pretty exhausted." And more often than not, especially in his first two years in office, the member would end up promising the president his support (LBJL). Indeed, by a variety of quantitative measures, Lyndon Johnson was what he seemed to be, an unusually ambitious and successful legislative leader in the White House (see Documents 5.2–5.5).

## Intellectuals, Dissenters, and Protesters

President Johnson became less effective in his sales pitches to Congress as dissent grew over the Vietnam War and over the pace of domestic change—too slow for some, too fast for others. In both his 1967 and 1968 State of the Union messages, the president was forced by the growing costs of the Vietnam War to ask Congress for a tax surcharge. When the first such surcharge finally made its way through a reluctant Congress, it did so in the form drafted not by Johnson's White House, but by Wilbur Mills, D-Ark., who chaired the House Ways and Means Committee. "I didn't want that additional money to be spent for new things," Mills recounted in his oral history for the Johnson library. Johnson tried arm twisting and pleading. "Walter Reuther would throw me out" of office if I gave in to you, the president told Mills, referring to a powerful labor leader from Detroit, who was influential in liberal circles (LBJL). Johnson even attempted to pressure Mills publicly, blaming him in press conferences for the failure of the tax measure. But the president could not budge Mills and finally accepted his demand that the tax surcharge be paid for by significant spending cuts on domestic programs.

Being humbled by Mills was difficult for Johnson to bear, but he and his former congressional colleague remained on good terms. They were both after all professional politicians. Johnson's relationship with some of his other critics, within and especially outside government, was altogether different.

President Johnson simply could not accept that members of Congress, such as Sen. William Fulbright, D-Ark., who publicly broke with the president over the U.S. response to turmoil in the Dominican Republic (see Chapter 3), were motivated by good intentions. Professionals, in Johnson's way of thinking, ultimately compromised their way to a resolution of their problems, and they did so privately if at all possible. Senator Fulbright did not play by these rules and thereby earned the wrath of the president. Fulbright, Johnson complained to Doris Kearns Goodwin, "couldn't find a president who would name him secretary of state," so he sought attention by criticizing the president (Goodwin 1991, 313).

Johnson also lamented to Goodwin that the country's intellectual elite, for whom he thought he had done so much, were "squawking" at him on Vietnam "because I never went to Harvard. That's why. Because I wasn't John F. Kennedy. Because I wasn't friends with all their friends. Because I was keeping the throne from Bobby Kennedy. Because the Great Society was accomplishing more than the New Frontier [the slogan President Kennedy used to describe his agenda]." "You see," a bitter former president continued, "they had to find some issue on which to turn against me and they found it in Vietnam" (Goodwin 1991, 313).

Johnson's insecurity with the people of ideas within and outside of his administration compelled him to worsen the situation. His naturally coarse language and manners would become outrageous in the presence of Ivy Leaguers, which only alienated them from him even more deeply.

Johnson's reaction to protest was actually more reserved than his response to criticism. The protestors in the inner cities, he believed, were responding to decades of frustration. They were, he reasoned, right to be upset and were manipulated into demonstrations and violence by vicious malcontents. Johnson also sympathized with the "kids" who took to the streets against the war. "Don't they realize I'm really one of them?" he asked Goodwin. Like them, Johnson reminded his young chronicler, he had dropped off the path to a college degree and tried his luck in California, had hated cops as a young man, and had rebelled against authority (Goodwin 1991, 333–334).

At his most depressed, Johnson speculated that the protestors were the dupes of the more treacherous dissenters, who themselves were in league— wittingly or not—with communists out to destroy the government. Why is it, he asked Goodwin once when he was in one of his dark moods, "That you could always find [Soviet Ambassador Anatoly] Dobrynin's car in front of [ *New York Times* editorialist James] Reston's house the night before Reston delivered a blast on Vietnam?" (Goodwin 1991, 317).

## CIVIL RIGHTS LEADERS

President Johnson had a mixed relationship with the leaders of civil rights organizations. His relationship with the single most prominent civil rights leader, Martin Luther King Jr., was never close, though it was constructive (see Document 5.6). Both men were used to holding center stage in any gathering and so never were at ease with each another. Moreover, their relationship soured in response to the Vietnam War. Before his death, King had begun to speak out against the war and to link the struggle for civil rights with that against the war. In addition to his difficult relationship with King, Johnson was unable, as presumably any president in his position would have been, to get on good terms with the more radical civil rights organizations, those that rejected nonviolence and sought confrontation, not compromise, with the political establishment.

In the summer of 1966 a militant minority within the Student Non-Violent Coordinating Committee (SNCC) elected Stokely Carmichael as chairman, removing John Lewis from the position. At the Congress of Racial Equality (CORE), a similar change in leadership presaged a move away from nonviolence and toward black nationalism. "Freedom Now" was replaced by "Black Power" as the ideal of younger, more militant, civil rights leaders.

With major civil rights groups that adhered to a nonviolent agenda, by contrast, Johnson came to be closely allied with many of their most prominent leaders. Sometimes this meant overcoming skepticism that the southern president who had engineered the historic but ineffectual Civil Rights Act of 1957 (see Chapter 3) was sincerely committed to expanding rights for minorities.

Johnson consulted extensively on the 1964 and 1965 civil rights acts with Roy Wilkins, executive secretary of the National Association for the Advancement of Colored People (NAACP), Whitney Young of the National Urban League, James Farmer, who headed CORE, and John Lewis, who led the SNCC at that time. The president also consulted regularly with King's organization, the Southern Christian Leadership Conference (SCLC), until King cut off his relationship with the White House in protest against the Vietnam War.

Lyndon Johnson was especially close to Roy Wilkins and Whitney Young. Wilkins and Young tried to separate the issues of civil rights and the war in Vietnam, and they did what little they or any "establishment" figures could do to dampen protests and riots in the cities. In Wilkins's estimation, it was important that Johnson remain politically strong so that the programs his administration was pursuing could have time to work. As Wilkins recalled in his oral history for the Johnson library, the Johnson administration stood for not just civil rights but the War on Poverty, model cities, the Job Corps, aid to education, Volunteers in Service to America, and other programs that provided help to, among others, African Americans.

In a reflective analysis of Johnson's common cause with the NAACP, Wilkins suggested that at the time, neither Johnson nor anyone else really knew what to do to end discrimination and improve conditions for poor and minority people in the United States. "But he knew that the federal government had to become more involved. He knew that opportunity had to be provided. . . . And he knew that the traditional political machinery, the traditional civil rights machinery, and the traditional social work machinery had not worked. . . . So he conceived the federal government's role to be to provide an opportunity for the inner cities, the crowded urban centers, to express themselves and to try to harness their own energy through corporations and agencies that would be financed by the government." "When the chips were down," Wilkins concluded, "he used the great power of the presidency on the side of the people who were deprived. And you can't take that away from him" (LBJL; see Document 5.7).

## THE GOVERNMENT

President Johnson's passion was legislation. He was aware of the problems of implementing all his new laws, but with only a limited time to make what he hoped would be revolutionary changes in the government's relationship with society, he never followed through on his occasional bursts of attention to the problems of agency overlap, underfunded programs, failed innovations, the chaotic organization of his own White House, or a host of other administrative issues. As the historian Vaughn Davis Bornet writes, Johnson almost let loose in a speech in 1966 about his problems of management. "I'm not funding all the programs I got action on last year. More than that, it takes trained personnel, you just can't mash a button and have the whole working operation" (Bornet 1984, 237). But the president ultimately decided to keep such complaints to himself. Although he knew that he was creating a bureaucratic behemoth that would eventually have to be tamed, he was too preoccupied with the quest for new programs to want to draw attention to the problems of the programs he had already passed through Congress.

The members of the Johnson administration were well aware of the president's priorities. As his aide, Harry McPherson, recounted shortly before the end of the Johnson presidency, in an oral history for the Johnson library, "on two or three occasions since I've been here, he's sent out a memorandum saying everybody is to put down exactly what he does, and we're really going to put this thing in boxes, just the way General Eisenhower had it. That either never lasts or never even gets done" (LBJL).

Like Kennedy before him, moreover, Johnson was enamored of the idea that too much organizational coherence stifled creativity. Like Franklin Roosevelt, neither Kennedy nor Johnson ever appointed a formal chief of staff. As George Reedy, a longtime Johnson aide, wrote in *Lyndon Johnson: A Memoir,* the FDR model was not as easy to copy as Johnson suspected. "The lesson that Johnson had failed to learn from FDR" Reedy believed, "was that an activist administration needs activist leaders as well as 'idea men.' There were no David Lilienthals, Harry Ickes, or Harry Hopkins in the Johnson administration. I suspect that some of his cabinet officers were capable of playing similar roles but they were kept too busy pushing new bills, new approaches, new panaceas dreamed up by the staff in the White House, which had discovered early in the administration that the road to presidential favor was paved with proposals" (Reedy 1982, 51).

## THE MILITARY

The president's relationship with the professional military was strained. In part, the strain was the outcome of heavy use. Not just in Vietnam but in a number of other spots around the world, President Johnson, like President Kennedy before him, called on the military to respond to crises (see Document 5.8). In larger part, however, his trouble with the leaders of the armed services stemmed ironically from the fact that Lyndon Johnson did not treat the military any differently from the way he treated any other segment of the permanent government. The president and his White House staff considered the military to be a pesky interest group, rather than the unique repository of professional skills that civilians, by definition, could not possess. Johnson and his staff worried about how to keep control of the uniformed military establishment, just as they worried about how to keep the bureaucrats in the social service agencies in line and how to prevent the president's civilian appointees from "going native," that is, transferring their loyalty from the White House to the agency they were assigned to lead.

President Johnson's first secretary of defense, Robert McNamara, was the ideal instrument for a president with a skeptical attitude toward the military. McNamara was confident of his and his civilian staff's ability to make sound decisions on military issues, including combat tactics and the procurement of weaponry. Emboldened by his own confidence and that of the president, McNamara became the strongest defense secretary in modern times. McNamara centralized power in the Office of the Secretary of Defense and implemented modern planning, programming, and budgeting systems throughout the Pentagon. Under McNamara, the Defense Department began to work from a master five-year defense blueprint, updated yearly. To create systemic pressure for the use of systems analysis, the defense secretary created a powerful new assistant secretary position—the assistant secretary of defense, systems analysis. The "whiz kids" who staffed this office influenced not just budgeting but the assessment of military success and failure in Vietnam as well.

In his relationship with the Joint Chiefs of Staff (JCS), the heads of the military services, McNamara was similarly intent on imposing presidential control. Until 1965 McNamara cleverly exploited interservice rivalries to secure the acquiescence of the JCS in major policy decisions. From 1966 on McNamara's position weakened, as Gen. Earle Wheeler unified the fractious JCS from his position as chairman.

The administration's offensive against its own military advisers does not mean that the president was bereft of military advice. Johnson did, however, struggle to keep the JCS from publicizing advice that he considered but rejected. According to its harshest critics (such as H. R. McMaster in

*Dereliction of Duty)*, the JCS, even under General Wheeler's leadership, comprised the "five silent men" who stood by while the president pursued a failing military strategy. From a more moderate perspective (Michael Lind in *Vietnam)*, the president accepted such military advice as he liked (such as that from his field commander, Gen. William Westmoreland) and purposely marginalized those military leaders who disagreed with his strategic decisions.

It is certainly true, however, that the president often excluded the military from sessions where vital decisions about the war in Vietnam were made. Starting in February 1964 the president began Tuesday lunch meetings with his secretary of state, Dean Rusk, his national security adviser, McGeorge Bundy, and his secretary of defense, Robert McNamara. Over the five years that followed, the Tuesday group met more than twice as often as the National Security Council, whose membership, established by law, includes the chairman of the JCS. If the Tuesday lunch sessions were significant as a means for circumventing the military, however, their significance diminished in 1967, when General Wheeler became a regular participant.

## THE MEDIA

President Johnson entered the White House paranoid about the media. He conjectured that a Texan who graduated from San Marcos Teacher's College could never get fair coverage in the elite press. To assuage the new president's anxiety, his longtime media aide, George Reedy, sent Johnson a handwritten note shortly before his first address to Congress. Reedy assured the president that the press was behind him. "They are in a mood now," Reedy wrote the president in a memorandum of November 27, 1963, "where they are merely looking for historical indications that you are going to be a good President and a strong President" (LBJL).

President Kennedy's assassination had created a honeymoon period between President Johnson and the White House press corps. During this time, Johnson attempted to befriend White House reporters, and, in return, the reporters refrained from criticizing the president. This brief period did not last. In the spring of 1964 the president exploded in anger at several media reports that seemed to him unfairly designed to hurt his young administration. *Time* magazine ran a story detailing the president's behavior at the ranch. He tore around the country roads of Texas, *Time* reported, at breakneck speed, sipping Pearl beer out of a paper cup. When a member of the press in the back seat of the presidential Lincoln Continental remarked at the president's driving, Johnson placed his hat over the speedometer. The *Wall Street Journal* ran an even more damaging story, raising questions about Johnson's use of political influence in building his family's fortune in the heavily regulated radio and television industries. As if these items were not enough, the White House had to reply at about the same time to protests from dog lovers when the president was photographed picking up his pet beagle by the dog's ears. The dog liked the treatment, the president indignantly asserted. For the remainder of Johnson's presidency, his relationship with the press was characterized by mutual suspicion.

Two factors led to Johnson's poor relations with the press. First, Johnson distrusted the media (see Document 5.9). He called the White House press corps the "Eastern press" and bluntly told journalists that someone from his part of the country would never receive fair treatment in their publications. Johnson frequently spoke of an "Ivy League" bias; on one occasion he told *Newsweek* reporter Charles Roberts that because Roberts's bureau chief, Ben Bradlee, was a Harvard alumnus, Johnson could not rely on *Newsweek* for unbiased coverage.

Second, Johnson attempted to control the press. He told Doris Kearns Goodwin that "Reporters are puppets. They simply respond to the pull of the most powerful strings. . . . And if you don't control the strings to that private story, you'll never get good coverage no matter how many great things you do for the masses of the people" (Goodwin 1991, 247). Charles Roberts recalled Johnson's "clumsiest effort" to control the press. Soon after he took office, Johnson told a group of reporters aboard *Air Force One*, "If you help me, I'll help you and make you all big men in your profession" (Thompson 1986, 107). Johnson's counterproductive efforts to play favorites and control the press resulted in an enormous amount of tension and hostility.

Johnson's relationship with the news media was, however, not unremittingly unpleasant. In 1964 the media aided Johnson in his effort to paint presidential rival Barry Goldwater in a negative light. A September 14 memo from Jack Valenti to other presidential aides underscored the importance of media attention on Goldwater's extremism. "Right now, the biggest asset we have is Goldwater's alleged instability in re atom and hydrogen bombs. WE MUST NOT let this slip away" (LBJL). By election day, most Americans held a negative view of Barry Goldwater. Johnson's landslide victory in the 1964 presidential contest is largely attributable to the unpopularity of Goldwater rather than overwhelming support for Johnson (see Chapter 2).

Without a Goldwater to rally against, however, Johnson's attempts to manage the press did him more harm than good. So that he could favor those who wrote friendly stories and punish those who wrote critical ones, Johnson ended the traditional practice whereby White House reporters took turns at detailed access to the president and his top people and then shared notes of their interviews with their peers. This practice, called the press pool, left the journalists in control, which Johnson did not like. Instead, he kept the horde of White House reporters at a distance and steered information to a select group to whom he would grant intimate, one-on-one interviews. Reporters who published unwelcome stories would find that the president would somehow always be "too busy" to talk to them, and the White House would "forget" to keep them informed of such vital items as changes in the president's schedule. By 1966 the antagonisms caused by such uneven treatment of the press had become so great that his press secretary, Bill Moyers, sent a letter to the president warning of serious discontent among the journalists. "The White House Press Corps has come to believe that we antagonize them deliberately, keep them as uninformed as possible, make their personal lives as difficult as we can, play games with them, are unduly secretive, massage them when we need them and kick them when we don't and generally 'downgrade the profession'" (LBJL).

Rather than accept this analysis, and its implicit criticism of Johnson's own decisions on press relations, the president decided that the problem was Moyers himself. Johnson accused Moyers of receiving too much personal attention from the press, detracting from attention to the president. Robert Dallek interprets Johnson's dissatisfaction with Moyers as little more than scapegoating. "However much Moyers may have contributed to the credibility gap, it was the President's own deceitfulness that stood at the center of the distrust that congressmen and senators, journalists, and ultimately people all over the country felt toward him." (Dallek 1998, 294).

Johnson was especially frustrated with media coverage of the Vietnam War. He anticipated the media would further his interests, much as they did during his 1964 bid for reelection and as they had for his idol, Franklin Roosevelt, during World War II. Although the press generally supported Johnson's decision to fight, he felt the coverage was imbalanced. On more than one occasion, Johnson lashed out at the press; according to the minutes of a cabinet meeting on December 17, 1965, he complained, "The Viet Cong atrocities never get publicized. Nothing is being written or published to make you hate the Viet Cong; all that is being written is to hate us" (LBJL).

During the final months of his presidency, Johnson granted an interview to United Press International reporter Helen Thomas. He told her that the tragic error of his presidency had been an "inability to establish a rapport and a confidence with press and television." Robert Dallek concludes, "the interview with Thomas suggests that he saw himself as a misunderstood and rejected leader who was given little credit for presidential gains" (Dallek 1998, 592).

After leaving office, Johnson agreed to sit down at his ranch with CBS journalist Walter Cronkite for a series of one-hour interviews. The seven topics to be addressed, one per interview, were the assassination of President Kennedy and Johnson's ascension to the presidency, the struggle for civil rights, America's space program, the war in Vietnam, presidential decision making in 1968, Harry Truman, and general politics. Cronkite envisioned a documentary that would detail the successes and failures of Johnson's presidency; Johnson foresaw a series highlighting the accomplishments of his administration. A protracted legal battle resulted in a compromise that left neither party fully satisfied, though the series did air in three prime-time segments and did address all topics agreed upon at the start of negotiations (see Document 4.14).

## THE COURTS

President Franklin Roosevelt proposed the New Deal, a comprehensive series of government programs to rescue the United States from the Great Depression. Much of Roosevelt's ambitious agenda passed through Congress within three months of his inauguration, setting the "hundred day" standard that all modern presidents are measured against. However, the New Deal was severely limited by a chain of Supreme Court rulings that declared many of the programs unconstitutional.

Fearing that the Supreme Court would limit the Great Society as it had the New Deal, Johnson wanted an ally on the Court who could provide inside information and support his domestic programs. He concocted an elaborate plan to get his close friend, Abe Fortas, on the Court. First, he recognized that Associate Justice Arthur Goldberg was ambitious for a position beyond the Court. He was, in fact, rumored to be interested in being Johnson's vice presidential candidate in 1964. Johnson therefore was able to persuade Goldberg to step down from the Supreme Court and assume a U.S. ambassadorship to the United Nations. Johnson convinced Goldberg that this move would best serve Goldberg's political career.

With an empty Supreme Court slot, Johnson lobbied Fortas, who in addition to being a trusted Johnson friend was a brilliant and well-known Washington attorney, to accept the nomination and round out the Court's membership (see Document 5.10). Fortas, however, had struggled financially by serving the public as a young New Deal attorney and now was a partner in a highly profitable Washington law firm. Fortas reported to the president that neither he nor his wife wanted an appointment to the Court at this time. Fortas thought the issue had been settled when he received a summons from the president to attend a White House press conference where Johnson would announce the deployment of 50,000 troops to Vietnam. Johnson announced at the press conference that Fortas had agreed to sacrifice for his country and accept the nomination. Biographer Robert Dallek adds that Fortas's wife hung up on the president when he called to tell her the "good news" (Dallek 1998, 235). Fortas's nomination was confirmed by a voice vote of the Senate on August 11, 1965.

In October 1964, well before Fortas was able to don judicial robes, the first major challenge to the Civil Rights Act reached the Supreme Court (see Document 5.11). The Heart of Atlanta Motel located in Atlanta, Georgia, refused to accept black customers. Title II of the Civil Rights Act passed earlier that year (see Chapter 3) forbade places of public accommodation from racially discriminating against patrons. The Heart of Atlanta claimed that the Civil Rights Act denied the motel its right, accorded to it in the Commerce Clause of the Constitution, to select customers. In a unanimous decision, the Court upheld the Civil Rights Act, by finding that the motel had no right to choose its customers free of government regulation.

The Court simultaneously considered a second challenge to the Civil Rights Act. The owner of Ollie's Barbecue in Birmingham, Alabama, refused to serve black customers. The owner claimed that Congress had overstepped its bounds in the civil rights law by interfering with interstate commerce. In another unanimous decision, the Court found that the Civil Rights Act did not overstep constitutional bounds and that restaurants that serve interstate travelers cannot discriminate on racial grounds.

In January 1966, with Fortas on the bench, the next major challenge to civil rights legislation reached the Supreme Court. In *South Carolina v. Katzenbach,* the Court considered whether the Voting Rights Act of 1965 violated South Carolina's right to control its own elections. In an 8–1 opinion, the Court declared that the act did not violate the state's rights. The decision explained that, "Congress had found that case-by-case litigation was inadequate to combat wide-spread and persistent discrimination in voting, because of the inordinate amount of time and energy required to overcome the obstructionist tactics invariably encountered in these lawsuits. After enduring nearly a century of systematic resistance to the Fifteenth Amendment, Congress might well decide to shift the advantage of time and inertia from the perpetrators of the evil to its victims" (383 U.S. 301, 1966).

Johnson got a second chance to influence the Supreme Court in 1967 when Associate Justice Tom Clark announced his retirement. At that time, the Supreme Court had never had a female or a black justice. Johnson decided that the appointment of a black to the Supreme Court could be a monumental statement. Johnson looked to Thurgood Marshall, a prominent black attorney whom Kennedy had named to the Second Circuit Court of Appeals in 1961 and whom Johnson had named solicitor general in 1965. Amid much suspense, Johnson announced the appointment on June 13, 1967. The Senate considered the appointment for an uncommonly long two-month period. Marshall was confirmed on August 30, 1967, by a vote of 69–11.

Johnson enjoyed a symbiotic relationship with the Supreme Court during his presidency. One of his greatest allies was Chief Justice Earl Warren, an Eisenhower appointee. Eisenhower's hope was that Warren, a Republican governor, would lead the Court as a moderate conservative. During the 1960s the Warren Court supported the Civil Rights Act of 1964, the Voting Rights Act of 1965, Great Society legislation, rapid integration of southern schools, and an expansion of rights for individuals accused of crimes. In *Miranda v. Arizona,* the Court established the requirement for police to read defendants their rights before submitting to questioning and, in *Gideon v. Wainwright,* it guaranteed the right of the accused to secure an attorney. To Eisenhower's dismay and Johnson's satisfaction,

Warren led the Supreme Court in a liberal direction. Unlike the New Deal, which was limited by judicial review, the Great Society flourished with Court protection and enforcement.

During the final year of Johnson's presidency, however, Johnson suffered his one serious setback in his relationship with the federal bench. Chief Justice Earl Warren announced his retirement. This departure seemingly gave Johnson the opportunity to protect Great Society legislation by appointing one of his closest associates to be the next chief justice. Johnson wanted Abe Fortas to take the job. To quell the commotion he knew would erupt by his proposed elevation of Fortas, an East Coast liberal, to the chief justiceship, Johnson nominated a Texas judge, Homer Thornberry, to fill Fortas's seat.

A protracted battle ensued over Fortas's appointment. In Senate testimony, questioning focused on the close ties between Johnson and Fortas. Senators expressed concern that Fortas had leaked confidential Court information to the president over the years Fortas had served as associate justice. The appointment debate was complicated by Johnson's framing of the nominations; his allies in the Senate had linked the fate of Fortas to that of Thornberry so the Senate had to approve or veto both nominations.

Johnson succeeded in securing majority support for the appointments. However, anticipating a Republican victory in the 1968 presidential election, Republican senators successfully filibustered so that the next president could nominate the chief justice. Democrats tried to invoke cloture and bring the nomination to a vote on the floor, but they fell short.

## THE PUBLIC

Lyndon Johnson enjoyed strong public support when he assumed the presidency. The shock of the Kennedy assassination impelled many Americans who otherwise would not have supported Johnson to rally around him at first. The Gallup Organization acknowledged Johnson to be its "most admired man" of 1963, and, by January 1964, 80 percent of Americans approved of his job performance (see Documents 5.12 and 5.13)

With such resounding support, Johnson became a close observer and true believer in the polls. Louis Harris, founder of the Harris Poll, shrewdly observed that Johnson was in fact the "truest believer of polls, but only when they tended to support what he was doing" (Harris 1973, 287). From 1963 to 1966 Johnson frequently carried the latest polls in his pocket so that he could share his popularity ratings with guests on a moment's notice.

Public support was used as a tool only in the first three years of his administration, however, because after that time the polls turned more negative. During Johnson's tenure in office, he experienced a steady decline in popular support (see Document 5.13). By the time his approval rating fell below 50 percent, the president changed his position on public opinion polls; he disregarded them as inaccurate and chose to support his actions on moralistic grounds rather than rooting them in popular support.

A key reason for the diminution of public support was Johnson's style before the public. The president excelled at behind-the-scenes politics. The famed "Johnson Treatment" was his method to convince legislators in one-on-one sessions to support him. Before larger audiences, and especially on television, by contrast, Johnson often appeared either wooden or so folksy as to lack credibility. As a result Johnson—who had been a confident and skillful public speaker in the electioneering environment of his younger days, when candidates for public office in his home state often engaged in on-stage histrionics—developed deep insecurities about addressing the nation as president.

In 1966, as Great Society legislation sailed through Congress in an unprecedented fashion and additional troops were deployed to Vietnam, the president remained mysteriously quiet. His only address to the nation that year was the mandatory State of the Union speech in January. Indeed, except for the occasion when he announced both that he would not stand for reelection and that he was halting bombing of North Vietnam, Johnson devoted only one major address to the war in Vietnam during his five years in office, at Johns Hopkins University in 1965, in which he promised a TVA–style development program for the Vietnamese if they would lay down their arms (see Document 4.16). By comparison, Richard Nixon delivered eleven major addresses on Vietnam in his first term alone.

Johnson did deliver some well-remembered and highly praised speeches as president. In the wake of police brutality against peaceful demonstrators in Selma, Alabama, an event that many would refer to as Bloody Sunday, Johnson's special message to Congress, entitled "The American Promise," turned public outrage into a mandate for the Voting Rights Act of 1965. And when he addressed the nation about the Vietnam War in a major speech for only the second time, on March 31, 1968, the president enjoyed a small surge in public approval.

The issue that most hurt Johnson's standing with the public was Southeast Asia. Initial support for the Vietnam War was strong. The public remained committed to the war through early 1966 despite the deaths of more than 2,000 U.S. soldiers (see Document 5.14). An early turning point in support came when Senator Fulbright, who chaired the Senate Foreign Relations Committee, began to speak out vehemently against the war and opened Senate hearings to scrutinize America's role in it.

Public approval of the Vietnam War declined in response to the hearings. Early in his presidency, Johnson promised Americans that the United States would quickly prevail in Vietnam with minimal costs. Seeing no end in sight by mid-1966, Americans began to doubt a meaningful victory could be achieved. Even if victory was attainable, many believed the benefits were incommensurate with the increasing costs and the growing loss of American lives.

Johnson's difficulty with the public was intensified by his continued silence. In a time of war, Americans expect the president to lead the nation by providing information and inspiration. Johnson, fearing what might happen if he inflamed public opinion and thereby built pressure for a wider war, chose to work in the shadows. When the president did provide information, many Americans doubted its validity. A "credibility gap" developed that undermined the integrity of the president. Recognizing the growing problems associated with the Vietnam War, Sen. George Aiken, R-Vt., suggested to Johnson that America "declare that we have achieved our objectives in Vietnam and go home" (Brace and Hinckley 1992, 125). Johnson disregarded Aiken, as he did public opinion, and continued to escalate the war.

Johnson's willingness to disregard public opinion in the pursuit of a major objective places him in a unique category of American presidents. Paul Brace and Barbara Hinckley argue in *Follow the Leader: Opinion Polls and the Modern Presidents* that Johnson, like Gerald Ford and Harry Truman, were the three "accidental" presidents of the modern era. They all assumed office without a general election. Intriguingly, all three took action against public opinion; Johnson's boldest action was the escalation of the Vietnam War as public support for the war plummeted. Brace and Hinckley posit that taking unpopular actions is a trait that unites these presidents because the normal election process screens out individuals who pursue personal convictions over the public will (Brace and Hinckley 1992, 139–140). An interesting paradox to Johnson's personality is his bewilderment at why more Americans did not support him. Although he disregarded public opinion on Vietnam, he still expected high approval ratings.

As Johnson told Doris Kearns Goodwin, "No matter what anyone said, I knew that the people out there loved me a great deal. All that talk about my lack of charisma was a lot of crap. There is no such thing as charisma. It's just the creation of the press and the pollsters. Deep down I knew—I simply knew—that the American people loved me. After all that I'd done for them and given to them, how could they help but love me?" (Goodwin 1991, 315).

BIBLIOGRAPHY

On Johnson's relationship with Congress, the government and the military, see the sources cited in Chapter 3 (which covers legislative accomplishments), Chapter 4 (which details Johnson's policies toward Vietnam and the influence of civil-military conflict on that war), and Appendix A (which includes coverage of Johnson's senior White House aides and other members of the government).

On the media, see Doris Kearns Goodwin, *Lyndon Johnson and the American Dream* (New York: St. Martin's Press, 1991); and George Reedy, *Lyndon B. Johnson: A Memoir* (New York: Andrews McMeel, 1982). Also note Kenneth W. Thompson, ed., *The Johnson Presidency: Twenty Intimate Perspectives of Lyndon B. Johnson* (Lanham, Md.: University Press of America, 1986).

Several important memoranda to the president on the topic of media relations are available at the Lyndon B. Johnson Library (LBJL) in Austin, Texas. See especially Reedy to LBJ, November 27, 1963, Handwriting file; and Moyers to LBJ, June 6, 1966, WHCF: Aides: Moyers. The notes to Johnson's cabinet room meeting quoted from in this chapter are from Cabinet Room Meeting, December 17, 1965, Meeting Notes file.

The most comprehensive volume on judicial appointments is Neil D. McFeeley, *Appointment of Judges: The Johnson Presidency* (Austin: University of Texas Press, 1987). For a discussion of the politics behind court appointments and decisions, see Robert Dallek, *Flawed Giant: Lyndon Johnson and His Times, 1961–1973* (New York: Oxford University Press, 1998). See also David Alistair Yalof's analytical history, *Pursuit of Justices: Presidential Politics and the Selection of Supreme Court Nominees* (Chicago: University of Chicago Press, 1999).

Johnson's relationship with the public is compared with that of other modern presidents in Paul Brace and Barbara Hinckley, *Follow the Leader: Opinion Polls and the Modern Presidents* (New York: Basic Books, 1992). Public opinion on the Vietnam War is analyzed in John E. Mueller, *War, Presidents, and Public Opinion,* (New York: Wiley, 1973).

Other works cited in this chapter include Vaughn Davis Bornet, *The Presidency of Lyndon B. Johnson* (Lawrence: University Press of Kansas, 1984); Louis Harris, *The Anguish of Change* (New York: Norton, 1973); Barbara Kellerman, *The Political Presidency: Practice of Leadership* (New York: Oxford University Press, 1984); Michael Lind, *Vietnam, the Necessary War: A Reinterpretation of America's Most Disastrous Military Conflict* (New York: Free Press, 1999); and H. R. McMaster, *Dereliction of Duty: Lyndon Johnson, Robert McNamara, the Joint Chiefs of Staff, and the Lies That Led to Vietnam* (New York: HarperCollins, 1997).

### Document 5.1     Relations with Congress

*Johnson applied the lessons he learned as a member of Congress to the presidency. In the excerpt below, Johnson discusses how an experience he had as a representative affected his presidential dealings with Congress.*

Throughout my Presidency I insisted that we brief the Congress fully before our messages were sent to the Hill. We made many mistakes, but failure to inform and brief Congress was not one of them. My insistence on this practice was rooted in an experience I had in the House in 1941, when I witnessed the negative impact of a failure to brief congressional leaders. I was standing in the back of the House behind the rail as Speaker Sam Rayburn listened to the House clerk read an important new administration message President Roosevelt had just sent to the Hill. Several dozen Democrats were gathered around him. As he finished, a unanimous chorus of complaints rushed forth: "Why, that message is terrible, Mr. Sam—we can't pass that" . . . "That last section is awful" . . . "Why didn't you warn us?"

Speaker Rayburn listened to all the criticisms and then responded softly: "We'll just have to look at it more carefully. That's all I can say now, fellows. We'll have to look at it more carefully." The crowd scattered. Mr.

Sam and I were left alone in the back. I could see that something was wrong. "If only," he said, "the President would let me know ahead of time when these controversial messages are coming up. I could pave the way for him. I could create a base of support. I could be better prepared for criticism. I could get much better acceptance in the long run. But I never know when the damned messages are coming. This last one surprised me as much as it did all of them." He shook his head sadly and walked slowly away.

I could see that his pride was hurt. So was the President's prestige and the administration's program. I never forgot that lesson.

*Source:* Lyndon B. Johnson, *Vantage Point* (New York: Holt, Rinehart, and Winston, 1971), 447–448.

## Document 5.2    Requests for Legislation

*The following table details the number of legislative requests that Presidents Kennedy, Johnson, Nixon, and Ford sent to Congress in State of the Union messages. "New requests" refer to new agenda items; "Repeats" refer to items also requested in the previous year's State of the Union address. As the table shows, many of Johnson's requests during his first year in office (1964) reiterated Kennedy's requests from 1963. The next four years depict the enormous number of new requests.*

| President (administration) | Years | New requests | Repeats |
|---|---|---|---|
| Kennedy/Johnson (first) | 1961–1964 | 53 | 31 |
| | 1961 | 25 | 0 |
| | 1962 | 16 | 8 |
| | 1963 | 6 | 12 |
| | 1964 | 6 | 11 |
| Johnson (second) | 1965–1968 | 91 | 31 |
| | 1965 | 34 | 4 |
| | 1966 | 24 | 7 |
| | 1967 | 19 | 8 |

*continued*

**Document 5.2** *continued*

| President (administration) | Years | New requests | Repeats |
|---|---|---|---|
| Johnson (second) | 1968 | 14 | 12 |
| Nixon (first) | 1969–1972 | 40 | 35 |
| | 1969 | 17 | 0 |
| | 1970 | 12 | 9 |
| | 1971 | 8 | 12 |
| | 1972 | 3 | 14 |
| Nixon (second)/Ford | 1973–1976 | 41 | 24 |
| | 1973 | 20 | 3 |
| | 1974 | 5 | 11 |
| | 1975 | 10 | 3 |
| | 1976 | 6 | 7 |

*Source:* Paul C. Light, *The President's Agenda: Domestic Policy Choice from Kennedy to Clinton,* 3d ed. (Baltimore: Johns Hopkins University Press, 1999), 42.

## Document 5.3    Presidential Requests for Legislation: Large Programs versus Small Programs

*The following table provides insight into the scope of presidential requests to Congress. Small programs, such as highway beautification, differ significantly from large programs, such as the Civil Rights Act. The table confirms the impression that Johnson was uniquely ambitious among presidents who held office in the 1960s and 1970s.*

| President | Large programs | | Small programs | |
|---|---|---|---|---|
| | Total | Average per year | Total | Average per year |
| Kennedy/Johnson | 28 | 7 | 25 | 6 |
| Johnson | 50 | 12 | 41 | 10 |
| Nixon | 23 | 4 | 42 | 7 |
| Ford | 8 | 4 | 8 | 4 |

*Source:* Paul C. Light, *The President's Agenda: Domestic Policy Choice from Kennedy to Clinton,* 3d ed. (Baltimore: Johns Hopkins University Press, 1999), 244.

## Document 5.4    Presidential Requests for Legislation:
## New Programs versus Old Programs

*The following table distinguishes between legislative requests to modify old government programs and requests to create new programs. Although the percentage of new programs Johnson requested does not stand out, the sheer number of requests he sent to Congress was unprecedented; his administration requested the greatest number of new programs and modifications to old programs in history.*

| President | New programs | | Old programs | | New programs as percentage of total |
|---|---|---|---|---|---|
| | Total | Average per year | Total | Average per year | |
| Kennedy/ Johnson | 33 | 8 | 20 | 5 | 62% |
| Johnson | 55 | 14 | 36 | 9 | 60 |
| Nixon | 46 | 12 | 19 | 5 | 71 |
| Ford | 6 | 3 | 10 | 5 | 44 |

*Source:* Paul C. Light, *The President's Agenda: Domestic Policy Choice from Kennedy to Clinton,* 3d ed. (Baltimore: Johns Hopkins University Press, 1999), 244.

## Document 5.5    Proposals versus Vetoes

*The separation of powers mandated in the Constitution constrains presidential choice once Congress passes a bill. A president can sign the bill, veto the bill, or take no action on the bill. The following table shows the number of proposals for legislation that presidents made to Congress versus the number of bills they vetoed. The small number of bills that Johnson vetoed is evidence of his close relationship with Congress.*

| President | Proposals | | Vetos | | Proposals as a percentage of totals |
|---|---|---|---|---|---|
| | Total | Average per year | Total | Average per year | |
| Kennedy/ Johnson | 53 | 13 | 29 | 7 | 65% |
| Johnson | 91 | 23 | 22 | 5 | 81 |
| Nixon | 65 | 11 | 43 | 7 | 58 |
| Ford | 16 | 8 | 66 | 33 | 20 |

*Source:* Paul C. Light, *The President's Agenda: Domestic Policy Choice from Kennedy to Clinton,* 3d ed. (Baltimore: Johns Hopkins University Press, 1999), 112.

## Document 5.6    Conversation between Johnson and
## Martin Luther King Jr., January 15, 1965

*Johnson's telephone conversations from 1965 were not released publicly until more than three decades after they were recorded. In the following excerpt, Johnson advises civil rights leader Martin Luther King Jr. on how to further his cause by gaining maximum media exposure.*

The longer the march is postponed, the greater the presence, the longer the people from outside are going to stay in Alabama and the more problem you are going to have, the more problem I am going to have, and the more problem the country is going to have.... If you take that one illustration and get it on the radio, get it on television, get it in the pulpits, get it in the meetings, every place you can, then pretty soon the fellow who didn't do anything but drive a tractor would say, "Well, that is not right, that is not fair."

*Source:* LBJ Library.

## Document 5.7    Roy Wilkins on Johnson

*Roy Wilkins was executive director of the NAACP during most of the Johnson administration. When Vice President Johnson became President Johnson, Wilkins perceived a clear change in the priority that Johnson gave to civil rights. In this excerpt from Wilkins' oral history interview for the Lyndon B. Johnson Library, he reminisced about Johnson's relationship with the civil rights movement.*

*Wilkins:* I didn't come to know [Johnson] for more than just passing acquaintance until 1957.

*Baker:* Did you classify him in those days in regard to his stand on civil rights? Did you, as the NAACP man, consider him a friend, foe, neutral?

*Wilkins:* We didn't consider him a friend. We considered him more dedicated to his concept of the role of a Majority Leader of the Senate than he was to the civil rights cause. That allegiance, of course, involved his relationship to the Senate via his election from Texas. So, Mr. Johnson's attitude towards civil rights legislation faithfully reflected, up until (he) voted for the civil rights bill in 1957, it became a reflection of his concern, and the concern of all persons elected under that system, for their reelection and continuance in office. I think that Mr. Johnson felt rather fairly, although he never expressed it in so many words, that it would be better for him to be reelected from Texas and be Majority Leader than it would be for him to come out flatly for civil rights, be defeated in Texas, and thus not be in a position of influence at all. Now he didn't say this, but this is what I gather. . . .

*Baker:* In 1960, after Mr. Kennedy was nominated by the Democratic Party and chose Mr. Johnson as his running mate, was there a certain amount of dismay among civil rights advocates at Mr. Johnson being on the ticket?

*Wilkins:* Oh, yes. Oh, yes. I think this too was a matter of history. Their attitude was one of dismay. They believed that probably Mr. Kennedy had gone too far [to the right, in balancing his ticket] just as a great many other Americans who were not Negroes felt that he might have overstepped the bounds. . . .

*Wilkins:* Five days after President Kennedy was murdered, [President Johnson] addressed a joint session of the Congress and he only asked for two measures. One was the pending tax bill and one was the civil rights law. The day after Thanksgiving he began his conferences on the civil rights bill with a conference with me.

*Baker:* What did you talk about at that conference?

*Wilkins:* We talked about the civil rights situation and the necessity for a law and Mr. Johnson's belief that such a law could be enacted if the people really wanted it. This was an echo of his Senate days—if the votes and support are there. He was asking us if we wanted it, if we would do the things required to be done to get it enacted. He said he could not enact it himself; he was the President of the United States; he would give it his blessing; he would aid it in any way in which he could lawfully under the Constitution; but that he could not lobby for the bill; and nobody expected him to lobby for the bill; and he didn't think we expected him to lobby for the bill. But in effect he said—he didn't use these words— "You have the ball; now run with it." He gave unmistakable notice that you had a friend not an enemy in the White House for this legislation.

*Source:* Roy Wilkins, interviewed by Thomas H. Baker, April 1, 1969, LBJ Library.

## Document 5.8   Major U.S. Military Interventions, 1961–1967

*The military action in Vietnam was just one of many uses of military force in the Kennedy/Johnson years. The following table details some of these interventions.*

| Year | Country | Intervention |
|---|---|---|
| November 1961 | Dominican Republic | Kennedy sends the navy offshore of the Dominican Republic as a show of force to discourage associates of the recently assassinated dictator, Rafael Trujillo, from trying to reclaim power. |
| May–July 1962 | Thailand | Five thousand marines land in Thailand to support the government against Chinese-backed communists. They depart nine weeks later. |
| October–December 1962 | Cuba | After discovering that Cuba is readying missile silos for nuclear weapons from the Soviet arsenal, Kennedy orders 180 U.S. Navy ships and a B-52 bomber force carrying A-bombs into the Caribbean to blockade Soviet ships. In return for a pledge never to invade Cuba and a private agreement to withdraw NATO missiles from Turkey, Soviet premier Nikita Khrushchev agrees to dismantle the missile sites. This web of events is known as the Cuban Missile Crisis. |
| May 1963 | Haiti and Dominican Republic | Domestic unrest against the corrupt Duvalier regime in Haiti brings about a threat of intervention from the Dominican Republic. To calm the situation, a U.S. Marine battalion is positioned off the coast of Haiti. |
| November 1964 | Congo | U.S. aircraft in the Congo carry Belgian paratroopers to rescue civilians—including sixty Americans—from antigovernment rebels. |
| May 1964–January 1973 | Laos | To retaliate for the downing of U.S. spy planes flying over Laos, U.S. Navy jets attack Pathet Lao communist strongholds. Air attacks on Laos—the site of the Ho Chi Minh Trail along which North Vietnamese brought supplies and troops into South Vietnam—continue throughout the Vietnam War. |

*continued*

**Document 5.8** *continued*

| Year | Country | Intervention |
|------|---------|--------------|
| April 1965 | Dominican Republic | Following a confusing set of events in the Dominican Republic, during which communist factions joined with others in a revolt against the government, Johnson dispatches 22,000 U.S. troops to protect Americans and to support anti-communist factions within the government. |
| June 1967 | Middle East | During the (Six Day) Arab-Israeli War, Johnson sends the Sixth Fleet to the coast of Syria, to counter movement toward possible intervention by the Soviet Union. |
| July–December 1967 | Congo | Johnson sends three C-130 transport planes with crews to aid government forces battling white mercenaries and Katangese rebels in the Congo. |

*Source:* Compiled by the author.

**Document 5.9    Media Problems**
*Booth Mooney was a speechwriter and assistant to President Johnson. In this excerpt from Mooney's unorthodox biography of Johnson, he speculates on the source of Johnson's problems with the media.*

Johnson could not or would not understand that his own personality had become an issue in itself—to many observers, the overriding issue. His vanity, his instant rages, his excessive use of four-letter words, his flagellation of loyal and hardworking employees had become legendary in Washington. None of these qualities really had anything to do with the major war going on in Asia or the major revolution under way in the United States. But they were idiosyncrasies, to put it mildly, that did nothing to endear LBJ to the men and women of the press—and, just as Reedy [White House press secretary, 1964–1965] said, what they wrote formed public opinion.

George Christian, the President's last press secretary, said one fundamental difficulty was that the press people sensed Johnson had no feeling at all about them as individuals. "They were unimportant to him as people," Christian observed, and since he showed them no consideration they felt no obligation to be considerate to him. . . .

"We created problems that we didn't have to have," Christian remarked after he was back with his public relations firm in Austin. "We had a reputation for never knowing whether we were going to do something or not, and the press never did believe our reasons for keeping these options open."

The press did believe, however, and joyously gave circulation to stories showing Johnson as a calculating, domineering, boorish Texan who had little regard for the truth when it did not serve his purposes. . . .

When he found fault with a telecast by CBS correspondent Daniel Schorr, as later reported by Thomas Whiteside in *The New Yorker*, he called the commentator one midnight and exclaimed, "Schorr, you're a prize son of a bitch." Schorr told Whiteside that he had also been bawled out by Kennedy for some of his comments about that President. "I've always found that sort of reaction understandably human," he said forgivingly.

Others were less tolerant. However, Malcolm Kilduff, an assistant White House press secretary, could laugh as he told of LBJ walking into his office one day, looking at his neat desktop, and remarking acidly, "Kilduff, I hope your mind is not as empty as your desk." A few days later he again came into the office and this time papers were spread out on the working surface. "Kilduff, clean up your desk!" Johnson barked and strode out of the room.

The significance of such gossipy stories, wholly unimportant in themselves, was that they reflected the nearly complete disenchantment of most press people with the president. They were ready to believe anything that made him look like an unfeeling clod. Johnson being Johnson, the more they jabbed at him the more he opened up additional targets for their sneers.

*Source:* Booth Mooney, *LBJ: An Irreverent Chronicle* (New York: Thomas Y. Crowell, 1976), 183–185.

## Document 5.10  Supreme Court Justices

*Johnson appointed two Supreme Court justices. He had the additional opportunity to appoint Earl Warren's successor as chief justice, but his controversial appointment of Abe Fortas never received Senate approval.*

| Name | State appointed from | President appointed by | Date judicial oath taken | Date service terminated |
|---|---|---|---|---|
| Earl Warren (chief justice) | California | Eisenhower | October 5, 1953 | June 23, 1969 |
| Hugo L. Black | Alabama | Roosevelt | August 19, 1937 | September 17, 1971 |
| Felix Frankfurter | Massachusetts | Roosevelt | January 30, 1939 | August 28, 1962 |
| William O. Douglas | Connecticut | Roosevelt | April 17, 1939 | November 12, 1975 |
| Tom C. Clark | Texas | Truman | August 24, 1949 | June 12, 1967 |
| John Marshall Harlan | New York | Eisenhower | March 28, 1955 | September 23, 1971 |
| William J. Brennan Jr. | New Jersey | Eisenhower | October 16, 1956 | July 20, 1990 |
| Charles E. Whittaker | Missouri | Eisenhower | March 25, 1957 | March 31, 1962 |
| Potter Stewart | Ohio | Eisenhower | October 14, 1958 | July 3, 1981 |
| Byron R. White | Colorado | Kennedy | April 16, 1962 | June 28, 1993 |
| Arthur J. Goldberg | Illinois | Kennedy | October 1, 1962 | July 25, 1965 |
| Abe Fortas | Tennessee | Johnson | October 4, 1965 | May 14, 1969 |
| Thurgood Marshall | New York | Johnson | October 2, 1967 | October 1, 1991 |

## Document 5.11 Landmark Supreme Court Cases and Important Constitutional Events

*Under the leadership of Chief Justice Earl Warren, the Supreme Court of the 1960s broadened the rights of individuals and upheld important components of the social agenda of the Johnson presidency. The following table lists major Supreme Court decisions and the ratification of constitutional amendments.*

| Year | Event | Result |
|---|---|---|
| 1964 | Twenty-fourth Amendment<br>Ratified January 23, 1964 | Bans poll taxes |
| | *New York Times v. Sullivan*, 376 U.S. 254<br>Decided March 9, 1964 | Protects media from loose claims of libel |
| | *Reynolds v. Sims*, 377 U.S. 533<br>Decided June 15, 1964 | Applies "one person, one vote" rule to state legislatures |
| | *Malloy v. Hogan*, 378 U.S. 1<br>Decided June 15, 1964 | Extends constitutional protection against self-incrimination to criminal defendants in state courts |
| | *Escobedo v. Illinois*, 378 U.S. 478<br>Decided June 22, 1964 | Makes inadmissible confessions made by suspect not advised of the right to counsel before questioning |
| | *Heart of Atlanta Motel v. United States*, 379 U.S. 241<br>Decided December 14, 1964 | Upholds Civil Rights Act of 1964 by banning discrimination in public places of accommodation |
| 1965 | *Pointer v. Texas*, 380 U.S. 400<br>Decided April 5, 1965 | Confirms defendants' right to cross-examine accusers |
| | *Griswold v. Connecticut*, 381 U.S. 479<br>Decided June 7, 1965 | Guarantees right to personal privacy that extends to use of contraceptives |

**Document 5.11** *continued*

| Year | Event | Result |
|------|-------|--------|
| 1966 | *South Carolina v. Katzenbach*, 383 U.S. 301<br>Decided March 7, 1966 | Court upholds Voting Rights Act of 1965 |
| | *Miranda v. Arizona*, 384 U.S. 436<br>Decided June 13, 1966 | Finds that police must read suspects their rights before questioning |
| 1967 | Twenty-fifth Amendment<br>Ratified February 23, 1967 | Specifies presidential succession procedures |
| | *In re Gault*, 387 U.S. 1<br>Decided May 15, 1967 | Requires that juveniles have some due-process protection in court proceedings |
| | *Loving v. Virginia*, 388 U.S. 1<br>Decided June 12, 1967 | Disallows states from banning interracial marriages |
| | *Washington v. Texas*, 388 U.S. 14<br>Decided June 12, 1967 | Allows defendants in state courts a right to access advantageous witnesses |
| 1968 | *Duncan v. Louisiana*, 391 U.S. 145<br>Decided May 20, 1968 | Upholds right to trial by jury for persons accused of serious crimes |
| | *Green v. County School Board*, 391 U.S. 430<br>Decided May 27, 1968 | Requires schools to propose a realistic and workable plan to desegregate "now" |
| | *Terry v. Ohio*, 392 U.S. 1<br>Decided June 10, 1968 | Upholds the police practice of "stop and frisk" |

*Source:* Joan Biskupic and Elder Witt, *Congressional Quarterly's Guide to the U.S. Supreme Court*, 3d ed. (Washington, D.C.: Congressional Quarterly: 1997), 2:976, 1138–1140.

## Document 5.12    Most Admired People, 1963

*At the end of every year, the Gallup Organization asks Americans: "What man (woman) that you have heard of or read about, living today in any part of the world, do you admire the most?"*

| Most admired people (in order of frequency of mention) | |
| --- | --- |
| Women[a] | Men[b] |
| Jacqueline Kennedy | Lyndon Johnson |
| Lady Bird Johnson | Dwight Eisenhower |
| Queen Elizabeth II | Winston Churchill |
| Margaret Chase Smith | Albert Schweitzer |
| Mamie Eisenhower | Robert Kennedy |
| Clare Boothe Luce | Billy Graham |
| Helen Keller | Adlai Stevenson |
| Princess Grace of Monaco | Pope Paul VI |
| Mme. Ngo Diem Nhu | Charles de Gaulle |
| Marian Anderson | Richard Nixon |

[a] Poll conducted December 25, 1963.
[b] Poll conducted December 27, 1963.

*Source: The Gallup Poll: Public Opinion 1935–1971, Volume Three: 1959–1971* (New York: Random House, 1972), 2885–2886.

## Document 5.13    Presidential Approval

*The table below indicates public approval for "the way President Johnson is handling his job as President." Johnson began with high ratings but endured a forty-five-point erosion of support that bottomed out during violent protests in Chicago outside the Democratic National Convention in August 1968.*

| Date | Approve | Disapprove | No opinion |
|------|---------|-----------|-----------|
| *1963* | | | |
| Early December | 78% | 2% | 20% |
| December 12 | 79 | 3 | 18 |
| | | | |
| *1964* | | | |
| January 2 | 80 | 5 | 15 |
| February 1 | 75 | 8 | 17 |
| Mid-February | 73 | 9 | 18 |
| February 28 | 79 | 9 | 12 |
| Mid-March | 77 | 9 | 14 |
| March 27 | 75 | 12 | 13 |
| April | 75 | 11 | 15 |
| May 6 | 75 | 11 | 14 |
| Late May | 74 | 13 | 13 |
| June 4 | 74 | 12 | 14 |
| Mid-June | 74 | 14 | 12 |
| Late June | 74 | 15 | 11 |
| November | 69 | 18 | 13 |
| December 11 | 69 | 18 | 13 |
| | | | |
| *1965* | | | |
| January 7 | 71 | 15 | 14 |
| Late January | 71 | 16 | 13 |
| February | 68 | 18 | 14 |
| Early March | 69 | 21 | 10 |
| Late March | 69 | 21 | 10 |
| Early April | 67 | 22 | 11 |
| April 23 | 64 | 22 | 14 |
| May 13 | 70 | 18 | 12 |
| June 4 | 69 | 19 | 12 |

*continued*

| Date | Approve | Disapprove | No opinion |
|------|---------|------------|------------|
| June 24 | 65 | 21 | 14 |
| July 16 | 65 | 20 | 15 |
| Early August | 65 | 22 | 13 |
| August 27 | 64 | 25 | 13 |
| September 16 | 63 | 24 | 13 |
| October | 66 | 21 | 13 |
| October 19 | 64 | 22 | 14 |
| November 18 | 62 | 22 | 16 |
| December 11 | 63 | 26 | 11 |
| | | | |
| *1966* | | | |
| Early January | 59 | 24 | 17 |
| January 21 | 61 | 27 | 12 |
| February 10 | 56 | 34 | 10 |
| March 3 | 58 | 28 | 14 |
| March 24 | 57 | 28 | 15 |
| April | 54 | 33 | 13 |
| May 5 | 46 | 34 | 20 |
| May 19 | 50 | 33 | 17 |
| June | 48 | 39 | 13 |
| July 8 | 56 | 30 | 14 |
| July 29 | 51 | 38 | 11 |
| August | 48 | 38 | 14 |
| September 8 | 46 | 39 | 15 |
| Early October | 44 | 42 | 14 |
| Late October | 44 | 41 | 15 |
| November 10 | 48 | 37 | 15 |
| December | 44 | 47 | 9 |
| | | | |
| *1967* | | | |
| Early January | 47 | 37 | 16 |
| January 26 | 46 | 38 | 16 |
| February | 45 | 42 | 13 |
| March | 45 | 41 | 14 |
| Late March | 46 | 38 | 16 |
| April 19 | 48 | 37 | 15 |
| May | 45 | 39 | 16 |

*continued*

**Document 5.13** *continued*

| Date | Approve | Disapprove | No opinion |
|---|---|---|---|
| June 2 | 44 | 40 | 16 |
| June 22 | 52 | 35 | 13 |
| July | 47 | 39 | 14 |
| Early August | 40 | 48 | 12 |
| August 24 | 39 | 48 | 13 |
| September | 38 | 47 | 15 |
| October | 38 | 50 | 12 |
| October 27 | 41 | 49 | 10 |
| December 7 | 46 | 41 | 13 |
| | | | |
| *1968* | | | |
| January 4 | 48 | 39 | 13 |
| February 1 | 41 | 47 | 12 |
| Late February | 41 | 48 | 11 |
| March 15 | 36 | 52 | 12 |
| April 4 | 42 | 47 | 11 |
| Early May | 46 | 43 | 11 |
| Late May | 41 | 45 | 14 |
| Early June | 42 | 45 | 13 |
| Late June | 40 | 47 | 13 |
| July | 40 | 47 | 13 |
| August 7 | 35 | 52 | 13 |
| September 26 | 42 | 51 | 7 |
| November 9 | 43 | 44 | 13 |
| December | 44 | 43 | 13 |
| | | | |
| *1969* | | | |
| January 1 | 49 | 37 | 14 |

*Source:* Lyn Ragsdale, *Vital Statistics on the Presidency, Washington to Clinton,* Rev. ed. (Washington, D.C.: Congressional Quarterly, 1998), 203–205.

## Document 5.14    Support for Vietnam as a Function of U.S. Battle Deaths

*The following public opinion poll shows Americans' responses to the following question: "In view of the developments since we entered the fighting in Vietnam, do you think the U.S. made a mistake sending troops to fight in Vietnam?" The cumulative hostile deaths column indicates deaths of U.S. troops only.*

| Date of poll | Cumulative hostile heaths | Percentage of respondents supporting |
| --- | --- | --- |
| August 1965 | 166 | 61% |
| November 1965 | 924 | 64 |
| March 1966 | 2,415 | 59 |
| May 1966 | 3,191 | 49 |
| September 1966 | 4,976 | 48 |
| November 1966 | 5,798 | 51 |
| February 1967 | 7,419 | 52 |
| May 1967 | 10,341 | 50 |
| July 1967 | 11,939 | 48 |
| October 1967 | 13,999 | 44 |
| December 1967 | 15,695 | 46 |
| February 1968 | 19,107 | 42 |
| March 1968 | 20,658 | 41 |
| April 1968 | 22,061 | 40 |
| August 1968 | 27,280 | 35 |
| October 1968 | 28,860 | 37 |
| February 1969 | 32,234 | 39 |
| September 1969 | 38,581 | 32 |
| January 1970 | 40,112 | 33 |
| March 1970 | 40,921 | 32 |
| April 1970 | 41,479 | 34 |
| May 1970 | 42,213 | 36 |
| January 1971 | 44,109 | 31 |
| May 1971 | 44,980 | 28 |

*Source:* Eric V. Larson, *Casualties and Consensus: The Historical Role of Casualties in Domestic Support for U.S. Military Operations* (Santa Monica, Calif.: Rand, 1996), 111.

*Johnson in retirement at his ranch near Stonewall, Texas, September 18, 1972.*

# CHAPTER SIX

# After the White House

## *Johnson in Retirement*

L yndon Johnson never acknowledged publicly that he was forced from the presidency by his political opponents. He spoke instead of concerns for his health and for issues that transcended partisan politics. Often during his career Johnson had worried about his family's history of heart disease and early death, and he seems to have felt in 1968, and even in 1964, that he might not serve out a long tenure in the presidency. When he announced his imminent departure from the presidency in March 31, 1968, Johnson spoke not of political troubles but diplomatic opportunities. Johnson presented himself to the public in that speech as a man who was willingly sacrificing his political future in order that he might bring peace to Vietnam (see Document 6.1). But to his friend, Robert Hardesty, Johnson said many times that he had left office "pretty much repudiated" (Hardesty 1990, 95).

Given Johnson's pride and sensitivity, and his high hopes for his time in the presidency, his was an especially difficult transition to private life. The president expressed his hopes and frustrations in his final State of the Union address. "Now it is time to leave," he said. "I hope it may be said a hundred years from now, that by working together we helped to make our country more just, more just for all of its people, as well as to insure and guarantee the blessings of liberty and of our posterity. That is what I hope. But I believe that at least it will be said that we tried." Fittingly, the president who had defined himself by effort and will took refuge in his departure in the thought that he would, at the least, be remembered as one who tried. As he looked back on his departure from office in his memoirs, Johnson echoed the theme of effort, and bravely asserted that he was happy to be heading into retirement. "The long, hard effort was over now," Johnson recollected, "and I was glad to see it end" (Johnson 1971, 566; see Document 6.2).

In his last day as president, there was a normal frenzy of work as well as some ceremonial moments. Medals of Freedom were bestowed on those who had stuck with the president on the Vietnam War (see Document 6.3), and lands were added to the national park system, including a Franklin Delano Roosevelt Memorial Park. That evening, the Johnsons hosted a small buffet reception for the White House staff. On inaugural day, Johnson stoically went through the motions of the transfer of power to the new president, Richard M. Nixon, before departing for Texas from Andrews Air Force Base. At the base, Texas representative George Herbert Walker Bush was among the handful of well-wishers. "A fine president and invariably courteous and fair to me and my people," Bush, the future president, remarked (Dallek 1998, 601).

Back along the Pedernales, it was the first time in thirty-two years that the Johnsons had lived anyplace other than Washington, D.C. In the words of one of his daughters, "My daddy committed political suicide for this war in Vietnam. And since politics was his life, it was like committing actual suicide" (Hardesty 1990, 138). The former president resumed chain smoking—he had given up cigarettes after his nearly fatal heart attack in the Senate—and resumed heavy eating and drinking as well. "By God, I'm going to do what I want to do," Johnson told his former press secretary, George Christian, and a great many other visitors to the LBJ ranch (Dallek 1998, 601). In a mark of rebelliousness, he let his now-silver hair grow until he looked like William Jennings Bryan, his parents' populist idol from the turn of the century, or like the protestors who had tormented him in the White House.

Lady Bird was there as always to tend to her husband's needs and to attempt to keep him somewhat in line. To those who asked how she could put up with an irascible former president, she would typically remark, "My dear, just think of it all as one big adventure" (Dallek 1998, 603–604). President Johnson took comfort in the visits of his grandchildren and umbrage at the impositions of occasional ceremonial chores, such as sitting in the bleachers for the launch of Apollo XI. He reminisced about the

New Deal and the Lower Colorado River Authority and left some who saw him at this time worried about his mental health.

Absolutely "psychopathic," thought Nixon's chief of staff, Bob Haldeman, of the former president's obsessive worries, which Johnson expressed on a visit to Camp David with his successor (Haldeman 1994, 82–83). Actually, the former president's behavior was well within normal bounds for Lyndon Johnson. His outsized manner was, however, no longer exhibited against a backdrop of presidential responsibilities and power and thus stood out more readily. Now, it was mere courtesy and respect, not fear, that compelled people to heed the president's temper.

When not tending to his wounds with worry or recreation, Johnson threw himself into what was at hand, which on most days meant the work of his ranch (see Document 6.4). He attempted to micromanage operations at the ranch as if it were the White House and its concerns the cares of the world. He tracked the number of eggs produced, the health of each new calf, and the condition of fence posts and water tanks. A water pump going out set the stage for a frantic effort to see to the delivery of a new pump. Airline presidents and truck company executives were swung into action following a phone call from the former president. When he was in a ranch-managing mood, there would be early morning conferences with his ranch foreman and ranch hands. They would be exhorted, criticized, and energized. They knew that as long as the mood held, they would get little rest on the LBJ ranch.

Often enough, when Johnson was devoting his manic energies to the work of the ranch, he was thereby taking himself off the hook for working on his memoirs. He was supposed to produce a two-volume autobiography, starting with the presidency and working his way backward. Only one volume was ever completed. The assistants working on Johnson's memoirs would research each section from materials being collected for the presidential library. The president would use the research of his associates to refresh his memory about various events and would then talk his way through each stage of his presidency. His ghostwriters would interview him thoroughly and record his answers. Once a chapter was drafted, Doris Kearns Goodwin recalls, the "sanitation" process would begin. "It's a presidential memoir, damn it, and I've got to come out looking like a statesman, not some backwoods politician" (Goodwin 1991, 355). To the regret of his aides working on the project, he insisted that the volume be written in formal and staid prose, with no touches of the famous LBJ humor.

Fortunately for posterity, one of his writers was also one of his earliest biographers, and many of Johnson's stories that he would not permit to appear in his own book appear in hers. Doris Kearns was a White House fellow in the final two years of Johnson's presidency. In the last months of the presidency, Johnson persuaded her to join his postpresidential staff. Johnson wanted the "Harvards" of the nation, such as Kearns (who fit extended stays at the ranch into her teaching schedule at the Kennedy School of Government at Harvard), to understand and appreciate him.

Fortunately for Johnson, he did not need the money that he missed out on by not completing the second volume of his memoirs. The Johnsons received over a million dollars in profit each year from their radio station. The former president devoted time in retirement to liquidating a large portion of his estate, to leave his family in comfort when he died without the worries of managing individual companies. With their fortune secure for their children and grandchildren, the Johnsons gave to the presidential library and the LBJ School of Public Affairs all the money they received for their postpresidential books ($1.2 million) and for his series of interviews with Walter Cronkite of CBS ($300,000). President Johnson also helped to raise funds from other sources for his library and school. When the Lyndon B. Johnson Presidential Library and Museum was dedicated in televised ceremonies, May 22, 1971, Johnson was described by one of his friends as being "in hog heaven" (Miller 1980, 670; see Document 6.5).

When confronted with a political question or a request for help from one of his former political associates, the president would often decline. "I'm not in that business anymore," Johnson would reply (Hardesty 1990, 97). His reluctance to get involved in politics in part reflected the movement of his party away from the president's positions in the Vietnam War. In the 1972 presidential election, the Democrats played the role that the Republicans had played in 1964, nominating a candidate who was easily depicted by the other side as being on the fringes of his own party. George McGovern got the formal endorsement of the former president, but Johnson made clear the limits of his support. Johnson would not campaign for McGovern, and he restricted media coverage of the candidate's meeting with Johnson at the ranch.

Behind the scenes, Johnson worked for the reelection of Richard Nixon, who had won the presidency in 1968 by defeating Hubert Humphrey, the

Democratic nominee. He did so primarily because he preferred Nixon's policy on the war to that of McGovern. But it did not hurt, as Bob Haldeman recounts in his diary, that President Nixon cultivated the former president. Nixon invited the Johnsons to the White House and to Camp David, and he helped the former president with unspecified issues involving the Secret Service. In addition, Johnson wanted the government's help in reviewing and declassifying his White House papers as rapidly as possible, and Nixon was accommodating in this matter (Haldeman 1994, 82, 114).

Their cordial relations, however, did not keep Nixon and Johnson from threatening each other in 1972. During the reelection year Congress was investigating Nixon for the White House's role in the presidency-shattering break-in at the Watergate offices of the Democratic National Committee. Nixon knew that Johnson still had influential friends on Capitol Hill and wanted the former president to help divert the investigation. Through intermediaries, Nixon threatened to reveal to the press that the Johnson campaign had electronically eavesdropped on Nixon's campaign plane in 1968 if Johnson did not cooperate. In reply, Johnson threatened to reveal the reason for the alleged bugging—Nixon's successful maneuvering to stall Vietnam peace talks. Johnson's biographer Robert Dallek speculates that Johnson may also have intended to reveal, if need be, the Nixon campaign's receipt of large cash contributions from the military government of Greece (Dallek 1998, 619). Amid the threats and counterthreats, peace was maintained between Johnson and Nixon during the campaign, and the investigation that eventually forced President Nixon from office continued.

In June 1972 Johnson suffered a severe heart attack. Insisting on returning to the ranch from the hospital in San Antonio, he repeated a familiar line that he had picked up from his father as a youth. He wanted to go back to the hill country, he said, as reported by numerous commentators, "where they know when you're sick, and they care when you die." Six weeks before his death, Johnson went to Austin for a conference on civil rights at the LBJ School, ignoring his health, an ice storm, and his wife's entreaties. At the conference, Johnson put on a classic performance (see Document 6.6).

In prepared remarks, Johnson told the conferees, "I am sort of ashamed of myself, that I had six years and couldn't do more than I did . . . So let no one delude themselves that our work is done" (Miller 1980, 561–562). Taking the stage to respond to an ill-willed criticism from the audience of the

Nixon administration's efforts on civil rights, the former president tried to explain the difficulties that the new president was under and the importance of working constructively with him. To illustrate his point, Johnson told one of his favorite stories. He and his Austin mentor, Alvin Wirtz, were in a contentious meeting with power company executives when Congressman Johnson lost his temper and told the corporate leaders where they could go. Afterward, Wirtz explained something to Johnson that he never forgot. "Lyndon," Wirtz instructed, "there's a difference between telling a man to go to hell, and making him go." "He doesn't want to go, Wirtz continued, and moreover, doesn't think he belongs there" (LBJL). The conference was a highlight of Johnson's retirement, though it cost him two days of bed rest to recover from the exertion.

On January 22, 1973, Lyndon Johnson suffered a heart attack and died alone in his bedroom at the LBJ ranch (see Documents 6.7 and 6.8).

BIBLIOGRAPHY

The most in-depth coverage of Johnson in retirement is offered in Doris Kearns Goodwin, *Lyndon Johnson and the American Dream* (New York: St. Martin's Press, 1991); Robert Hardesty, "With LBJ in Retirement," in *Farewell to the Chief: Former Presidents in American Public Life,* ed. Richard Norton Smith and Timothy Walch (Worland, Wyo.: High Plains Publishing, 1990); and Leo Janos, "The Last Days of the President: LBJ in Retirement," *Atlantic* 232 (July 1973): 35–41.

See also Robert Dallek, *Flawed Giant: Lyndon Johnson and His Times, 1961–1973* (New York: Oxford University Press, 1998); Lyndon B. Johnson, *Vantage Point* (New York: Holt, Rinehart, and Winston, 1971); Merle Miller, *Lyndon: An Oral Biography* (New York: Ballantine, 1980); and Jan Jarboe Russell, *Lady Bird: A Biography of Mrs. Johnson* (New York: Scribner's, 1999).

H. R. Haldeman, *The Haldeman Diaries: Inside the Nixon White House* (New York: Putnam, 1994) is also cited in this chapter.

## Document 6.1    Limiting the War in Vietnam and the Decision Not to Seek Reelection

*Johnson rarely addressed the nation during his presidency. His only major speech in support of the Vietnam War was delivered at Johns Hopkins University on April 7, 1965 (see Document 4.17). The next major televised address on Vietnam came three years later when the president announced a de-escalation of the war. At the end of the speech, he announced he would not seek reelection.*

Tonight I want to speak to you of peace in Vietnam and Southeast Asia.

No other question so preoccupies our people. No other dream so absorbs the 250 million human beings who live in that part of the world. No other goal motivates American policy in Southeast Asia.

For years, representatives of our Government and others have traveled the world—seeking to find a basis for peace talks.

Since last September, they have carried the offer that I made public at San Antonio. That offer was this:

That the United States would stop its bombardment of North Vietnam when that would lead promptly to productive discussions—and that we would assume that North Vietnam would not take military advantage of our restraint.

Hanoi denounced this offer, both privately and publicly. Even while the search for peace was going on, North Vietnam rushed their preparations for a savage assault on the people, the government, and the allies of South Vietnam.

Their attack—during the Tet holidays—failed to achieve its principal objectives.

It did not collapse the elected government of South Vietnam or shatter its army—as the Communists had hoped.

It did not produce a "general uprising" among the people of the cities as they had predicted.

The Communists were unable to maintain control of any of the more than 30 cities that they attacked. And they took very heavy casualties.

But they did compel the South Vietnamese and their allies to move certain forces from the countryside into the cities.

They caused widespread disruption and suffering. Their attacks, and the battles that followed, made refugees of half a million human beings.

The Communists may renew their attack any day. . . .

This much is clear:

If they do mount another round of heavy attacks, they will not succeed in destroying the fighting power of South Vietnam and its allies.

But tragically, this is also clear: Many men—on both sides of the struggle—will be lost. A nation that has already suffered 20 years of warfare will suffer once again. Armies on both sides will take new casualties. And the war will go on.

There is no need for this to be so. . . .

Tonight, I renew the offer I made last August—to stop the bombardment of North Vietnam. We ask that talks begin promptly, that they be serious talks on the substance of peace. We assume that during those talks Hanoi will not take advantage of our restraint. . . .

So, tonight, in the hope that this action will lead to early talks, I am taking the first step to deescalate the conflict. We are reducing—substantially reducing—the present level of hostilities.

And we are doing so unilaterally, and at once. . . .

I cannot promise that the initiative that I have announced tonight will be completely successful in achieving peace any more than the 30 others that we have undertaken and agreed to in recent years.

But it is our fervent hope that North Vietnam, after years of fighting that have left the issue unresolved, will now cease its efforts to achieve a military victory and will join with us in moving toward the peace table.

And there may come a time when South Vietnamese—on both sides— are able to work out a way to settle their own differences by free political choice rather than by war.

As Hanoi considers its course, it should be in no doubt of our intentions. It must not miscalculate the pressures within our democracy in this election year.

We have no intention of widening this war.

But the United States will never accept a fake solution to this long and arduous struggle and call it peace. . . .

Our reward will come in the life of freedom, peace, and hope that our children will enjoy through ages ahead.

What we won when all of our people united just must not now be lost in suspicion, distrust, selfishness, and politics among any of our people.

Believing this as I do, I have concluded that I should not permit the

Presidency to become involved in the partisan divisions that are developing in this political year.

With America's sons in the fields far away, with America's future under
challenge right here at home, with our hopes and the world's hopes for
peace in the balance every day, I do not believe that I should devote an hour
or a day of my time to any personal partisan causes or to any duties other
than the awesome duties of this office—the Presidency of your country.

Accordingly, I shall not seek, and I will not accept, the nomination of
my party for another term as your President.

But let men everywhere know, however, that a strong, a confident, and
a vigilant America stands ready tonight to seek an honorable peace—and
stands ready tonight to defend an honored cause—whatever the price,
whatever the burden, whatever the sacrifice that duty may require.

*Source:* "The President's Address to the Nation Announcing Steps to Limit the War
in Vietnam and Reporting His Decision Not to Seek Reelection," March 31, 1968.
In *Public Papers of the Presidents of the United States: Lyndon B. Johnson, 1968–69*
(Washington, D.C.: U.S. Government Printing Office), 1:704–707.

## Document 6.2    Reflections
*In the following excerpt from Johnson's memoirs, he reflects on his time in the
White House.*

The long, hard effort was over now, and I was glad to see it end. I did not
believe that I had ever flinched from the responsibilities or the demands of
the office. I had used its powers and prerogatives as fully as I could to
accomplish what I thought ought to be done. I had lived thoroughly every
hour of those five years. I had known sorrow and anger, frustration and
disappointment, pain and dismay. But more than anything else, I had experienced a towering pride and pleasure at having had my chance to make
my contribution to solving the problems of our times. I had tried to face
up to them all, without dodging any of them, and to provide solutions
whenever I could. When we made mistakes, I believe we erred because
we tried to do too much too soon, and never because we walked away from
challenge. If the Presidency can be said to have been employed and to have

been enjoyed, I had employed it to the utmost, and I had enjoyed it to the limit. Now I was putting aside the burden that no President can adequately explain or describe and that no citizen can fully understand.

I heard Richard Nixon conclude his oath of office with the words "so help me God." To me, they were welcome words. I remember two thoughts running through my mind: first, that I would not have to face the decision any more of taking any step, in the Middle East or elsewhere, that might lead to world conflagration—the nightmare of my having to be the man who pressed the button to start World War III was passing; and second, that I had fervently sought peace through every available channel and at every opportunity and could have done no more.

Now my service was over, and it had ended without my having had to haul down the flag, compromise my principles, or run out on our obligations, our commitments, and our men who were upholding those obligations and commitments in Vietnam. I repeated these thoughts to Lady Bird as we walked up the steps toward a room inside the Capitol after the inauguration. I repeated them later to President Nixon. I realize that it may be difficult for people to understand how I felt. As discerning and perceptive as the American people are, I believe that very few of them have ever been able to grasp what transpired in the minds and hearts of the thirty-seven men who have served them in the Presidency. The recognition of unrelenting responsibility reminds me of the truth of a statement I heard my father repeat many times: "Son, you will never understand what it is to be a father until you *are* a father."

*Source:* Lyndon B. Johnson, *The Vantage Point: Perspectives on the Presidency, 1963–1969* (New York: Holt, Rinehart, and Winston, 1971), 566–567.

## Document 6.3    Presidential Medals of Freedom

*The Presidential Medal of Freedom is America's highest civilian honor. President Kennedy established the award in 1963. Since then, honorees have come from a broad spectrum of professions including music, politics, academia, religion, the military, and civil rights. Johnson gave eighty-eight medals during his presidency. Among the most controversial recipients were some of the twenty last-minute honorees whom Johnson thanked for supporting his position on Vietnam.*

| Date of award | Recipient | Position |
|---|---|---|
| December 6, 1963 | Marian Anderson | Opera singer; first black opera singer to perform at New York's Metropolitan Opera House |
| | Ralph Bunche | U.N. undersecretary general for special political affairs; civil rights activist |
| | Ellsworth Bunker | Ambassador to Argentina, Italy, India, Nepal, and at-large; sugar company executive |
| | Pablo Casals | Celloist |
| | Genevieve Caulfield | Teacher; established schools for the blind abroad |
| | James B. Conant | Scientist; educator; diplomat |
| | John F. Enders | Physician whose work led to polio vaccine |
| | Felix Frankfurter | Supreme Court justice; Harvard law professor; founder of the American Civil Liberties Union |
| | Karl Holton | Innovator in criminal rehabilitation; focused on juvenile delinquency as head of Los Angeles probation department |
| | John F. Kennedy | Thirty-fifth president of the United States |
| | Robert J. Kiphuth | Yale University and U.S. Olympic Team swim coach |
| | Edwin H. Land | Inventor of the Polaroid camera; chief executive officer of Polaroid Co. |
| | Herbert H. Lehman | Governor of New York |

*continued*

**Document 6.3** *continued*

| Date of award | Recipient | Position |
|---|---|---|
| | Robert A. Lovett | Undersecretary of state |
| | J. Clifford MacDonald | Teacher; president of the National Association for Retarded Children |
| | John J. McCloy | World Bank president; presidential advisor |
| | George Meany | AFL-CIO president |
| | Alexander Meiklejohn | Amherst College president |
| | Ludwig Mies van der Rohe | Architect; director of the Illinois Institute of Technology. |
| | Jean Monnet | Diplomat who authored Monnet Plan to rebuild France after World War II; promoted creation of European economic community |
| | Luis Muñoz Marin | First elected governor of Puerto Rico |
| | Pope John XXIII | Pope; Led Second Vatican Council in 1962 |
| | Clarence B. Randall | Steel company executive; Truman advisor |
| | Rudolf Serkin | Pianist |
| | Edward Steichen | American photographer |
| | George W. Taylor | Labor arbitrator to five presidents |
| | Alan T. Waterman | First director of the National Science Foundation |
| | Mark S. Watson | Military correspondent for the *Baltimore Sun* during World War II |
| | Annie D. Wauneka | First woman elected to the Navajo Tribal Council |
| | E. B. White | Essayist for the *New Yorker;* author of *Elements of Style* |
| | Thornton Wilder | Playwright; novelist, wrote *Our Town* |
| | Edmund Wilson | Literary critic; essayist |
| | Andrew Wyeth | Painter of the American scene |
| September 14, 1964 | Dean Acheson | Secretary of state; architect of the North Atlantic Treaty Organization. |
| | Detlev W. Bronk | Johns Hopkins University president; presidential advisor |

| Date of award | Recipient | Position |
|---|---|---|
| | Aaron Copland | "Dean of American composers" |
| | Willem de Kooning | Abstract expressionist painter |
| | Walt Disney | Cartoon animator; motion picture producer; theme park pioneer |
| | J. Frank Dobie | Folklorist; leading writer on culture of the American southwest |
| | Lena F. Edwards | Pioneering black physician; provided medical care to migrant workers |
| | Thomas Stearns Eliot | Poet; author of *The Waste Land* |
| | John W. Gardner | Carnegie Corporation president; secretary of health, education, and welfare |
| | Theodore M. Hesburgh | Notre Dame University president |
| | Clarence L. "Kelly" Johnson | Aircraft designer |
| | Frederick Kappel | U.S. Postal Service chairman; head of AT&T. |
| | Helen Keller | Educator of the handicapped |
| | John L. Lewis | United Mine Workers president; founder of Congress of Industrial Organizations |
| | Walter Lippmann | Journalist for *New Republic, Washington Post, Newsweek,* and *New York Herald Tribune* |
| | Alfred Lunt and Lynne Fontanne | Husband and wife theater acting team |
| | Ralph McGill | Editor of the *Atlanta Constitution* |
| | Samuel Eliot Morison | "Dean of American historians" |
| | Lewis Mumford | Urban planner |
| | Edward R. Murrow | World War II journalist; director of the U.S. Information Agency |
| | Reinhold Niebuhr | Theologian |
| | Leontyne Price | Pioneering black opera singer |
| | A. Philip Randolph | AFL-CIO vice president; civil rights activist |
| | Carl Sandburg | Biographer of President Lincoln; poet |
| | John Steinbeck | Novelist; author of *The Grapes of Wrath* |

*continued*

**Document 6.3** *continued*

| Date of award | Recipient | Position |
|---|---|---|
| | Helen B. Taussig | Physician who pioneered pediatric cardiology |
| | Carl Vinson | Democratic representative from Georgia who served fifty years in Congress |
| | Thomas J. Watson Jr. | IBM president |
| | Paul Dudley White | Physician who pioneered heart disease research and brought public awareness to disease |
| December 23, 1967 | Ellsworth Bunker | Ambassador to Argentina, Italy, India, and Nepal |
| | Robert W. Komer | Presidential advisor |
| | Eugene Murphy Locke | Ambassador to Pakistan |
| February 28, 1968 | Robert S. McNamara | Secretary of defense |
| December 9, 1968 | James E. Webb | NASA director |
| January 16, 1969 | Dean Rusk | Secretary of state |
| January 20, 1969 | Eugene R. Black | World Bank president |
| | McGeorge Bundy | National security adviser |
| | Clark McAdams Clifford | Johnson adviser |
| | Michael DeBakey | Surgeon who pioneered open-heart surgery |
| | David Dubinsky | International Ladies Garment Workers Union president |
| | Ralph Ellison | Novelist; author of *Invisible Man* |
| | Henry Ford II | Chief executive officer of Ford Motor Company |
| | W. Averell Harriman | Ambassador to the United Kingdom.; secretary of commerce; governor of New York |
| | Bob Hope | Entertainer; comedian |
| | Edgar Kaiser | Kaiser Industries president |

*continued*

| Date of award | Recipient | Position |
|---|---|---|
| | Mary Lasker | Philanthropist who lobbied for increased government spending on cancer and other diseases |
| | John Macy | Civil Service Commission chairman |
| | Gregory Peck | Movie actor |
| | Laurance Rockefeller | Rockefeller Center president |
| | Walt Whitman Rostow | Economic historian; Presidential adviser |
| | Merriman Smith | *UPI* White House correspondent |
| | Cyrus Vance | Deputy secretary of defense |
| | William S. White | *New York Times* Washington correspondent |
| | Roy Wilkins | NAACP executive director |
| | Whitney M. Young Jr. | National Urban League executive director |

*Source:* Bruce Wetterau, *The Presidential Medal of Freedom: Winners and Their Achievements* (Washington, D.C.: CQ Press, 1996).

## Document 6.4    Johnson's Solace in Retirement

*During Sen. Wayne Morse's, D-Ohio, twenty-four years in the Senate, he switched party affiliation from Republican to Independent to Democratic. He was born on a farm in Wisconsin and was quick to reply with his own stories to Johnson's stories of childhood hardship in Texas. Sen. Robert Kerr, D-Okla., similarly liked to regale listeners with his tales of growing up in the Chickasaw Nation, Indian territory, as the son of a tenant farmer and pioneer. Sen. Clinton Anderson, D-N.M., also had stories to share as the son of a storekeeper and farmer in South Dakota. In the excerpt below, Senate Majority Secretary Bobby Baker recalls the informal but heated debates of these senators. Johnson's passion for his ranch stayed with him after he left Congress, and was his solace in retirement.*

*Baker:* I remember [Johnson] talking to Senator Russell and Senator Kerr about Lady Bird (having) spent some of her money buying a ranch. I don't think at that particular time I had ever been to Texas. This was

his hobby; this was his love. This did more for him mentally than anything, because with the way he drove himself, he needed some hobby.
. . . Some of the fiercest debates I have ever heard in my life were
between Johnson and Morse and Clint Anderson and Kerr about who
knew more about cattle. There were big fights about Hereford, Black
Angus. . . .

*Gillette:* Someone has recalled that they actually traded cattle on the floor
of the Senate, that they would sit there and—

*Baker:* Oh, sure they did. They're trading. One day, to show you what took
place on the Senate floor, Senator Kerr came to me one day. Johnson—
you know, (he) start(ed) talking about the Ranch and (how) he bought
it and so forth. Kerr, he really liked Johnson, but he didn't want Johnson to have something he didn't have. Kerr didn't know a damn thing
about cattle, so he went out to the University of Oklahoma and he
made a speech. He asked to meet the head of the veterinary department, and it was a fellow named Dr. Kazee, K-A-Z-E-E. He said,
"Kazee, what do they pay you?" He said, "Senator, they pay me fifteen
thousand dollars a year and they give me a house and an automobile."
Kerr, said, "Kazee, I'll give you fifty thousand dollars and you have your
wife pick out whatever floor plan you want and I'll build you a house,
and I'll buy you two cars if you'll come to work for me." But he said,
"I want to be one of the best cattlemen in America, because between
Lyndon Johnson and Clinton Anderson and Wayne Morse, they're driving me crazy about how smart they are." So Dr. Kazee agreed to go to
work for Senator Kerr.

So Senator Kerr told me one day, he said, "I'm going to get a call
and I told a man to ask for you. He's out in South Dakota looking to
buy a bull for me." So Dr. Kazee called and asked for me and I got Senator Kerr off the floor. He and Johnson were talking. I said, "Gentlemen, I got an emergency for Senator Kerr." So Kerr came to the phone.
When he got off the phone he grabbed me by the lapels, he said, "I just
paid twenty thousand dollars for a bull called Highland Marshall. The
bull has got clap." I said, "I never heard of that. I never thought it possible for an animal to have gonorrhea." He said, "Kazee says in six
months he thinks that he can cure him. I'm rolling the dice." Senator
Kerr bought that bull. He's the first man to ever syndicate a [bull]. He
syndicated that bull, Highland Marshall, for about three hundred and

thirty-three thousand dollars. The bull was so good that before Senator Kerr died they had to change the rules. . . .

So he and Johnson used to talk about "how's that old bull doing that's got the clap." That's what they talked about on the Senate floor. It was hilarious. They were jabbing each other all the time, and Johnson talking about (how) that old Hill Country around Johnson City was so much better for cows because it has more minerals. It did look like those old cows did weigh more, but I didn't know a damn thing about cows, could have cared less. But he and Kerr, they'd just sit there and talk about how many they had and how many they lost. But that was his hobby; he loved it.

*Source:* Robert H. Baker, interviewed by Michael L. Gillette, December 9, 1983, LBJ Library.

## Document 6.5    Johnson's Remarks at the LBJ Library Dedication, May 22, 1971

*Johnson strove to create the foremost presidential library to house documents from his administration. Former president Gerald Ford at the Harry Middleton lecture in 1997 said, "The next time someone in the Washington bureaucracy or on Capitol Hill says, 'let's build a centralized facility inside the Beltway to house presidential papers,' I'll tell him: go to Austin, and see what Harry Middleton and the Johnson Foundation have created."*

Mr. President [Nixon], we are delighted that you, the Vice President, the Members of Congress, and these distinguished guests have come here today.

We are all partners in this hopeful undertaking. The people of Texas built this library. The National Archives will manage the Library. The documents I have saved since the 1930s are being given, along with the documents of many others who served with me. Those documents contain millions and millions of words. But the two that best express my philosophy are the words, "Man can." . . .

The Library records reflect the Nation for 40 years—from the '30s through the '60s. They picture a sweep of history beginning with the depression and ending with the most prosperous era we have ever known.

They record a drive for change and social reform unparalleled in its energy and scope—and a World War unmatched in its destruction. They chronicle the end of colonialism—and the beginning of the Cold War and the Atomic Age which still threaten mankind. They cover the time when liberty was challenged in Europe and Latin America and Asia—and record America's response to those challenges.

It is all here: the story of our time—with the bark off.

A President sees things from a unique perspective. No one can share his responsibility. No one can share the scope of his duties or the burden of his decisions. . . .

There is no record of a mistake, nothing critical, ugly, or unpleasant that is not included in the files here. We have papers from my 40 years of public service in one place, for friend and foe to judge, to approve or to disapprove.

I do not know how this period will be regarded in years to come. But that is not the point. This Library will show the facts . . . not just the joy and triumphs, but the sorrow and failures, too.

So, Mr. President, here are 31 million documents, to be preserved for the Nation—for all to review and evaluate—which reflect what man can do and cannot do in one life.

*Source:* LBJ Library.

### Document 6.6  Civil Rights Symposium

*Soon after the Johnson presidential library opened, Johnson told library director Harry Middleton that the library should host symposiums that address issues of public concern. The second symposium, held in December 1972, addressed civil rights; the two-day event would be Johnson's last public appearance. The following are excerpts from Johnson's speech, interwoven with descriptions of the event by Middleton and Hugh Sidey,* Time *magazine correspondent, columnist, and Washington bureau chief.*

*Middleton:* It came time for the president to speak. He had slipped in and was sitting on a front seat.

And I don't suppose that anybody who saw him come up will ever forget it. He was very slow on those steps. He had a good speech to make—he went further in this speech than he had ever gone before. He began slowly; he warmed up to it.

At one point Lyndon took a nitroglycerin pill out of his pocket and popped it into his mouth, the first time, and the last, that he did that in public. He talked in a low but steady voice for about twenty minutes. Among the things he said were:

*Johnson:* I didn't want this symposium to spend two days talking about what we have done. The progress has been much too small; we haven't done nearly enough. I'm kind of ashamed of myself that I had six years and couldn't do more.... So let no one delude himself that his work is done.... as I see it, the black problem is not one of just regions or states or cities or neighborhoods. It is a problem, a concern, and responsibility of this whole nation. Moreover, and we cannot obscure this blunt fact, the black problem remains what it has always been, the simple problem of being black in a white society. That is the problem which our efforts have not addressed.

To be black, I believe, to one who is black or brown, is to be proud, is to be worthy, is to be honorable. But to be black in a white society is not to stand on level and equal ground. While the races may stand side by side, whites stand on history's mountain and blacks stand in history's hollow. We must overcome unequal history before we overcome unequal opportunity....

This is precisely the work which we must continue. This is the whole important part of this meeting. Not what we have done, what we can do. So little have we done. So much we must do....

It's time we get down to the business of trying to stand black and white on level ground....

We know there's injustice. We know there's intolerance. We know there's discrimination and hate and suspicion. And we know there's division among us. But there is a larger truth. We have proved that great progress is possible. We know how much still remains to be done. And if our efforts continue and if our will is strong and if our hearts are right and if courage remains our constant companion, then, my fellow Americans, I am confident we shall overcome.

*Sidey:* When he was done he acknowledged the applause and stepped off the stage to take a seat in the auditorium. Then squabbling broke out among the black factions.

*Merle Miller:* The more radical of the blacks present wanted the symposium to express their views, particularly their views of the Nixon administration. The Reverend Kendall Smith of the National Council of Churches in New York, and Roy Innes, chairman of the Congress of Racial Equality, had composed a statement, which Smith then delivered: "Racism under the administration of Richard Nixon has increased. This gathering of great Americans must not leave without an organized, ongoing structure dedicated to reconvening and to combating injustice in America, as was done by your Administration. . . ."

*Middleton:* The President bounded back up the steps then, and by this time it was the old LBJ of vintage times, and he put on this splendid performance that everybody remembers. Totally impromptu. Totally impromptu! The formal speech had ended; now it was just Lyndon Johnson from the courthouse square.

*Sidey:* The fatigue of the night before seemed to drop away, the old adrenaline machine pumping back into action. Going to the microphone with his hands molding the air, he delivered one of his sermons on brotherhood and reason, flavoring it with one of those marvelous stories about a backwoods judge and the town drunk, reminiscences of when he arrived in Hoover's Washington and the bonus marchers were driven down Pennsylvania Avenue.

*Johnson:* Now I want you to go back all of you, and counsel together—the way Burke and Marshall used to in the Kennedy days and later in the Johnson days—in that soft, kind way. Just cool and push off wrath, indulge, tolerate, and finally come out with a program with objectives, with organization. . . . Let's try to get our folks reasoning together and reasoning with the Congress, with the Cabinet! Reason with the leadership and with the President. There's not a thing in the world wrong— as a matter of fact, there's everything right—about a group saying, "Mr. President, we would like you to set aside an hour to let us talk." And you don't need to start off by saying he's terrible, because he doesn't think he's terrible. Start talking about how you believe that he wants to do what's right and how you believe *this* is right, and you'll be surprised how many who want to do what's right will try to help you. . . .

While I can't provide much go-go at this period of my life, I can provide a lot of hope and dream and encouragement, and I'll sell a few wormy calves now and then and contribute.

Let's watch what's been done and see that it's preserved, but let's say we have just begun, and let's go on. Until every boy and girl born into this land, whatever state, whatever color, can stand on the same level ground, our job will not be done!

*Sidey:* People came to the stage and crowded around him as he tried to leave. They were all reaching for a bit of the old magic. But nobody got as much of it as Mr. Youngblood, a thin, aging black who used to wait on tables in Austin's ancient Driskill Hotel, where Johnson sweated out election night returns. The former president and the former waiter stood there for a few seconds gripping hands, and if any questions lingered about what Lyndon Johnson had tried to do for his country, they were answered right then.

*Source:* Merle Miller, *Lyndon: An Oral Biography* (New York: Putnam's Press, 1980), 561–562.

## Document 6.7    Eulogizing Johnson

*Barbara Jordan, the first African American to represent Texas in the U.S. Congress, eulogized the president for his leadership in advancing civil rights and the interests of ordinary Americans.*

Mr. Speaker, the death of Lyndon B. Johnson diminished the life of every American involved with mankind.

He was a great man and a great President of the United States. Historians may regard that judgment as premature. But those of us who felt the power of his compassion and were the beneficiaries of his legislative prowess and effectiveness cannot await the historian's judgment. We know and see clearly . . . that Lyndon B. Johnson's life and work stripped the Federal Government of its neutrality and made it the actor on behalf of America's old, poor, and black citizens.

The depth of Lyndon B. Johnson's concern for people cannot be quantified. It was big and all encompassing. Old men straightened their backs because he lived. Little children dared look forward to intellectual achievement because he lived.

Black Americans became excited about a future of opportunity, hope, justice and dignity during his Presidency. Lyndon B. Johnson reminded this country shortly before his death that the problem of being black in a white society remains and that the problem of unequal opportunity cannot be overcome until unequal history is overcome. He wanted America to get on with the business of removing the vestiges of racial discrimination wherever found. . . .

Lyndon B. Johnson left us a legacy of courage and commitment.

Let us today resolve to protect and defend this inheritance. He was counting on us and we must not let him down.

*Source:* The Honorable Barbara Jordan of Texas, "Memorial Services in the Congress of the United States and Tributes in Eulogy of Lyndon B. Johnson Late a President of the United States," Ninety-Third Congress, first session, House document no. 93-111 (Washington, D.C.: U.S. Government Printing Office, 1973), 74.

### Document 6.8    Bill Moyers on Johnson

*Bill Moyers was one of the most influential aides in the Johnson White House. In this remembrance of Johnson after his death, Moyers recounts how he first came to work for Johnson, and what public service meant to Johnson, and Moyers.*

I was drawn to him early. To a generation of ambitious Texans Lyndon Johnson was as big as the state itself and just as promising. To a small-town kid with an overwrought Baptist conscience he showed how to get things done in a hurry. We were short on philosophy in Texas, short on history and philosophy, too. On the frontier, which Texas remained until late, life was its own reason for living, action its own justification. And you didn't read a textbook on how to climb the greasy pole; you just started climbing. How often I would hear him say: "Don't just stand there, son, get busy."

But power had a purpose for L.B.J. It was the way to deliver the goods. If you shared in the rewards (his mother, he told me, insisted that "If you do good, you'll make good"), so be it: the "folks" were always the real winners. The greatest good for the greatest number, he preached, and the largesse was pouring in: rural electricity, dams, highways, defense contracts, space projects, aerospace plants. "This is what your government did," he told his hill-country friends as he patted a new R.E.A. building as if it were a new-born calf.

His critics smirked when he said that what most people want "is a rug on the floor, a picture on the wall and music in the house." Their criticism bothered him least of all. "Those S.O.B.'s got it all," he said. "The folks I'm talking about don't even have the simple decencies, and they out-number that slicked-down crowd"—here he would wrinkle his nose as if squinting through pince-nez— "ten million to one."

So I wrote him for a summer job. Later he told me the letter was imper-tinent, my suggesting that he was out of touch with Texas young voters and offering to help him reach them, but maybe because he had also been brash and not a little cocky when he was 18: he told me to come to Wash-ington, sight unseen.

I flew there aboard an old twin-engine Convair, my first trip east of the Red River, and landed expecting to counsel the mighty. Instead I wound up in a tiny airless room so deep in the basement labyrinth of the Capitol that one old Senator who had stashed his mistress in a nearby hideaway got lost coming back from a quorum call and couldn't find her for hours.

I spent my first night in Washington—from 5 P.M. to the following noon—completing my first assignment for Lyndon B. Johnson: address-ing 100,000 letters to Texas voters one at a time on an ancient machine operated by pumping the right foot up and down, like a sewing machine. I stopped only to go to the bathroom and to assure Senator _____'s girl friend, who kept poking her tearful face in the door to inquire how long quorum calls lasted (I didn't know), that he was certain to return (I didn't know that, either).

I emerged the next day squinting in the light, hobbling on my now-stunted right foot, and wondering how L.B.J. would reward me. I soon found out. "I'm going to promote you to an upstairs room," he announced. I reported there immediately—and got to put stamps on all those letters I had just addressed. Some reward.

Years later I told him how my illusions had suffered those first two days in Washington. "Politics is stamps, spit and shakin' hands," he said. Then he smiled: "Besides, whom the Lord liketh, He chasteneth." Not quite a literal translation, but I got the point.

Throughout his career, Lyndon Johnson carried on that kind of love affair with the country, a one-time school teacher from Cotulla, Texas, for-ever trying to instruct his charges.

He taught us that the country is a "peepul," with names, faces, and dreams. He came to despise the bureaucracy his own programs created because they started dealing in "categories" and assigning numbers to human beings whose names were Hathie, Joe Henry, Fritz or Betty Lou— people who lived down the road, across the Pedernales. Once he cut an H.E.W. official off in mid-sentence with the outburst: "godamit, you make those folks sound like subjects instead of citizens."

Another time he ripped into a group of Government lawyers who had drafted an Appalachian assistance bill. "Who the hell can read this gob-bledy-gook?" he thundered. "But that's a technical document, Sir," one of the men replied. The President gave him a long, merciless stare, then with his own black felt pen he rewrote the establishing clause. "There!" he said, holding the document out before him with a flourish. "Now they'll know down in Morgantown what we're talking about."

As the Manila Conference droned to a close in 1966 the President was handed a draft on the final memorandum of agreement. He was aghast at its flat, sterile, polysyllabic prose: "Come on," he whispered pulling at my sleeve, and we left without so much as an "excuse me" to the dignitaries around the table. At the door he stopped long enough to whisper to the Secret Service agent: "Don't let one of em out until I get back."

In the next room he handed me a pad and his own pen. "Now I want to rewrite that preamble so it can be read in the public square at Johnson City," he said. We labored for an hour while Marshall Ky, President Thieu, Dean Rusk and other assorted, perplexed personages waited in the next room. The President dictated, edited, looked over my shoulder as I added what I could, finally picked up the pad, read silently, nodded, and stalked back toward the conference room. He stopped at the door and winking at me, said: "I want you to leak this to Smitty (Merriam Smith of UPI) first. It gets home first that way, and when ol' Judge Moursund reads this he'll know what we're trying to do out here with his money."

He taught us there's no progress without some giving up, that a nation of 200 million will stagnate without compromise. Some people scoffed as he reached for consensus, charging him with trying to please all the people all the time. But to him politics meant inclusion—"Noah wanted some of all the animals on board," he said, "not just critters with four legs." If consent of the governed is essential to a democracy, to L.B.J. compromise was its lubricant.

On the day I resigned, we rode around his ranch for hours. "You were born over there with those Choctaw Indians," he said. "Bet you don't know where the word 'okay' came from."

I didn't.

"Right from the Choctaws themselves," he said. "It meant 'we can agree now, if you aren't so all-fired set on perfection.'" If he had been born in another time, I thought, he would have made his living as a horse trader. Instead, he bent this remarkable talent for getting agreement from disparate men to making things happen. He taught us, after years of stalemate, that the legislative process can function.

Why, then, wasn't he willing to compromise in Vietnam? The irony is, though he was. "Well, boys, I've gone the second, third and fourth mile tonight," he said after his Johns Hopkins speech in 1965. He had proposed a multibillion-dollar rehabilitation program for Indochina, including North Vietnam, and he was convinced that it was a bargain Ho Chi Minh couldn't turn down. Another time he made another offer, in secrecy, and Ho again said no. "I don't understand it," he said, with a note of sadness in his voice. "George Meany would've grabbed at a deal like that."

Therein may be the biggest lesson Lyndon Johnson may inadvertently have taught us. We think of ourselves as broad-minded, good-intentioned, generous people pursuing worthy goals in a world we assume is aching to copy us. "Surely," the logic goes, "all we have to do is offer them what we would want if we were in their place."

This is not a lesson in the limits of power. Lyndon Johnson knew better than most the fragile nature of power, its shortcomings, the counterattitudes it inevitably provokes. "Hurry, boys, hurry," he would implore his staff after his great electoral triumph of '64. "Get that legislation up to the Hill and out. Eighteen months from now ol' Landslide Lyndon will be Lame-Duck Lyndon."

He knew the limits of power. What he had to learn the hard way, and teach us as he went along, was something about the limits of perception. What made Lyndon Johnson such a unique and authentic figure—half the Texas hill country, half Washington—may have also been his undoing. He was so much a creature of those places that he may have shaped the world in their image. And this image would hem him in, causing him to see others as he saw himself. It was this that made him such an American man when the world was in reality reaching for other models.

*Source:* Bill Moyers, "Across the Pedernales," *New York Times,* January 26, 1973.

*Appendix A*
# Notable Figures of the Johnson Presidency

**Albert, Carl (b. May 10, 1908, McAlester, Oklahoma)**
*Democratic representative, Oklahoma, 1947–1977; House majority leader, 1962–1971*
Albert, the son of a cotton farmer and coal miner, studied at Oxford University on a Rhodes scholarship. During Johnson's presidency he devised Democratic floor strategy and used power and pressure to move the president's agenda through the House. To speed passage of the 1964 Economic Opportunity Act, Albert threatened to cut off public works funding to Democrats who opposed the legislation. On foreign policy, Albert backed the U.S. war in Vietnam through Johnson's terms and into the Richard Nixon presidency.

**Baker, Bobby (b. November 12, 1928, Pickens, South Carolina)**
*Secretary to the Senate majority, January 1955–October 1963*
Baker came to the Senate as a page at the age of fifteen. Officially Senate majority secretary during Johnson's term as Senate majority leader, Baker was better known as the "ninety-seventh senator." (As Alaska and Hawaii were not yet states, there were only ninety-six elected senators.) Baker knew everyone in the Senate and knew all there was to know about them. His knowledge made him an excellent vote counter and go-between for Johnson. In 1964 the Senate Rules and Administration Committee opened investigations into Baker's alleged violation of conflict of interest statutes. Baker, on a salary of under $20,000, had become a millionaire through business deals undertaken with "fellow" senators. Despite the closeness of their relationship, only one charge against Baker in these election-year hearings directly involved Johnson. Don Reynolds, a Baker associate, claimed that in 1957, in return for the privilege of selling Johnson life insurance, he was asked to buy advertising on Senator Johnson's television station and to give the Johnsons a hi-fi set they

281

had allegedly been coveting. During the 1964 campaign, President Johnson denied these charges and distanced himself from Baker. Baker eventually served eighteen months in prison.

### Ball, George (b. December 21, 1909, Des Moines, Iowa)
*Undersecretary of state, November 1961–September 1966*
A trade specialist in the State Department in the Kennedy administration, Ball took on a broader portfolio in the Johnson presidency. Ball was at first a cautious hawk on the war in Vietnam. Like Johnson, he feared that withdrawal would damage American credibility but worried that escalation might bring China into the war. Gradually, Ball became more pessimistic about U.S. prospects in the war. The enemy, he realized, was more resilient, and the South Vietnamese allies more hapless, than U.S. planners had assumed. Ball voiced his opinions in a number of memoranda that became public after the 1971 publication of *The Pentagon Papers,* a secret history of the Vietnam War written by Pentagon experts and leaked to the *New York Times.*

### Bundy, McGeorge (b. March 30, 1919, Boston, Massachusetts)
*Special assistant to the president for national security affairs, better known as national security adviser, January 1961–February 1966*
An American aristocrat, Bundy graduated first in his class from Yale in 1940 and, at just thirty-four years of age, was named dean of arts and sciences at Harvard University. Bundy joined the Kennedy administration as national security adviser and stayed on after Kennedy's death. He played a key role in devising plans for increased U.S. assistance to South Vietnam, supporting systematic bombing against North Vietnam in Operation Rolling Thunder. After leaving the White House to assume the presidency of the Ford Foundation, one of the nation's most influential nonprofit research and advocacy organizations, Bundy gradually came to speak out against the war.

### Califano, Joseph (b. May 15, 1931, New York City)
*White House special assistant, July 1965–January 1969*
Califano made his way from Flatbush, Brooklyn, to Wall Street, with a degree from Harvard Law School, before entering government as a Pentagon attorney at the age of thirty-two. When Bill Moyers, who had been coordinating the president's busy legislative agenda, took over the press secretary position in the White House, Califano moved from the Pentagon, where he was a top aide to Secretary of Defense Robert McNamara, to join the White House as legislative coordinator. In his new role, Califano championed modern administrative processes, such as planning, programming, and budgeting (PPB) and cost-benefit analysis, while promoting the Great Society. Because he focused on domestic policy at a time when Johnson became increasingly consumed by the war in Vietnam, Califano became a virtual subpresident for domestic affairs. He was, wrote White House aide Harry McPherson, "smart, indefatigable, unafraid of responsibility or of making demands upon highly placed men in government and industry" (McPherson 1995, 254).

### Carpenter, Liz (b. September 1, 1920, Salado, Texas)
*Staff director and press secretary to the first lady, 1963–1969*
Carpenter went to Washington, D.C., after her graduation from the University of Texas with a degree in journalism. She became a friend of the Johnsons and served as executive assistant to Mr. Johnson and press aide to Mrs. Johnson in the 1960 vice presidential campaign. Aboard *Air Force One*, on its return to Washington following the Kennedy assassination, she penned the new president's first words to the nation. Carpenter was the first professional newswoman to be press secretary to a first lady, and she successfully promoted Mrs. Johnson's beautification campaign to clean up the nation's public spaces. During the 1964 campaign, she was Lady Bird's top aide on a whistle-stop tour of the South.

### Cater, Douglass (b. August 24, 1923, Montgomery, Alabama)
*White House special assistant, May 1964–October 1968*
A Harvard graduate, Cater was editor of *Reporter*, a trade magazine for journalists, in the 1950s and wrote sympathetically of Senate majority leader Johnson. Johnson first hired Cater as a speechwriter for his 1964 campaign. His forward-looking speeches on health and education led Johnson to regard Cater as his specialist in those fields. When Cater was brought into the White House as a special assistant, he was told merely to "think ahead." Cater did so and in the process helped to assemble and digest the work of numerous task forces and had a hand in shaping Great Society legislation until he went to work for Vice President Humphrey's 1968 presidential campaign.

### Christian, George (b. January 1, 1927, Austin, Texas)
*Special assistant to the president, May 1966–December 1966; White House press secretary, January 1967–January 1969*
A journalist and political confidante of Gov. John Connally of Texas, Christian joined the White House staff in 1966, working for Bill Moyers. When Moyers left the White House at the end of 1966, Johnson appointed Christian to succeed him as press secretary. Christian, loyal and hard working, did his best to defend the president against his many critics in the media as the Vietnam War dragged on.

### Clark, (William) Ramsey (b. December 18, 1927, Dallas, Texas)
*Assistant attorney general, 1961–1965; deputy attorney general, 1956–1966; acting attorney general, 1966–1967; attorney general, 1967–1969*
Son of a former attorney general and Supreme Court justice, Clark was appointed attorney general by President Johnson. During his tenure, Clark took a leading role in the administration's push for civil rights. He worked on the 1968 Civil Rights Act and used the courts to enforce school desegregation and fair employment laws. He also created the Bureau of Narcotics and Dangerous Drugs to fight drug abuse, used strike forces to battle organized crime, and advocated a number of controversial causes including gun control, opposition to the death penalty, and—after he left office—opposition to the Vietnam War.

**Clifford, Clark (b. December 25, 1906, Fort Scott, Kansas)**
*Secretary of defense, January 1968–February 1969*
As an adviser to President Truman, Clifford wrote the landmark 1947 National Security Act. He served the Kennedy administration as chairman of the president's Foreign Intelligence Advisory Board. He was a close adviser to President Johnson on domestic scandals including Walter Jenkins's arrest and the investigation of Bobby Baker. After traveling to Southeast Asia in 1966, Clifford believed the United States would prevail in Vietnam. By the time he was appointed secretary of defense and chairman of the president's ad hoc Task Force on Vietnam, he had developed reservations about America's Vietnam policy, straining his relationship with the president.

**Cohen, Wilbur (b. June 10, 1913, Milwaukee, Wisconsin)**
*Assistant secretary, Department of Health, Education, and Welfare,*
*April 1961–April 1965; undersecretary, Department of Health, Education,*
*and Welfare, April 1965–February 1968; secretary, Department of Health,*
*Education, and Welfare, March 1968–January 1969*
Cohen guided more legislation through Congress than any other leader of the Department of Health, Education, and Welfare. He played a key role in the passage of Medicare, the expansion of Social Security, and the Elementary and Secondary Education Act of 1965. On Social Security issues, Johnson turned to Cohen as the administration's chief expert.

**Cronkite, Walter (b. November 4, 1916, St. Joseph, Missouri)**
*CBS News correspondent*
A graduate of the University of Texas at Austin, Cronkite began his career in journalism as the Texas state capital reporter for Scripps-Howard news service. He became respected nationally as a United Press International reporter during World War II, earning distinction in public opinion polls as "the nation's most trusted person." After Johnson left office, Cronkite conducted seven one-hour television interviews with the former president. Cronkite envisioned a documentary including the successes and failures of the Johnson administration; Johnson envisioned a showcase for his achievements. After a protracted battle between Johnson and CBS, the documentary was filmed and televised. Its content and coverage left neither party fully satisfied.

**Dillon, (Clarence) Douglas (b. August 21, 1909, Geneva, Switzerland)**
*Secretary of the Treasury, January 1961–March 1965*
The son of a Wall Street banker, Dillon assumed a seat on the New York Stock Exchange after graduating from Groton preparatory school and Harvard College. He assisted in Nixon's 1960 presidential campaign; so his selection as secretary of the Treasury in 1961, under President Kennedy, surprised many observers. Dillon proved his value to the Kennedy and Johnson presidencies when he became a driv-

ing force behind the Kennedy-Johnson tax cut. After resigning as secretary of the Treasury in 1965, Dillon became part of Johnson's Senior Advisory Group (known popularly as the "Wise Men") that recommended the president de-escalate the war in Vietnam.

**Dirksen, Everett (b. January 4, 1895, Pekin, Illinois)**
*Republican senator from Illinois, 1951–1969; Senate minority leader, 1959–1969*
Senator Dirksen was a powerful and accommodating Republican leader. His influence with his colleagues was instrumental to the 1964 Civil Rights Act, which needed Republican support to overcome the opposition of southern Democrats. Under President Kennedy, Dirksen had opposed the bill, but for President Johnson, he engineered the vote of twenty-four GOP senators for the landmark civil rights act. Moreover, Dirksen, though he occasionally opposed the president on domestic policy, gave the commander in chief strong support for the war in Vietnam.

**Farmer, James (b. January 12, 1920, Marshall, Texas)**
*National director, Congress of Racial Equality, February 1961–March 1966*
Farmer founded the Congress of Racial Equality (CORE), an interracial civil rights group committed to nonviolent protests, in 1942. He became its national director in 1961 and launched a series of effective demonstrations. Also in 1961, he organized the Freedom Rides, a national protest against the segregation of mass transportation facilities. Farmer helped to lobby for the civil rights legislation passed during the Johnson presidency. When other civil rights leaders turned against the president because of the Vietnam War or in protest against accommodation with establishment authority figures, Farmer remained steadfast in his support of Johnson. In 1998 he was awarded the Presidential Medal of Freedom by President Bill Clinton.

**Fortas, Abe (b. June 19, 1920, Memphis, Tennessee)**
*Associate justice, U.S. Supreme Court, 1965–1969*
The top graduate in his class at Yale Law School, Fortas took the lead in devising a risky all-or-nothing strategy for quashing legal opposition to Johnson's contested victory in the 1948 Senate election. Fortas continued to advise Johnson as a friend and legal confidante over the years but declined an offer from President Johnson to become attorney general. In 1965 Johnson just barely persuaded Fortas to accept nomination to the Supreme Court. When Chief Justice Earl Warren resigned in 1968, Johnson nominated Fortas to that post, but Republican senators, and some Democrats as well, were upset about the possibility of Fortas's elevation. It was an open secret in Washington that Fortas had been working behind the scenes to serve the president's political interests from the first night of the Johnson presidency. A Senate filibuster prevented Fortas from assuming the position. Fortas resigned from the Court in 1969 under heavy public pressure surrounding questionable financial transactions (see Chapter 5).

**Fulbright, (James) William (b. April 9, 1905, Sumner, Missouri)**
*Democratic senator from Arkansas, 1945–1975; chairman,*
*Senate Foreign Relations Committee, 1959–1975*
Born to a prominent Arkansan family, Fulbright studied at Oxford University on
a Rhodes scholarship. He was an early supporter of Johnson's foreign policy, intro-
ducing the Gulf of Tonkin Resolution in the Senate and defending it against
amendment. Viewing the president's armed intervention in the Dominican
Republic as a mistake, Fulbright broke with the administration and publicly questioned the president's credibility (see Document 3.8). A 1966 televised committee investigation into the Vietnam War brought pressure on the administration to
reassess its policy. In a series of lectures in 1966, published the next year under
the title *The Arrogance of Power*, Fulbright decried the administration's alleged self-
righteousness and questioned whether it was mere pride that kept the United States
from negotiating an end to the war. By the last year of the Johnson presidency,
Fulbright was one of the most outspoken critics of Johnson's foreign policy.

**Gardner, John (b. October 8, 1912, Los Angeles, California)**
*Secretary of health, education, and welfare, August 1965–January 1968*
Gardner graduated from the University of California with a doctorate in psychol-
ogy. After working in academia, he served as president of the Carnegie
Corporation, a nonprofit foundation that sponsored far-reaching research and edu-
cational initiatives. At the request of President Johnson, Gardner, a liberal
Republican, headed a task force looking into the problems of American education.
In a report to the president, the task force recommended proportional federal aid
to elementary and secondary schools based on the level of poverty in a community. The report served as the foundation for the Elementary and Secondary
Education Act of 1965. As secretary of health, education, and welfare, Gardner
withheld federal funds from schools that did not adhere to the desegregation guidelines he established to comply with the 1964 Civil Rights Act, which barred federal assistance to institutions that practiced racial discrimination.

**Goldman, Eric (b. June 17, 1915, Washington, D.C.)**
*White House special consultant, February 1964–September 1966*
A Princeton University historian, Goldman joined the White House as the unofficial historian in residence following the departure of President Kennedy's aide, the
historian Arthur M. Schlesinger Jr. Goldman organized the June 14, 1965, White
House Festival of the Arts, which became a public relations disaster when invited
guests circulated a petition denouncing the president's foreign policy, and other invi-
tees publicly sent their regrets through the editorial pages of the nation's newspapers.
Out of favor, Goldman tendered his resignation to the president, only to have it
answered by the first lady. Goldman's book on the Johnson presidency, *The Tragedy
of Lyndon Johnson*, criticized the president as "the wrong man from the wrong place
at the wrong time under the wrong circumstances" (Goldman 1969, 531).

## Goldwater, Barry (b. January 1, 1909, Phoenix, Arizona)
*Republican senator from Arizona, 1953–1965, 1969–1987*

Goldwater was a leader of the conservative movement during the Kennedy administration. A devout anticommunist, he opposed arms control negotiations and any conciliatory diplomatic measures with the Soviet Union. His prominence as a conservative came at the expense of cooperation with the liberal wing of his party. He was one of only six Republican senators who voted against the 1964 Civil Rights Act. Despite the division in his party, Goldwater won the 1964 Republican presidential nomination. Johnson ran an effective campaign against Goldwater. He painted the Republican as a reckless extremist whose dangerous ideology could result in a nuclear war with the Soviet Union. Domestically, Goldwater's opposition to Social Security and civil rights left him with little support outside of the conservative Republican base. He lost in a landslide defeat by carrying only 38.4 percent of the popular vote.

## Goodwin, Doris Kearns (b. January 4, 1943, Rockville Center, New York)
*Special assistant to the president, 1968; special consultant to the former president, 1969–1973*

Doris Kearns was a graduate student at Harvard University when she entered the competition to join the prestigious White House Fellows program. At a reception for those selected for the program, President Johnson suggested that she work directly for him in the White House. The untimely publication of an article by Kearns in *The New Republic*, suggesting ways to dump Johnson from the Democratic ticket in 1968 because of his stand on the war in Vietnam led her to be exiled to the Labor Department instead. Despite this inauspicious start, Johnson brought Kearns into the White House in his final year as president and, after his presidency ended, persuaded her to spend her weekends and vacations at the ranch in Texas. Johnson seemed to relish the challenge of winning Kearns's support. As he told her, and she recounted in *Lyndon Johnson and the American Dream*, "I want to do everything I can to make the young people of America, especially you Harvards, understand what this political system is all about." On the ranch, Kearns helped Johnson with his memoirs and collected material for her own interpretive biography of Johnson. In 1975 she married Richard Goodwin, a former Kennedy–Johnson aide.

## Goodwin, Richard (b. December 7, 1931, Boston, Massachusetts)
*Presidential special assistant, December 1964–September 1965*

Goodwin, valedictorian of both his undergraduate class and his Harvard Law School class, was a Kennedy aide who became one of President Johnson's favorite speechwriters. He coined the term *Great Society* and was the principal draftsman of the president's best-remembered speech, the March 15, 1965, address to Congress and the nation in support of the Voting Rights Act. Disturbed by Johnson's policy on Vietnam, Goodwin left the White House and worked for both the Eugene

McCarthy and Robert Kennedy campaigns in 1968. While serving in the White House, Goodwin and his friend Bill Moyers shared with each other their anxiety that, under the burdens of the Vietnam War, the president was becoming clinically paranoid and depressed and even discussed the Twenty-fifth Amendment, which authorizes replacing an incapacitated president.

### Humphrey, Hubert (b. May 27, 1911, Wallace, South Dakota)
*Democratic senator from Minnesota, 1949–1964, 1971–1978; vice president of the United States, 1965–1969*
Like Johnson, Humphrey developed his passion for politics from his father, a South Dakota politician who admired Democratic president Woodrow Wilson and his Populist secretary of state, William Jennings Bryan. Humphrey gained national prominence when he delivered a strong civil rights speech at the 1948 Democratic National Convention; the same year he was elected to the Senate from Minnesota. During Humphrey's first sixteen years in the Senate, he introduced nearly 1,500 bills and worked as majority whip to ensure the passage of the Civil Rights Act of 1964, the Kennedy-Johnson tax cut, and the Nuclear Test-Ban Treaty of 1963. Elected vice president in 1964, he chaired the President's Council on Economic Opportunity, the Peace Corps Advisory Council, and the National Aeronautics and Space Council. In his 1968 presidential campaign, Humphrey received only weak support from Johnson.

### Jenkins, Walter (b. March 23, 1918, Jolly, Texas)
*White House special assistant, November 1963–October 1964*
According to the Johnson library's oral history of Deke DeLoach, the FBI's liaison in the Johnson White House, President Johnson worked Jenkins "like a slave" (LBJL). Jenkins developed his work habits when he joined Representative Johnson's staff in 1939. As a presidential staff member, he did anything and everything that Johnson wanted him to do, from delivering delicate messages to political allies or enemies to overseeing complicated scheduling and logistics during the campaign. His loyalty kept him in Johnson's good graces until Jenkins was arrested on a morals charge for homosexual conduct in a public restroom in October 1964. Angered at what he thought was a Republican sting operation during a presidential campaign season, Johnson nevertheless accepted Jenkins's resignation. The Republican candidate, Sen. Barry Goldwater, declined to exploit Jenkins's misfortune to its fullest potential. Jenkins returned to Texas to work for the Johnson family media corporation. Looking forward to retirement, Johnson told his old-time associate and White House lawyer, Larry Temple, as recounted in Temple's oral history, that one of the first things Johnson intended to do upon leaving office was "just throw his arms around him [Jenkins] and hug him . . . Jenkins had been as dear a friend working for him as he ever had" (LBJL).

**Johnson, Lady Bird (b. December 22, 1912, Karnack, Texas)**
*First Lady, 1963–1969*

Lady Bird, so named by her nanny, grew up in a seventeen-room mansion, the daughter of the undisputed "Cap'n" and "Boss" of a small East Texas town. She studied journalism at the University of Texas, professing a desire to see the world and meet interesting people. She met Lyndon Johnson shortly after her graduation, while visiting a friend in Austin. Johnson proposed marriage on their first date. Ten weeks later, Johnson, a congressional secretary at the time, proposed again. They were married November 17, 1934, in a rushed ceremony in San Antonio, Texas. Occasionally embarrassed and even publicly humiliated by her domineering husband, Mrs. Johnson nevertheless was devoted to him and developed an inner poise that earned her the esteem of the Johnsons' friends over the years.

In 1937 Lyndon needed cash to begin his campaign in a special election for a House seat. Mrs. Johnson secured $10,000 from her father and pitched in to help. She provided her husband with similar help in 1942, combining her money with his influence to purchase a struggling radio station in Austin. KTBC became the core of a highly successful media empire, making the Johnsons one of the wealthiest first families in presidential history.

Of her role as a politician's wife, her biographer recounts Mrs. Johnson saying, "His life became my life. I respected it. I wanted to learn from it, excel in it" (Russell 1999, 143). While serving as first lady, Lady Bird focused attention on beautification and conservation, important issues in the Great Society program that were central to the president's domestic policy (see Chapter 3). In a 1982 poll of historians undertaken by the Sienna Research Institute, Loudonville, New York, Lady Bird was ranked number three among first ladies.

**Jordan, Vernon (b. August 15, 1935, Atlanta, Georgia)**
*Director, Voter Education Project, Southern Regional Council, 1964–1968*

A civil rights activist, Jordan escorted the first black student at the University of Georgia through a mob of protestors. In 1964 he became the director of the Voter Education Project, an initiative sponsored by a coalition of major civil rights organizations. Jordan succeeded in keeping the coalition together, despite the differences in opinion that developed between militant and moderate civil rights groups in the late 1960s. During President Johnson's time in office, the Voter Education Project registered nearly two million southern black voters. After 1968 Jordan served as director of the United Negro College Fund and the National Urban League and was a friend and adviser to President Bill Clinton.

**Kappel, Frederick (b. January 14, 1902, Albert Lea, Minnesota)**
*Chairman and chief executive, American Telephone and Telegraph*
*Corporation (AT&T), August 1961–January 1967*
Kappel rose through the corporate ranks of the company Alexander Graham Bell
established in 1885 to become president of the company in 1961. During his presidency, AT&T had more employees, more stockholders, and made more money
than any other company relative to that time in the history of the world. Kappel
was often contacted by President Johnson for advice on business and economic
issues, such as budgeting, taxes, and the specter of inflation. After retiring from
AT&T, Kappel served as head of a presidential commission to review the U.S.
Postal Service.

**Katzenbach, Nicholas (b. January 17, 1922, Philadelphia, Pennsylvania)**
*Deputy attorney general, 1962–1964; acting attorney general, 1964–1965;*
*attorney general, 1965–1966, undersecretary of state, 1966–1969*
A Rhodes scholar with degrees from Princeton University and Yale Law School,
Katzenbach received a call from the newly elected president Johnson with a mandate to draft and secure passage for a comprehensive voting rights bill. When the
bill Katzenbach drafted became law one year later, he successfully defended its constitutionality before the Supreme Court and proceeded to enforce it. As attorney
general, Katzenbach also enforced school desegregation laws and directed government agencies to cease funding discriminatory programs. He resigned his position after a bitter struggle with FBI director J. Edgar Hoover over the legality of
wiretapping. He subsequently was appointed undersecretary of state.

**Kennedy, Robert F. (b. November 20, 1925, Brookline, Massachusetts)**
*Attorney general, January 1961–September 1964; Democratic senator from*
*New York, 1965–1968*
A graduate of Harvard University and the University of Virginia Law School,
Robert (Bobby) F. Kennedy successfully managed his brother John F. Kennedy's
1952 Senate campaign and 1960 presidential campaign, earning him an appointment as attorney general. In that position, he fought organized crime and pushed
for racial equality in the South. The relationship between Johnson and Bobby
Kennedy was strained. In *My Brother Lyndon*, Lyndon's younger brother Sam
Houston observed simply that "Lyndon hated Bobby" and "Bobby hated
Lyndon" (Johnson 1969, 159). After John F. Kennedy's assassination in 1964,
Bobby Kennedy wanted the vice presidential nomination, but Johnson selected
Hubert Humphrey. Kennedy successfully ran for Senate from New York and
became a vocal critic of Johnson's policy in Vietnam. Kennedy was assassinated in
1968 while campaigning for the Democratic presidential nomination.

**King, Martin Luther Jr. (b. January 15, 1929, Atlanta, Georgia)**
*President, Southern Christian Leadership Conference, 1957–1968*
A Baptist minister and civil rights activist, King was the first president of the Southern Christian Leadership Conference (SCLC). In that position, he advocated desegregation and voting rights through nonviolent protests including sit-ins and marches. Among the most famous protests were a sit-in at a segregated lunch counter in Birmingham, Alabama, that resulted in King's arrest and a march on Washington, in 1963, at which King delivered his famous "I have a dream" speech. King was instrumental in leading the protests for voting rights in Selma, Alabama, that gave President Johnson the opportunity he had hoped for to introduce far-reaching voting rights legislation. When President Johnson signed the Voting Rights Act, King was one of the principal guests in attendance. Despite the fact that they shared a similar vision of activist government, King and Johnson were never on close terms. The distance between the two was heightened when King began speaking out against the war in Vietnam in 1966. King was shot by an assassin April 3, 1968.

**Mann, Thomas (b. November 11, 1912, Laredo, Texas)**
*Assistant secretary of state for inter-American affairs, special assistant to the president, director of the Alliance for Progress, December 1963–February 1965; undersecretary of state for economic affairs, February 1965–April 1966*
A self-described pragmatist from a Texas border town, Mann joined the State Department as a way to get involved in World War II. He was assigned to Latin America and worked his way up the ranks of the Foreign Service. President Kennedy's ambassador to Mexico, Mann became "Mr. Latin America," in the words of Secretary of State Dean Rusk, with his simultaneous appointment to three positions for Latin American policy in 1963 under President Johnson. Mann steered Latin American policy in a controversially pragmatic direction, putting the United States on the side of nondemocratic, anticommunist governments in Latin America. In the spring of 1965, Mann joined a high-level diplomatic team sent by the United States to establish a new government in the Dominican Republic. The mission failed, and Mann was blamed for his allegedly high-handed treatment of the Organization of American States. Under strong press criticism, Mann left the government in April 1966.

**Mansfield, Mike (b. March 16, 1903, New York, New York)**
*Democratic senator from Montana, 1953–1977; Senate majority leader, 1961–1977*
A scholarly moderate, Mansfield was chosen by Senate Majority Leader Johnson to be his whip in 1957. When Johnson moved to the vice presidency, Mansfield became majority leader. During the Johnson presidency, the president often worked around Mansfield rather than through him in the Senate. The arrangement suited Mansfield because, unlike Johnson as majority leader, Mansfield diffused his power broadly among committee chairs, whips, and leaders of the opposition party.

## Marshall, Thurgood (b. July 2, 1908, Baltimore, Maryland)

*U.S. circuit judge, Second Circuit Court of Appeals, 1961–1965; solicitor general, 1965–1967; associate justice, U.S. Supreme Court, 1967–1991*

As director-counsel of the National Association for the Advancement of Colored People Legal Defense and Educational Fund from 1940 to 1962, Thurgood Marshall brought thirty-two cases before the Supreme Court. He successfully argued twenty-nine of those cases, including *Brown v. Board of Education* (1954), which banned racial segregation in public schools. Appointed the first black solicitor general by President Johnson, Marshall convinced the Supreme Court that eavesdropping was unconstitutional and the Voting Rights Act of 1965 was constitutional. Marshall was nominated to the Supreme Court in 1967 and served as the first black member of the Court.

## McCarthy, Eugene (b. March 29, 1916, Watkins, Minnesota)

*Democratic-Farmer-Labor representative from Minnesota, 1949–1959, Democratic senator from Minnesota, 1959–1971*

Senator McCarthy gained prominence when Johnson looked toward him as a potential running mate in 1964. As a Catholic Democrat with a solid liberal voting record, McCarthy appeared to complement Johnson well. Although he was not picked as the vice presidential nominee, McCarthy sailed through reelection and was placed on the Senate Foreign Relations Committee. Initially supportive of U.S. policy toward Vietnam, he voted for the Gulf of Tonkin Resolution, which gave the president power to use the military in Vietnam to protect troops and gain peace. Over the next four years, however, McCarthy became a vocal critic of the president's policy and competed unsuccessfully for the Democratic nomination for president in 1968.

## McCormack, John (b. December 21, 1891, Boston, Massachusetts)

*Democratic representative, Massachusetts, 1928–1971; Speaker of the House, 1962–1971*

A member of the House of Representatives for almost his entire adult life, McCormack succeeded Sam Rayburn as Speaker of the House in January 1962. During Johnson's presidency, McCormack promoted the president's agenda and backed his foreign policy. McCormack's age and aggressive anticommunism earned the enmity of younger, more liberal Democrats in the House, and the *New York Times* criticized McCormack for never developing the control over the House that the legendary Rayburn had achieved.

## McNamara, Robert (b. June 9, 1916, San Francisco, California)

*Secretary of defense, January 1961–February 1968*

McNamara was a scholar with degrees from the University of California, Berkeley, and Harvard Business School. He was a member of the Harvard faculty before joining the Ford Motor Company, where he became the first person outside the Ford family to be named president. After one month in that post, President Kennedy appointed McNamara secretary of defense, a position from which he implemented significant changes. McNamara increased the importance of the secretary's office by centralizing control of all military operations in his office, taking back power that his predecessors had delegated to generals and admirals. He created new budgetary procedures that diminished the power of the service chiefs. He also modernized the military to prepare for a "flexible response" to any crisis.

Several trips to Vietnam from 1962 to 1966 left McNamara optimistic that the United States could achieve its goals in Indochina. Vietnam might have to remain divided indefinitely, like Korea, but the United States, he reasoned, could surely prevent a communist victory in South Vietnam. However, by 1967 McNamara was less optimistic and commissioned a study on U.S. involvement in Vietnam that was leaked to the press in 1971 as *The Pentagon Papers*. McNamara's growing doubts about the U.S. role in Vietnam culminated with a recommendation to cease the bombing campaign that had been ongoing almost daily since the summer of 1965. President Johnson nevertheless remained greatly respectful of McNamara's intelligence, energy, and loyalty and eased his departure from the cabinet. In February 1968 McNamara left government service to become president of the World Bank.

### McPherson, Harry (b. August 22, 1929, Tyler, Texas)
*Assistant secretary of defense for education and cultural affairs, July 1964–August 1965; special assistant to the president, August 1965–February 1966; special counsel to the president, February 1966–January 1969*
An urbane man from the east Texas countryside, McPherson was motivated to enter law school to protect the civil liberties that he saw threatened by Sen. Joseph McCarthy. After he graduated from law school, a relative who had worked on Capitol Hill suggested that he apply for a vacant job with the Senate Democratic Policy Committee, chaired by Johnson. McPherson took the position of assistant counsel to the committee in 1956 and stayed until 1963, when he took an appointive position in the Pentagon. Two years later McPherson rejoined Johnson's staff, drafting executive orders and acting as liaison to the Justice Department. His most consequential work for the president was performed as a speechwriter.

### Middleton, Harry (b. October 24, 1921, Centerville, Iowa)
*Executive director, Lyndon Baines Johnson Presidential Library, March 1971–October 31, 2001*
Middleton was in the outer rings of the speechwriting department in the final years of the Johnson presidency. During Johnson's retirement, Middleton assisted in compiling the president's memoirs. Johnson chose him to head his presidential library and museum in 1970. In 1990, at about the time that Robert Caro published the second of his highly critical biographical volumes about Johnson and Oliver Stone excoriated the president from Texas in his film *JFK*, Middleton and Mrs. Johnson made an important decision. Rather than abide by the late president's wish that secret White House recordings from his telephone conversations remain sealed from the public for another thirty years, they would have the library release the recordings. This way, the public could hear for themselves how Johnson struggled with the war in Vietnam.

## Mills, Wilbur (b. May 24, 1909, Kensett, Arkansas)
*Democratic representative from Arkansas, 1939–1977; chairman, House Ways and Means Committee, 1957–1974*

Johnson was fond of saying that Congress was divided between whales and minnows, show horses and work horses. Wilbur Mills, to combine metaphors, was a whale of a work horse. As chairman of the powerful Ways and Means Committee, he controlled tax legislation and committee assignments. During the Johnson administration, he took center stage twice. First, he reversed his long-standing opposition to Medicare and became the chief House architect of the complex bill that created Medicare and Medicaid. Next, he fought the administration over a White House proposed tax surcharge to finance the war in Vietnam. After almost a year, the administration finally had no choice but to give in to Mills's demand to cut $10 billion from the budget in exchange for the tax surcharge. As Johnson had long feared, conservative members of Congress, like Mills, traded support for the Vietnam War for a scaling-back of Johnson's liberal domestic programs.

## Moyers, Bill (b. June 5, 1934, Hugo, Oklahoma)
*White House special assistant, November 1963–June 1965; White House press secretary, July 1965–December 1966*

Moyers, a former aide to Senator Johnson, was in Austin when he heard the news that President Kennedy had been shot in Dallas. Chartering a jet to Dallas and commanding a stunned police officer to drive him to *Air Force One,* Moyers made his way to Johnson's side, passing a note to Johnson that said, simply, "I'm here if you need me." From that moment until the end of the year, 1966, Moyers was the president's most valued White House aide. During the transition to the new presidency, Moyers was an unofficial ambassador to the Kennedy circle in government. In the campaign, he organized the 1964 task force operation and was the architect of the devastating negative advertising campaign against Barry Goldwater in 1964. As special assistant and, later, press secretary, Moyers was highly effective, building a network of associates throughout the government and handling delicate matters with both tact and cunning. A veteran journalist, Patrick Anderson, in a book about White House aides, termed Moyers "the most powerful White House assistant of modern times."

Johnson's relationship with Moyers was close, sometimes being described as father-son. Johnson admired the way the former farm boy and ordained Baptist minister handled himself in the rarified atmospheres of New York and Hyannis Port, Mass. Moyers, despite his youth, could also handle Johnson better than anyone else, except for the first lady. Moyers left Washington at the end of 1966 to become publisher of the nation's largest suburban daily, *Newsday,* and has enjoyed a long career in television journalism since 1976.

**O'Brien, Lawrence (b. July 7, 1917, Springfield, Massachusetts)**
*Special assistant to the president for congressional relations, January 1961–August 1965; postmaster general, November 1965–April 1968*
O'Brien was one of the most successful holdovers from the Kennedy White House. After helping the president win passage of an unrivalled volume of reform legislation, he accepted appointment as postmaster general. It was O'Brien's office, when he was chairman of the Democratic National Committee, that was burgled in the Watergate complex in 1972, leading eventually to the resignation of President Richard Nixon.

**Reedy, George (b. August 5, 1917, East Chicago, Illinois)**
*White House press secretary, March 1964–July 1965*
Reedy served on Senator Johnson's staff in the 1950s and stayed on with Johnson during his vice presidency and presidency. Reedy's tenure as press secretary came to an end when he became the scapegoat for polls indicating that the president had an image problem with voters. Reedy wrote two books on the presidency. In *Lyndon Johnson's White House, A Memoir* (1982), Reedy tried to come to terms with his abusive but accomplished former employer. Reedy's portrayal is of a pathological but heroic man, someone with a penchant for abusive personal behavior but the willpower to work himself sick and to inspire others to do the same. Reedy's prose is often bitter but always thoughtful.

**Reuther, Walter (b. September 1, 1907, Wheeling, West Virginia)**
*President, United Automobile Workers, 1946–1970; president, Congress of Industrial Oranizations (CIO), 1952–1955; vice president, American Federation of Labor/Congress of Industrial Organizations, 1952–1967*
Reuther began his working career as a tool and die maker. In 1936 he joined the executive board of his local union, the United Auto Workers. After organizing a 30,000-person strike on Detroit's west side, the union gained considerable power. Reuther later became president of the union where he successfully fought for higher wages, better working conditions, an annual cost-of-living wage increase, and health care benefits. At first distrustful of Johnson's alleged conservatism, Reuther became a strong supporter of President Johnson's domestic activism. His influence was felt especially in the development of the Model Cities program (see Chapter 3).

**Rostow, Walt Whitman (b. October 7, 1916, New York, New York)**
*Chair, State Department Planning Council, 1961–1966; special assistant to the president for national security affairs, April 1966–January 1969*
As a member of President Kennedy's administration, Rostow analyzed the problems of less-developed countries. He argued that during the transition of such nations to economic "take-off," modernization created opportunities for communist insurgents. Rostow believed that only the use of escalating military force

could forestall communist victory under such conditions. From his position in the State Department, he became identified with Johnson's policy on Vietnam. Succeeding McGeorge Bundy as national security adviser in 1966, Rostow remained hawkish on Vietnam to the end of the Johnson presidency, after which he followed Johnson to Texas, accepting a position on the faculty of the Lyndon Johnson School of Public Affairs at the University of Texas.

### Rusk, Dean (b. February 9, 1909, Cherokee County, Georgia)
*Secretary of state, January 1961–January 1969*
A Rhodes scholar, Dean Rusk was the president of the Rockefeller Foundation for nearly a decade. President Kennedy appointed Rusk secretary of state, but Kennedy's desire to handle foreign policy matters personally reduced Rusk's role. Under President Johnson, however, Rusk became a key adviser on Vietnam and other foreign policy issues. Rusk advised Johnson on all important foreign and military affairs. He viewed the Vietnam War as a battle for the hearts and minds of the people of the third world, who would lose confidence in the United States if North Vietnam and its powerful patrons in Beijing and Moscow were permitted to conquer South Vietnam. As Secretary of Defense Robert McNamara drifted to a dovish position on the war, Rusk believed it was his duty to stand all the more resolutely behind Johnson's hard-line position. When preliminary peace talks began in Paris in May 1968, the secretary of state played little part in them.

### Shriver, (Robert) Sargent Jr. (b. November 9, 1915, Westminster, Maryland)
*Director, Office of Economic Opportunity, February 1964–February 1968;*
*ambassador to France, February 1968–March 1970*
As a young man, Shriver worked for the Kennedy family patriarch, Joseph Kennedy, as assistant manager of the Chicago Merchandise Mart, a property management and trade-show production corporation. In 1953 he married Eunice Kennedy, sister to John, Robert, and Ted Kennedy. When the Peace Corps was established by his brother-in-law's administration, Shriver became its first director. Johnson persuaded Shriver to leave that position to become the director of the War on Poverty, part of Johnson's Great Society program (see Chapter 3). Shriver's enthusiasm and administrative competence were highly regarded in the Johnson White House, as were his credentials as a Kennedy in-law outspoken in his support of the Johnson presidency.

### Valenti, Jack (b. September 5, 1921, Houston, Texas)
*White House special assistant, November 1963–May 1966*
Valenti was a Houston public relations executive who handled Democratic advertising in Texas in the 1960 presidential campaign. On hand when President Kennedy was assassinated, Valenti accompanied the new president to Washington on board *Air Force One*. At Johnson's request, Valenti stayed in Washington and

became an important aide to the president. He was with the president constantly during the hectic early months of the Johnson presidency. Unfortunately for Valenti, his worshipful praise of the president made him a laughingstock to the sophisticates of the press corps. He left the White House to take a well-paid position as president of the Motion Picture Association of America, a job he still held thirty-five years later.

### Warren, Earl (b. March 19, 1891, Los Angeles, California)
*Chief Justice, U.S. Supreme Court, 1953–1969*

Warren was elected attorney general in California and was three times the state's governor before running unsuccessfully for vice president in 1948 on the Republican ticket. As chief justice, Warren presided over the unanimous *Brown v. Board of Education* decision, which barred racial segregation in public schools. The Supreme Court he presided over also established the "one man, one vote" foundation for reapportionment of voting districts, guaranteed rights for criminal suspects in the *Miranda* ruling (see Document 5.11), and supported Great Society legislation by affirming the Civil Rights Act of 1964 and Voting Rights Act of 1965 (see Chapter 3). In 1963 he accepted an appointment by President Johnson to investigate the death of President Kennedy; the Warren Commission found that Lee Harvey Oswald acted alone as the assassin.

### Watson, Marvin (b. June 6, 1924, Oakhurst, Texas)
*White House special assistant, January 1965–March 1968, postmaster general, April 1968–January 1969*

As executive assistant to the president of a Texas steel company, Watson established one of the first Johnson for president clubs in Texas. After successfully coordinating the Democratic convention in Atlantic City in 1964, Watson became gatekeeper to the Oval Office. Because President Johnson had no formal chief of staff, Watson's position as appointments secretary was of unusual importance in the Johnson years.

### Weaver, Robert (b. December 29, 1907, Washington, D.C.)
*Secretary, Department of Housing and Urban Development, January 1966–January 1969*

Weaver earned a Ph.D. in economics in 1934 and began government service in the New Deal, becoming a leading member of President Roosevelt's so-called Negro Brain Trust. As administrator of the precursor agency to the Department of Housing and Urban Development (HUD), Weaver was a principal lobbyist for the elevation of the housing post to cabinet status. On January 13, 1966, he became the first African American appointed to a president's cabinet. As HUD secretary, he implemented the controversial Model Cities program, a component of the Great Society (see Chapter 3). Weaver described the effort in a 1967 magazine article for

*The Nation's Cities* as "a revolutionary mechanism to show us how to mobilize vast federal, state, and local forces and direct them to the economic, social, and physical reorganization of the neglected areas in our cities" (Weaver 1967, 9). He was also a key figure in lobbying Congress to pass the 1968 Fair Housing Act.

**Westmoreland, William (b. March 26, 1914, Spartanburg County, South Carolina)**
*Commander, U.S. Military Assistance Command, South Vietnam, une 1964–June 1968; Army chief of staff, June 1968–June 1972*
General Westmoreland, a graduate of the U.S. Military Academy at West Point, was the principal architect of American strategy in Vietnam. Under his command, the United States fought a war of attrition, in which U.S. forces sought patiently to kill enemy soldiers until the other side realized their cause was futile. Eager to "attrit" the enemy in firefights, Westmoreland sent his soldiers on large-scale search-and-destroy operations in South Vietnam. In response to the Tet offensive (see Chapter 4), he requested an additional 200,000 troops. Bitter that his request was not honored, Westmoreland nevertheless kept his critical opinions to himself until his retirement, when he lashed out at Secretary of Defense Robert McNamara and other civilians who, he believed, had lost the war by second-guessing the military and giving up too soon.

**Wheeler, Earle (b. January 13, 1908, Washington, D.C.)**
*Army chief of staff, 1962–1964; chairman, joint chiefs of staff, July 1964–July 1970*
As chairman of the Joint Chiefs, Wheeler acted on his belief that the nation's top military leaders had become overly deferential to the civilian secretary of defense. Wheeler's predecessor, Gen. Maxwell Taylor, was tremendously loyal to President Kennedy and had not sought to interfere when Secretary of Defense Robert McNamara provoked interservice rivalries so as better to dominate military policy. Under Wheeler, the chiefs were encouraged to work out their differences in private and present McNamara with a united front of military expertise. When McNamara testified before Congress that U.S. bombing was ineffective in the war in Vietnam and that no wider war was called for, Wheeler and the other members of the Joint Chiefs agreed to resign en masse the next day. Wheeler, suffering chest pains and agonizing over his military oath of obedience, called off the press conference at which the chiefs were to announce their unprecedented move. McNamara had won.

**Wilkins, Roy (b. August 30, 1901, St. Louis, Missouri)**
*Executive secretary, National Association for the Advancement of Colored People (NAACP), 1955–1964; executive director, NAACP, 1965–1976*
While working for a black weekly newspaper in Kansas City, Wilkins gained the attention of the NAACP. After serving nearly a decade as its executive secretary, he became the executive director of the organization. Under his leadership, the

NAACP sponsored voter registration drives, created legal clinics across the nation to advance legal access for African Americans, and furthered the civil rights movement through marches, legislation, and lobbying. Wilkins' actions were important in the implementation of the Voting Rights Act of 1965 (see Chapter 3). In the struggle of the mid- to late 1960s over the future of the civil rights movement, Wilkins remained a steadfast moderate, condemning the use of violence as immoral and the dreams of black separatists as deluded. For the duration of his presidency, Johnson sought his advice and counsel.

### Young, Whitney Jr. (b. July 31, 1921, Lincoln Ridge, Kentucky)
*Executive director, National Urban League, 1961–1971*
A civil rights activist, Young was the executive director of the National Urban League, the world's largest civil rights organization at the time. Under his leadership, the organization focused its efforts on ameliorating the lack of social, political, and economic power held by blacks who lived in ghettos. President Johnson frequently consulted Young on the administration's War on Poverty; he served on seven presidential commissions during the Johnson presidency.

BIBLIOGRAPHY

The most valuable single resource on the lives of those who worked for, with, and against the president is the oral history collection of the Lyndon B. Johnson Presidential Library. Numerous interviews are available online. (Navigate to the oral histories from the Johnson presidential library home page at www.lbjlib.utexas.edu/.) The best published resource is *Political Profiles: The Johnson Years*, ed. Nelson Lichtenstein and Eleanor W. Shoenebaum (New York: Facts on File, 1976).

On the people in the Johnson White House, see the following books by veteran Washington reporters: Patrick Anderson, *The Presidents' Men: White House Assistants of Franklin D. Roosevelt, Harry S Truman, Dwight D. Eisenhower, John F. Kennedy, and Lyndon B. Johnson* (Garden City, N.Y.: Doubleday, 1968); and Charles Roberts, *LBJ's Inner Circle* (New York: Delacorte, 1965). Also valuable is Richard Tanner Johnson, *Managing the White House: An Intimate Study of the Presidency* (New York: Harcourt and Brace, 1974).

Johnson's wife and one of his brothers have added personal accounts of the people involved in the Johnson presidency. The first lady's memoir, Lady Bird Johnson, *A White House Diary* (New York: Holt, Rinehart and Winston, 1970), is a condensed version of the voluminous journal that Mrs. Johnson kept of her years in the White House. On Mrs. Johnson herself, see Jan Jarboe Russell, *Lady Bird: A Biography of Mrs. Johnson* (New York: Scribner's, 1999); and Liz Carpenter, *Ruffles and Flourishes: The Warm and Tender Story of a Simple Girl Who Found Adventure in the White House* (Garden City, N.Y.: Doubleday, 1969). The president's brother adds his distinctive voice in Sam Houston Johnson, *My Brother Lyndon*, ed. Enrique Hank Lopez (New York: Cowles, 1969). His observations about the people who worked for, and against, his brother are astute and frank.

Two of the most revealing and informative books by former Johnson associates involved most heavily in domestic affairs are Joseph A. Califano Jr., *The Triumph and Tragedy of Lyndon Johnson: The White House Years* (New York: Simon and Schuster, 1991); and George Reedy, *Lyndon B. Johnson: A Memoir* (New York: Andrews McMeel, 1982). Speechwriter Richard Goodwin caused a media stir with his book *Remembering America: A Voice from the Sixties* (Boston: Little, Brown, 1988), in which he recounted his concern for the president's sanity. Harry McPherson's entertaining and literate account of his service for Senator and President Johnson is entitled *A Political Education: A Washington Memoir* (Austin: University of Texas Press, 1995).

Two of Johnson's highest-ranking foreign policy associates offer contrasting perspectives on the Johnson presidency in Robert S. McNamara, with Brian VanDeMark, *In Retrospect: The Tragedy and Lessons of Vietnam* (New York: Times Books, 1995); and Dean Rusk, as told to Richard Rusk, *As I Saw It*, ed. Daniel S. Papp (New York: Norton, 1990).

Other works cited in this appendix are Eric F. Goldman, *The Tragedy of Lyndon Johnson* (New York: Knopf, 1969); and Robert C. Weaver, "HUD at Two," *Nation's Cities*, November 1967, 9.

## Document A.1   Executive Department Heads

| Title | Executive | Years served |
| --- | --- | --- |
| Secretary of agriculture | Orville L. Freeman | 1961–1969 |
| Secretary of commerce | Luther H. Hodges | 1961–1964 |
| | John T. Connor | 1965–1967 |
| | Alexander B. Trowbridge | 1967–1968 |
| | Howard J. Samuels (acting) | 1968 |
| | Cyrus R. Smith | 1968–1969 |
| Secretary of defense | Robert S. McNamara | 1961–1968 |
| | Clark M. Clifford | 1968–1969 |
| Secretary of health, education, and welfare | Anthony J. Celebrezze | 1962–1965 |
| | John W. Gardner | 1965–1968 |
| | Wilbur J. Cohen | 1968–1969 |
| Secretary of housing and urban development | Robert C. Weaver | 1966–1968 |
| | Robert C. Wood | 1969 |
| Secretary of the interior | Stewart L. Udall | 1961–1969 |
| Attorney general | Robert F. Kennedy | 1961–1964 |
| | Nicholas de B. Katzenbach | 1965–1966 |
| | Ramsey Clark | 1967–1969 |

*continued*

| Title | Executive | Years served |
|---|---|---|
| Secretary of labor | W. Willard Wirtz | 1962–1969 |
| Postmaster general | John A. Gronouski | 1963–1965 |
| | Lawrence F. O'Brien | 1965–1968 |
| | W. Marvin Watson | 1968–1969 |
| Secretary of state | Dean Rusk | 1961–1969 |
| Secretary of transportation | Alan S. Boyd | 1967–1969 |
| Secretary of the Treasury | Douglas Dillon | 1961–1965 |
| | Henry H. Fowler | 1965–1968 |
| | Joseph W. Barr | 1968–1969 |

*Source:* Nelson Lichtenstein, ed., *Political Profiles: The Johnson Years* (New York: Facts on File, 1976).

## Document A.2    Regulatory Commissions and Independent Agencies

| Agency | Board/commission member | Years served |
|---|---|---|
| Atomic Energy Commission | Mary I. Bunting | 1964–1965 |
| | Francesco Costagliola | 1968–1969 |
| | Wilfrid E. Johnson | 1966[a] |
| | Samuel M. Nabrit | 1966–1967 |
| | John G. Palfrey | 1962–1966 |
| | James T. Ramey | 1962[a] |
| | Glenn T. Seaborg | 1961[a] Chairman 1968–1969 |
| | Gerald F. Tape | 1963–1969 |
| | Robert E. Wilson | 1960–1964 |
| Civil Aeronautics Board | John G. Adams | 1965[a] |
| | Alan S. Boyd | 1959–1965 Chairman 1961–1965 |
| | John H. Crooker, Jr. | 1968–1969 Chairman 1968–1969 |
| | Whitney Gilliland | 1959[a] |

*continued*

**Document A.2** *continued*

| Agency | Board/commission member | Years served |
|---|---|---|
| | Chan Gurney | 1951–1965<br>Chairman<br>1968–1969 |
| | G. Joseph Minetti | 1956[a] |
| | Charles S. Murphy | 1965–1968<br>Chairman<br>1965–1968 |
| | Robert T. Murphy | 1961[a] |
| Federal | Robert T. Bartley | 1952[a] |
| Communications | Kenneth A. Cox | 1963[a] |
| Commission | Frederick W. Ford | 1957–1965<br>Chairman<br>1960–1961 |
| | E. William Henry | 1962–1966<br>Chairman<br>1963–1966 |
| | Rosel H. Hyde | 1949–1966<br>Chairman<br>1953–1954,<br>1966–1969 |
| | Nicholas Johnson | 1966[a] |
| | H. Rex Lee | 1968[a] |
| | Robert E. Lee | 1953[a] |
| | Lee Loevinger | 1963–1968 |
| | James J. Wadsworth | 1965–1969 |
| Federal Power | Carl E. Bagge | 1965[a] |
| Commission | David S. Black | 1963–1966 |
| | Albert B. Brooke Jr. | 1968[a] |
| | John A. Carver Jr. | 1966[a] |
| | Lawrence J. O'Connor Jr. | 1962[a] |
| | Charles R. Ross | 1961–1968 |
| | Joseph C. Swidler | 1961–1965<br>Chairman<br>1961–1965 |
| | Lee C. White | 1966–1969<br>Chairman<br>1966–1969 |
| | Harold C. Woodward | 1962–1964 |

*continued*

| Agency | Board/commission member | Years served |
|---|---|---|
| Federal Reserve Board | C. Canby Balderston | 1954–1966 |
| | Andrew F. Brimmer | 1966[a] |
| | J. Dewey Daane | 1963[a] |
| | Sherman J. Maisel | 1965[a] |
| | William M. Martin Jr. | 1951[a] |
| | | Chairman 1951[a] |
| | A. L. Mills Jr. | 1952–1965 |
| | George Mitchell | 1961–AJ |
| | James L. Robertson | 1952[a] |
| | Charles N. Shepardson | 1955–1967 |
| | William W. Sherrill | 1967[a] |
| Federal Trade Commission | Sigurd Anderson | 1955–1964 |
| | Paul R. Dixon | 1961[a] |
| | | Chairman 1961[a] |
| | Phillip Elman | 1961[a] |
| | A. Leon Higginbotham | 1962–1964 |
| | Mary G. Jones | 1964[a] |
| | A. Everette MacIntyre | 1961[a] |
| | James M. Nicholson | 1967–1969 |
| | John R. Reilly | 1964–1967 |
| Securities and Exchange Commission | Hamer H. Budge | 1964[a] |
| | | Chairman 1969[a] |
| | William L. Cary | 1961–1964 |
| | Manuel F. Cohen | 1961–1969 |
| | | Chairman |
| | | 1964–1969 |
| | Hugh F. Owens | 1964[a] |
| | Richard B. Smith | 1967[a] |
| | Francis M. Wheat | 1964–1969 |
| | Jack M. Whitney II | 1961–1964 |
| | Byron D. Woodside | 1960–1967 |

[a] Member maintained seat after Johnson administration.

*Source:* Nelson Lichtenstein, *Political Profiles: The Johnson Years* (New York: Facts on File, 1976).

## Document A.3   Military Leaders during the Johnson Years

| Title | Executive | Years served[a] |
|---|---|---|
| Secretary of defense | Robert S. McNamara | 1961–1968 |
| | Clark M. Clifford | 1968–1969 |
| Chairman of the Joint Chiefs of Staff | Gen. Maxwell D. Taylor (U.S. Army) | 1962–1964 |
| | Gen. Earle G. Wheeler (U.S. Army) | 1964[b] |
| Joint Chiefs of Staff | Chief of staff, U.S. Army | |
| | Gen. Earle G. Wheeler | 1963–1964 |
| | Gen. Harold K. Johnson | 1965–1968 |
| | Gen. William C. Westmoreland | 1969[b] |
| | Chief of Naval operations | |
| | Adm. George W. Anderson Jr. | 1962–1963 |
| | Adm. David L. McDonald | 1964–1967 |
| | Adm. Thomas H. Moorer | 1968[b] |
| | Chief of Staff, U.S. Air Force | |
| | Gen. Curtis E. LeMay | 1962–1964 |
| | Gen. John P. McConnell | 1965[b] |
| | Commandant of the Marine Corps | |
| | Gen. Wallace M. Greene Jr. | 1964–1968 |
| | Gen. Leonard F. Chapman Jr. | 1969[b] |

[a] Years served indicate first full calendar year of service at time of congressional directory publication.

[b] Member maintained seat after Johnson administration.

*Source:* Compiled by the author.

## Document A.4  Tenure of Cabinet Secretaries, Multiterm Administrations, 1953–1977

*In an effort to maintain continuity after President Kennedy's assassination, Johnson kept Kennedy's cabinet intact for nearly a year. In retrospect, Johnson thought he had gone too far and should have started off with his own personnel. "I wanted them all to stay," he recalled later. "Frankly, if I'd been picking a cabinet, fresh from an election myself, I don't think I would have done that. And, in retrospect, I don't think I would do it again" (Miller 1980, 402). The table suggests that Johnson's cabinet was not as static as he perceived it to be. Compared with cabinets in comparable multiterm administrations, his and Kennedy's cabinet had a slightly higher than average turnover rate but more members who served for the entire administration.*

| Administration | Number of departments | Number serving (average) | Average months of service | Median months of service | Number serving whole administration |
|---|---|---|---|---|---|
| Eisenhower (1953–1961) | 10 | 20 (2.0) | 47.3 | 40.5 | 2 |
| Kennedy/Johnson (1961–1969) | 12 | 27 (2.3) | 36.5 | 25 | 3 |
| Nixon/Ford (1969–1977) | 11 | 43 (3.8) | 27.1 | 24 | 0 |

*Source:* Charles O. Jones, "Clinton's Cabinet: Stability in Disorder," *PRG Report* 24 (fall 2001): 15; Merle Miller, *Lyndon: An Oral Biography* (New York: Ballantine Books, 1980); Michael Nelson, ed., *Congressional Quarterly's Guide to the Presidency,* 2d ed. (Washington, D.C.: Congressional Quarterly, 1996), 2:1689–1697.

## Document A.5  Cabinet Members of Kennedy and Johnson Administrations

*Robert Kennedy's resignation as attorney general on September 3, 1964, marked the first change in Johnson's cabinet since President Kennedy's assassination. As the table details, the attorney general's departure prompted a rapid exodus of Kennedy appointees in 1965. Johnson, however, maintained key Kennedy cabinet members for much of his presidency, chief among them Dean Rusk and Robert McNamara. He told an interviewer in 1965, "They know everything there is to know about their departments because they've been there a long time. I needed them" (Goodwin 1991).*

| Position | Kennedy | | | Johnson | | | | | |
| | 1961 | 1962 | 1963 | 1964 | 1965 | 1966 | 1967 | 1968 | 1969 |
|---|---|---|---|---|---|---|---|---|---|
| Secretary of state | Dean Rusk | | | | | | | | |
| Secretary of the Treasury | C. Douglas Dillon | | | | | Henry Fowler | | | Joseph Barr |
| Secretary of defense | Robert S. McNamara | | | | | | | | Clark Clifford |
| Attorney general | Robert Kennedy | | | | | Nicholas Katzenbach | | Williams Clark | William Watson |
| Postmaster general | *James Day* | | John A. Gronowski Jr. | | Lawrence O'Brien | | | | |
| Secretary of the interior | Stewart Udall | | | | | | | | |
| Secretary of agriculture | Orville Lothrop Freeman | | | | | | | | |
| Secretary of commerce | Luther Hodges | | | | John Connor | | Alexander Trowbridge | Cyrus Rowlett Smith | |
| Secretary of labor | *Arthur Goldberg* | | | | | William Wirtz | | | |
| Secretary of health, education, and welfare | *Abraham Ribicoff* | Anthony Celebrezze | | | | John Gardner | | | Wilbur Cohen |

*Note:* Italics indicate cabinet members appointed by Kennedy.

*Source:* Michael Nelson, ed., *Congressional Quarterly's Guide to the Presidency*, 2d ed. (Washington, D.C.: Congressional Quarterly, 1996), 2:1694; Doris Kearns Goodwin, *Lyndon Johnson and the American Dream* (New York: St. Martin's Press, 1991), 177.

## Appendix B
# Key Events in Johnson's Life

**1908**

*August 27* LBJ is born in his family's farmhouse on the Pedernales River in Stonewall, Texas.

**1913**

The Johnson family moves to Johnson City, Texas.

**1917**

*April* Joseph Baines, LBJ's maternal grandfather, resigns his seat in the Texas state house. Sam Ealy Johnson Jr., LBJ's father, runs for the seat at the urging of his brother-in-law, Clarence Martin, who held the seat from 1893 to 1895.

**1924**

*May 24* LBJ graduates from Johnson City High School. To his mother's displeasure, he decides not to attend college. Instead, he heads to California with friends.

**1925**

LBJ returns from California and begins working as a manual laborer on a road construction crew.

**1927**

LBJ enrolls in Southwest Texas State Teacher's College at San Marcos (now Southwest Texas State University).

After going broke, LBJ leaves college and takes a job as a principal and teacher at the Wellhausen School in Cotulla, Texas. He continues his studies by correspondence, faces down a threatened teacher strike, and organizes extracurricular activities for his students. After one year, he returns to college.

**1930**

*August 19* LBJ graduates from college with a bachelor of science degree. His first job is teaching at Pearsall High School in Pearsall, Texas.

After a few weeks at Pearsall High School, LBJ leaves for Sam Houston High School in Houston, where an uncle secured him a job as the public speaking instructor.

**1931**

*November 24* U.S. representative Richard "Dick" Kleberg of Texas's Fourteenth District appoints LBJ as his congressional secretary.

**1933**

*March 4* Franklin D. Roosevelt is sworn in as the thirty-second president of the United States and launches the New Deal.

*March 4–June 16* President Roosevelt signs an unprecedented amount of legislation, setting a standard known as the Hundred Days, which all future presidents will be measured against.

*April* LBJ is elected speaker of the "Little Congress," a group composed of congressional aides.

**1934**

*September 19* LBJ enrolls at Georgetown University Law Center in Washington, D.C., while working for Representative Kleberg.

*September* LBJ meets Claudia Alta Taylor (Lady Bird) on a trip to Texas.

*November 17* Two months after meeting, LBJ and Lady Bird are wed in San Antonio, Texas. They travel to Mexico on their honeymoon.

**1935**

*June 26* President Roosevelt signs an executive order establishing the National Youth Administration (NYA), an employment program for Americans ages sixteen to twenty-five.

*July 25* Roosevelt names LBJ the Texas director of the NYA. He becomes the youngest state director in the nation.

**1937**

*March 1* LBJ resigns from the NYA to run for Congress in a special election after the death of Rep. James Buchanan.

*April 10* LBJ wins the Tenth Congressional District election and heads to Washington, D.C.

*May 14* LBJ assumes his seat in the U.S. House of Representatives and, due to the personal interest taken in the young congressman by President Roosevelt, takes his place on the powerful Naval Affairs Committee.

*July 7* China and Japan begin full-scale war against each other.

*October 23* Sam Ealy Johnson, LBJ's father, dies in Austin, Texas, at age sixty.

**1938**

*March 12* Germany invades Austria.

*September 27* LBJ's efforts to bring electricity to the Texas hill country are successful; the Pedernales Electric Co-operative receives a letter from the Rural Electrification Administration granting over a million dollars to build electric lines.

*September 30* Great Britain, France, Italy, and Germany sign the Munich Agreement, which divides Czechoslovakia.

*November 8* LBJ is reelected as the Tenth District representative from Texas.
## 1939
*March 15–16* Germany breaks the Munich Agreement by invading all of Czecho-slovakia.

*July* President Roosevelt asks LBJ to become administrator of the Rural Electrification Administration. He declines the offer to remain in Congress.

*August 23* Germany and the U.S.S.R. sign a nonaggression pact.

*September 1* Germany invades Poland.

*September 3* France and Great Britain declare war on Germany.
## 1940
*May 12* Germany invades France.

*June 10* Italy declares war against France and Great Britain. Italy then invades France.

*June 21* LBJ is commissioned a lieutenant commander in the U.S. Naval Reserve.

*June 22* France surrenders to Germany.

*November* LBJ is reelected as the Tenth District representative from Texas.
## 1941
*March 11* The United States establishes the Lend-Lease plan to aid the Allies.

*June 22* Germany invades the Soviet Union.

*June 28* LBJ narrowly loses a special election for the Senate after the death of Sen. Morris Sheppard. His campaign's early release of ballot totals from districts they control allows the opposition to "discover" just enough new votes in counties *they* control to seal the victory. LBJ maintains his seat in the House of Representatives.

*December 7* The Japanese attack Pearl Harbor naval base.

*December 8* The United States declares war on Japan.

*December 9* Two days after the attack on Pearl Harbor, reservist Johnson reports for active duty in the navy.

*December 11* Germany and Italy declare war on the United States.
## 1942
*June 9* LBJ is awarded a Silver Star for his participation as an observer on a bombing run over New Guinea.

*July 16* LBJ returns to Washington, when President Roosevelt releases all members of Congress from active duty.

*November* LBJ is reelected as the Tenth District representative from Texas.
## 1943
*January* Lady Bird Johnson files an application with the Federal Communications Commission to buy Austin radio station KTBC.

*March 19* Lynda Bird Johnson is born.
## 1944
*June 6* D day. Allied forces invade Normandy.

*August 25* Allied troops liberate Paris.

*November* LBJ is reelected as the Tenth District representative from Texas.

*December 16* The Battle of the Bulge begins.

*December 24* Allied troops force German soldiers to retreat across German border.

**1945**

*January 12* America liberates the Philippines from Japanese occupation.

*April 12* President Roosevelt dies. Harry S. Truman is sworn in as the thirty-third president of the United States.

*May 7* Germany surrenders unconditionally.

*May 8* Allies declare V-E Day.

*June 26* The United Nations is established.

*August 6* The United States drops the first atomic bomb on Hiroshima, Japan.

*August 9* The United States drops the second atomic bomb on Nagasaki, Japan.

*September 2* Japan unconditionally surrenders to the United States, ending World War II.

**1946**

*April 18* The League of Nations is disbanded and cedes its role to the United Nations.

*November* LBJ is reelected as the Tenth District representative from Texas.

**1947**

*June 22* President Truman forms a committee to administer Marshall Plan aid to Europe.

*July 2* Luci Baines Johnson is born.

**1948**

LBJ risks his secure place in the House by announcing he will run for the Senate.

*May 14* The nation of Israel is established. The First Arab-Israeli war begins.

*August 28* LBJ wins the Democratic primary and earns the derisive nickname "Landslide Lyndon" because of the slim, eighty-seven-vote margin.

*November* LBJ is elected to the U.S. Senate.

**1949**

*April 4* The North Atlantic Treaty Organization (NATO) is established.

**1950**

*February 9* Sen. Joseph McCarthy announces in a speech in Wheeling, West Virginia, that the State Department has been infiltrated by communists.

*June 25* North Korea invades South Korea, beginning the Korean War.

**1951**

*January 2* LBJ is elected majority whip of the Senate. He becomes the youngest person to hold this position.

**1953**

*January 3* LBJ is elected minority leader of the Senate.

**1954**

*April 22–June 17* LBJ orchestrates the public humiliation of Senator McCarthy, ending McCarthy's four-year anticommunist crusade.

*May 17* The U.S. Supreme Court determines segregated schools are unconstitutional in *Brown v. Board of Education*.

*November 2* LBJ is reelected to the Senate.

*December 2* LBJ votes for condemnation of Senator McCarthy.

**1955**

*January 5* LBJ is elected majority leader of the Senate. He is once again the youngest person to hold this position of power.

*May 14* The Warsaw Pact is signed, creating a Soviet-bloc counterpart to NATO.

*July 2* LBJ is rushed to Bethesda Naval Hospital after suffering a severe heart attack.

*August 7* After a month in the hospital, LBJ is released and returns to his ranch three weeks later.

*December 1* The Montgomery, Alabama, bus boycott begins following the arrest of Rosa Parks, who refused to sit in the "colored section" of a public bus.

*December 5* The American Federation of Labor and Congress of Industrial Organizations consolidate into one organization, the AFL-CIO.

**1956**

*July 26* Egypt nationalizes the Suez Canal, seizing control from Great Britain.

*August 16* LBJ is nominated for president at the Democratic National Convention in Chicago. Adlai Stevenson wins the nomination.

**1957**

*September 9* As majority leader of the Senate, LBJ oversees passage of the Civil Rights Act of 1957.

*September 24* Desegregation begins in public schools as the "Little Rock Nine" become the first black students to enter a white school in Arkansas.

*October 4* LBJ opens hearing on America's space program as a reaction to the Soviet launching of the earth's first artificial satellite, *Sputnik*.

**1958**

*March 27* Nikita Khrushchev becomes Soviet premier.

*April 14* LBJ cosponsors a bill to create the National Aeronautics and Space Administration (NASA) and oversees its passage.

*September 12* LBJ's mother, Rebekah Baines Johnson, dies in Austin, Texas at age seventy-seven.

**1959**

*January 1* Fidel Castro assumes power in Cuba.

*January 3* Alaska becomes the forty-ninth state admitted to the United States.

*August 21* Hawaii becomes the fiftieth state admitted to the United States.

**1960**

*February 1* The first civil rights sit-in takes place at a lunch counter in the F. W. Woolworth store in Greensboro, North Carolina.

*May 1* An American U-2 plane on a reconnaissance flight over Russia is shot down. The pilot is captured and imprisoned for two years.

*May 6* President Eisenhower signs the Civil Rights Act of 1960.

*July 13* LBJ is nominated for president at the Democratic National Convention in Los Angeles. He loses on the first ballot to John F. Kennedy.

*July 14* LBJ is nominated for vice president at the Democratic National Convention.

*November 6* Kennedy and Johnson are victorious in the general election; LBJ becomes vice president of the United States.

**1961**

*January 20* LBJ takes the oath of office as vice president.

*April 17* An anti-Castro force aided by the United States launches a failed invasion of Cuba at Bahia de Cochinos, the Bay of Pigs.

*April 20* LBJ becomes chairman of the Space Council and declares eight days later that America can put a man on the moon.

*May* LBJ travels to meet with President Ngo Dinh Diem of South Vietnam and other Asian leaders.

*May 4* The freedom rides, organized by the Congress on Racial Equality, leave Washington, D.C., bound for southern cities. Interracial participants disobey the segregated seating rules and sit together on buses.

*May 5* Alan Shepard becomes the first U.S. astronaut. He completes a fifteen-minute trip to space.

*May 20* Freedom riders are attacked by a mob in Montgomery, Alabama.

*August 6* The Soviet Union launches its first astronaut into space.

*August 13* A barbed wire fence that eventually becomes the Berlin Wall is erected between East and West Germany.

*September* LBJ travels to West Berlin and meets with Chancellor Konrad Adenauer and Mayor Willy Brandt.

**1962**

*February 20* John Glenn becomes the first person to orbit Earth.

*June 25* The U.S. Supreme Court finds school prayer is unconstitutional.

*August–September* LBJ travels to the Middle East to meet with heads of state in Iran, Turkey, Greece, and Cyprus.

*October 14* An American spy plane takes pictures of Soviet workers building missile bases in Cuba.

*October 22* President Kennedy informs America that the Soviet Union is building missile bases in Cuba. He also announces that naval and air "quarantines" are in effect.

*October 26* Khrushchev offers to remove missiles from Cuba if the United States removes missiles from Turkey and agrees not to invade Cuba.

**1963**

*April 12* Martin Luther King Jr. is arrested in Birmingham, Alabama, for organizing civil rights protests.

*June* LBJ travels to Rome to represent the United States at the funeral of Pope John XXIII.

*August 28* Civil rights groups march on Washington, D.C., to support the civil rights bill proposed by President Kennedy. Martin Luther King Jr. delivers his "I have a dream" speech.

*August 30* Moscow and Washington establish a "hot line" to facilitate emergency communications.

*November 22* President Kennedy is assassinated in Dallas, Texas. LBJ is sworn in as president aboard *Air Force One.*

*November 27* LBJ addresses Congress for the first time as president.

*November 29* LBJ appoints a commission to investigate Kennedy's assassination. Chief Justice Earl Warren is selected as its chairman.

## 1964

*January 8* LBJ delivers his first State of the Union address to Congress. He declares "unconditional war on poverty."

*February 26* LBJ signs a tax-reduction act to spur economic growth.

*May 22* LBJ uses the term "Great Society" in a speech at the University of Michigan.

*June 11* Nelson Mandela is sentenced to life in prison in South Africa.

*July 2* LBJ signs the Civil Rights Act of 1964 in a televised White House ceremony.

*August 2* The U.S.S. *Maddox* is attacked in the Gulf of Tonkin by North Vietnamese torpedo boats.

*August 4* The United States announces a second attack on the U.S.S. *Maddox* and the U.S.S. *Turner Joy.* (An ongoing debate exists as to whether the second attack ever took place.)

*August 5* Three civil rights workers on a mission to register black voters in Mississippi are reported missing. Three members of the Ku Klux Klan are eventually charged with their murders.

*August 7* Congress passes the Gulf of Tonkin Resolution authorizing the president to use force to protect U.S. troops.

*August 20* LBJ signs the Economic Opportunity Act, the foundation of his war on poverty.

*August 26* LBJ becomes the Democratic nominee for president at the Democratic National Convention.

*September 7* LBJ travels to Detroit, Michigan, to begin his campaign for president.

*November 3* LBJ is elected president of the United States. He soundly defeats Barry Goldwater by a margin of 486 to 52 electoral votes.

LBJ is named *Time* magazine's man of the year.

## 1965

*January 4* LBJ delivers the first nationally televised, prime-time State of the Union address. He outlines the components of the Great Society.

*January 20* LBJ again takes the presidential oath of office.

*February 7* LBJ orders air strikes against North Vietnam to retaliate for the attack on an American installation.

*February 21* Malcolm X is assassinated in Harlem, New York.

*March 7* Voting rights activists stage a march from Selma to Montgomery, Alabama. When the marchers reach a bridge on U.S. Route 80, police in riot gear attack them. The media captures the entire incident, which becomes known as Bloody Sunday.

*March 8–9* The first U.S. military combat troops arrive in South Vietnam.

*March 15* LBJ addresses Congress on the need for voting rights legislation. He submits a bill two days later.

*March 26* LBJ announces federal investigation of the Ku Klux Klan for murders and crimes against civil rights activists.

*April 2* The United States increases foreign aid to South Vietnam.

*April 7* LBJ delivers an address at Johns Hopkins University entitled, "Peace without Conquest." He discusses America's goals in Vietnam.

*April 11* LBJ signs the Elementary and Secondary Education Act of 1965 at his former elementary school in Johnson City, Texas.

*April 17* Students for a Democratic Society hold the first major antiwar rally in Washington, D.C.

*April 28* LBJ sends marines to the Dominican Republic after a coup overthrows the government.

*June 8* LBJ authorizes the use of ground troops in South Vietnam. He sends 21,000 additional troops to the region.

*July 28* LBJ announces an escalation of the war in Vietnam. He commits to send 50,000 additional troops. He also appoints Abe Fortas to the Supreme Court.

*July 30* LBJ signs the Medicare Bill at the Harry S. Truman Library in Independence, Missouri, with former president Truman present.

*August 6* LBJ signs the Voting Rights Act of 1965 in the Capitol Rotunda.

*August 11–16* Riots break out in the Watts neighborhood of Los Angeles; more than thirty people die.

*August 20* LBJ denounces the Watts riots, calling them baseless.

*October 4* LBJ becomes the first president to visit with a pope on U.S. soil.

*November 8* LBJ signs the Higher Education Act of 1965 in San Marcos, Texas, at his alma mater, Southwest Texas State College.

**1966**

*January 12* LBJ delivers his third State of the Union address to Congress. He announces a continuation of the Great Society and continued involvement in Vietnam until goals are met.

*January 31* LBJ announces a resumption of aerial bombing in North Vietnam because of failed peace efforts.

*March 15* Riots break out again in Watts, Los Angeles. Two people are killed and dozens are wounded.

*June 13* The U.S. Supreme Court rules in *Miranda v. Arizona* that individuals must be read their legal rights at the time of their arrest.

*June 30* LBJ announces an escalation of the war in Vietnam and the first bombing raids of Hanoi, the capital of North Vietnam.

*August 6*  Luci Baines Johnson marries Patrick Nugent at the Shrine of the Immaculate Conception in Washington, D.C.

*October 26*  While on a trip to Asia, LBJ makes a surprise visit to Cam Ranh Bay, South Vietnam. He becomes the first U.S. president to visit South Vietnam.

**1967**

*January 10*  LBJ delivers his fourth State of the Union address to Congress. He suggests a tax surcharge is necessary to stave off inflation and pay for the war in Vietnam. For the first time, NBC, CBS, and ABC all carry the address live.

*January 27*  LBJ signs a space treaty with Great Britain and the Soviet Union to preserve the autonomy of outer space and restrict its use for military aims.

*June 5*  The Six-Day War begins in the Middle East.

*June 13*  LBJ appoints Thurgood Marshall to the Supreme Court. Marshall is the highest court's first African American justice.

*July 13*  LBJ announces that additional troops will be sent to Vietnam.

*July 23*  Race riots break out across the nation.

*July 24*  LBJ sends federal troops to Detroit, Michigan, to subdue rioters.

*August 3*  LBJ sends a message to Congress asking for a 10 percent surcharge on personal and corporate income tax rates to pay for the war in Vietnam and stave off inflation. He also announces additional troops will be sent to Vietnam.

*December 9*  Lynda Bird Johnson marries Charles S. Robb at the White House.

*December 23*  LBJ again visits Cam Ranh Bay military base in South Vietnam. Johnson is named *Time* magazine's man of the year.

**1968**

*January 1*  LBJ travels to Johnson City, Texas, to report a negative balance of payments deficit in 1967. In a press conference, he requests Americans to limit investments abroad and postpone nonessential travel outside the hemisphere.

*January 17*  LBJ delivers his fifth State of the Union address. He promises an immediate end to the bombing in North Vietnam if peace talks can be scheduled.

*January 30*  The Tet offensive begins in Vietnam.

*March 16*  In seizing the Vietnamese village of My Lai, U.S. troops indiscriminately kill civilians in the "My Lai Massacre."

*March 31*  LBJ announces a de-escalation of the war in Vietnam and stuns a live television audience with his announcement that he will not seek reelection.

*April 4*  James E. Ray assassinates Martin Luther King Jr. in Memphis, Tennessee. LBJ makes a brief television statement expressing outrage over the assassination of King.

*April 5*  LBJ orders National Guard troops to Washington, D.C., to subdue rioters who emerge in the wake of King's assassination.

*April 11*  LBJ signs the Civil Rights Act of 1968, a measure aimed at housing discrimination.

*June 5*  Presidential candidate Robert F. Kennedy is assassinated. LBJ orders the Secret Service to protect all presidential candidates in the wake of the assassination.

*June 13*  The *New York Times* begins publishing the "Pentagon Papers."

*June 26*  LBJ appoints Abe Fortas as chief justice and Homer Thornberry as associate justice to the U.S. Supreme Court. Both men fail to receive Senate confirmation.

*July 1*  At a White House ceremony, LBJ signs the Nuclear Nonproliferaton Treaty and announces he will work with the Soviet Union to limit missile systems.

*August 21*  LBJ denounces the Soviet Union's occupation of Czechoslovakia.

*August 29*  LBJ announces his support for Vice President Hubert Humphrey for president, but he works behind the scenes for the election of the more hawkish Richard Nixon.

*October 31*  LBJ orders a unilateral cease-fire in Vietnam effective November 1.

*November 5*  Richard Nixon is elected president.

*November 11*  LBJ welcomes president-elect Nixon to the White House.

**1969**

*January 14*  LBJ delivers his sixth State of the Union address to Congress. He cites the challenges facing America and highlights the accomplishments of his administration.

*January 20*  Nixon is sworn in as the thirty-seventh president of the United States. Johnson returns to the LBJ ranch in Texas.

*July 20*  Neil Armstrong becomes the first person to walk on the moon.

*December 27*  LBJ appears in a television interview with Walter Cronkite. In the interview, he expresses confidence that he could have won reelection.

*December 31*  President Nixon begins U.S. troop withdrawal from Vietnam.

**1970**

*June 13*  LBJ attends the dedication of his birthplace as a national historical site.

*June 24*  The Senate repeals the Gulf of Tonkin Resolution.

*August 29*  LBJ attends the dedication of LBJ State Park.

*October 28*  Lady Bird Johnson's *A White House Diary* is published.

**1971**

*May 22*  The Lyndon Baines Johnson Presidential Library opens at the University of Texas at Austin.

*November 1*  LBJ's memoirs, *The Vantage Point: Perspectives of the Presidency, 1963–1969,* are published.

*December 11–12*  LBJ attends a civil rights conference at the LBJ library. He declares that the civil rights progress during his administration was too small.

**1973**

*January 22*  Lyndon Baines Johnson dies at his ranch.

# Index

317

Taiwan, 129
taxes, 172
Tet offensive, 175-177, 178
Vietnam War Memorial (Washington, D.C.), 168
Volunteers in Service to America, 110, 224
Voting Rights. *See* Civil rights
Voting Rights Act of 1965, 32, 115, 147-153, 232

Wallace, George, 77-78
*Wall Street Journal,* 44, 45, 73, 228
War on Poverty. *See also* Great Society; Poverty
  background of, 109-110
  declaration of, 71, 139
  economic effects of, 110
  legislative involvement of LBJ, 220
  political factors, 111-112
*War, Presidents, and Public Opinion* (Mueller), 10
Warren Commission, 167
Warren, Earl, 167, 232-233, 297
*Washington Post,* 113
Wasileski, Vincent T., 92

Watergate. *See* Scandals
Watkins, Arthur, 59
Watson, Marvin, 297
Weaver, Robert, 116, 297-298
Westmoreland, William, 171, 174, 197-202, 227, 298
Wharton Econometric Forecasting Associates, 133
Wheeler, Earle, 176, 197, 200, 201, 226-227, 298
*Wheeling and Dealing* (Baker), 29
Whiteside, Thomas, 245
White, Theodore, 15, 75
Wilkins, Roy, 224, 241-242, 298-299
Wilson, Woodrow, 67, 90
Wirtz, Alvin, 23, 260
Woodrow Wilson Center for Scholars, 118
Woodward, Warren, 4
World War II, 7, 25-26, 167, 229
World War III, 264
Wright, Zephyr, 108

Youngblood, Rufus, 164
Young, Whitney Jr., 224, 299

# Text Credits

Bartlett, Bruce R., "The Impact of Federal Tax Cuts on Economic Growth," April 1999, The Lexington Institute, http://www.lexingtoninstitute.org/whatworks/whtwrks1.htm.

DeCell, Ken, and Allan J. Lichtman, *The Thirteen Keys to the Presidency* (Lanham, Md.: Madison, 1990), 7, 310, 323, 334. Reprinted by permission of the publisher.

Dugger, Ronnie, *The Politician, the Life and Times of Lyndon Johnson: The Drive for Power, from the Frontier to Master of the Senate* (New York: Norton, 1982), pp. 112–114.

From THE GALLUP POLL, 1935–1971 by George Gallup, copyright © 1972 by American Institute of Public Opinion. Used by permission of Random House, Inc.

"How the President's Wife Built $17,500 Into Big Fortune in Television," by Louis M. Kohlmeiher, *The Wall Street Journal, Eastern Edition,* March 23, 1964.

"The Humor of LBJ: 25th Anniversary Edition," audio recording, LBJ Museum Store; "The Man and His Humor Are Recalled," *New York Times,* January 25, 1973. Copyright © 1973 by the New York Times Co. Reprinted by permission.

*Lady Bird Johnson: A White House Diary* (New York: Holt, Rinehart, and Winston, 1970), pp. 3–6. Courtesy of the LBJ Library.

Larson, Eric V., *Casualties and Consensus: The Historical Role of Casualties in Domestic Support for U.S. Military Operations* (Santa Monica, Calif.: Rand, 1996), p. 111. Copyright RAND 1996. Reprinted by permission.

Light, Paul, *The President's Agenda: Domestic Policy Choice from Kennedy to Clinton.* pp. 42, 244, 112. © 1999. Reprinted with permission of The Johns Hopkins University Press.

"McNamara Asks Giap: What Happened in Tonkin Gulf?" *Houston Chronicle,* November 19, 1995. Reprinted with permission of the Associated Press.

Miller, Merle, *Lyndon: An Oral Biography* (New York: Putnam's Press, 1980), pp. 561–562. Reprinted by permission.

Mooney, Booth, *LBJ: An Irreverent Chronicle* (New York: Thomas Y. Crowell, 1976), pp. 183–185.

Moyers, Bill, "Across the Pedernales," *New York Times,* January 26, 1973. Copyright © 1973 by the New York Times Co. Reprinted by permission.

Mueller, John *War, Presidents, and Public Opinion* (New York: Wiley, 1973), 54–55, 107, 275.

"Taxes, Inflation and the Rich," by Michael K. Evans, *The Wall Street Journal, Eastern Edition,* August 7, 1978.